The Myth of Left and Right

D1570203

The Myth of Left and Right

How the Political Spectrum Misleads and Harms America

HYRUM LEWIS
and
VERLAN LEWIS

OXFORD
UNIVERSITY PRESS

OXFORD
UNIVERSITY PRESS

Oxford University Press is a department of the University of Oxford. It furthers
the University's objective of excellence in research, scholarship, and education
by publishing worldwide. Oxford is a registered trade mark of Oxford University
Press in the UK and certain other countries.

Published in the United States of America by Oxford University Press
198 Madison Avenue, New York, NY 10016, United States of America.

© Oxford University Press 2023

CIP data is on file at the Library of Congress

ISBN 978–0–19–768062–9 (pbk.)
ISBN 978–0–19–768021–6 (hbk.)

DOI: 10.1093/oso/9780197680216.001.0001

Paperback printed by Marquis, Canada
Hardback printed by Bridgeport National Bindery, Inc., United States of America

CONTENTS

ACKNOWLEDGMENTS

We thank Mark A. Smith of the University of Washington for carefully reading over the manuscript and offering insightful feedback and encouragement. Thanks also to the members of the American Politics Working Group at Harvard for their critiques and support. Others who helped sharpen our ideas were Frances Lee, Hans Noel, Richard Bensel, David Mayhew, Terry Moe, David Pulsipher, John Thomas, Matt Miles, and the anonymous reviewers for Oxford University Press. Thanks to Dave McBride for his hard work in bringing this book to publication. And, of course, a big thanks to all of our teachers and mentors over the years who helped hone our thinking and taught us to challenge conventional wisdom on political matters.

Introduction

American politics is at a breaking point. This became obvious when a mob of American citizens, upset with the results of the 2020 presidential election, stormed the Capitol Building in Washington, DC, to stop Congress from tabulating the election results. In order to work, democracies require citizens who respect the rights of individuals, defer to the outcomes of elections, and abide by the rule of law. But today's toxic political culture has caused many Americans to abandon these vital norms. Ideological tribalism and partisan hatred have become so rampant that frightening numbers of American citizens countenance violence against their political opponents to get their way.[1]

How did we get to this point? The standard explanations—media echo chambers, party polarization, racism, status anxiety, internet misinformation, demographic sorting, fear, and social homophily—tell only part of the story. An important but overlooked contributor to American political dysfunction today is a widespread misunderstanding of ideology.[2]

Ideology dominates American politics, and since we are thinking about ideology all wrong, we are thinking about politics all wrong. Concepts have consequences, and when a society adopts an incorrect political model, the results can be devastating.

The standard view of ideology says that politics is largely a clash between two worldviews that can be modeled on a political spectrum.[3] The left-wing worldview, we are told, is expressed in a preference for greater government control of the economy, social permissiveness, and foreign policy dovishness, while the right-wing worldview is expressed in a preference for free markets, social restriction, and foreign policy hawkishness.[4] Taking these worldviews to extremes leads to totalitarianism—fascism at the far right or communism on the far left—while the more respectable positions exist at the center left ("liberalism" or "progressivism") and center right ("conservatism").[5]

This model of politics frames our thinking, shapes our language, and sets the terms of public debate. It creates a sense of personal identity for millions of

The Myth of Left and Right. Hyrum Lewis and Verlan Lewis, Oxford University Press. © Oxford University Press 2023.
DOI: 10.1093/oso/9780197680216.003.0001

Americans, is taught in classrooms across the country, and is used in nearly every political discussion, whether on social media, in the halls of Congress, on cable news, or around the dinner table. It is, without question, the most influential political paradigm of twenty-first-century America.

It is also completely wrong.

The political spectrum does not tell us where someone stands in relation to a fundamental worldview or philosophy (or disposition, temperament, belief, value, or any other "essence"); it only indicates a commitment to a tribe. As long as binary coalitions characterize our politics, the political spectrum can be useful for modeling commitment to those coalitions and what they stand for at a specific place and time, but it becomes misleading as soon as we assume that it is modeling a commitment to an underlying essence.

In the following chapters we will show how a mistaken understanding of ideological categories causes confusion and threatens to dissolve the "bonds of affection" that should unite us as citizens.[6] We challenge the static, "essentialist" conception of ideology that currently dominates public and academic discourse alike, and instead propose a "social" conception in which the political spectrum and the ideological terms associated with it ("left," "right," "liberal," "progressive," "conservative," and "reactionary") are socially constructed, historically contingent, context-dependent, and constantly in flux. Although America has two dominant ideological tribes, there is no essence uniting all of the positions of each side. Our two political teams have coalesced around the concepts of left and right, but the concepts themselves are fictions.[7]

While most people acknowledge that politics has become increasingly tribal, they generally assume that there must be some bedrock philosophy or value that each tribe rallies around. There is not. Terms are useful inasmuch as they are predictive, and it turns out that ideological terms are only predictive across contexts in describing *who* people support (tribe) but not *what* they support (a philosophy). The single biggest fallacy in politics today is that the political spectrum refers to divergent worldviews when, in reality, it refers only to divergent tribes.

Clearly, there are many issues in politics and yet we model politics using a unidimensional spectrum as if there were just one. Why? The answer, for most people, is that there is *something* that unites them. That *something* is the "essence" (e.g., the anti-abortion, low tax, and pro–Iraq War positions are all connected by a philosophy or disposition we call "conservative" and so we place conservatives on the "center right" of a political spectrum). Our task in this book is to demonstrate that such an essential unity does not exist, and that the various dimensions of politics don't have an intrinsic connection. Why do we refer to both Milton Friedman (a Jewish, pro-capitalist pacifist) and Adolf Hitler (an anti-Semitic, anti-capitalist militarist) as "right wing" when they had opposite policy views on every point? We shouldn't. Placing both Hitler and Friedman on the same side of a spectrum as if they shared some fundamental essence is both misleading and destructive. It shuts down productive discourse and stokes irrational prejudices.

Our thesis is simply this: left–right ideologies are bundles of unrelated political positions connected by nothing other than a group. A conservative or liberal is not someone who has a conservative or liberal philosophy, but someone who belongs to the conservative or liberal tribe. This means that ideologies do not define tribes, tribes define ideologies; ideology is not about what (worldviews), it is about who (groups); there is no liberalism or conservatism, only liberals and conservatives; and the political spectrum does not model an essential value, but only tribes and what they stand for at a specific time and place.[8] Ultimately, we are saying that nearly all of the incessant talk about "liberal," "conservative," "progressive," "left wing," and "right wing" is a lot of sound and fury signifying nothing.

We understand that this is a bold claim. It challenges a century of conventional wisdom and goes against the prevailing consensus of elite opinion in the United States.[9] Virtually all Republican politicians say that they agree with their party's platform because they are conservatives who share their party's conservative philosophy, while virtually all Democratic politicians say they agree with their party's platform because they are liberals (or "progressives") who share their party's liberal (or progressive) philosophy. Almost all of our academic colleagues say that they agree with "the left" on a wide array of issues (abortion, wealth redistribution, affirmative action, military intervention, environmentalism, etc.) because left-wing positions promote their single value of "social justice." Avid Fox News watchers say they agree with what Sean Hannity says because both they and Hannity are "on the right." Nearly every politician, partisan voter, pundit, journalist, or public intellectual believes that they agree with the many issues associated with their side of the political spectrum because they agree with the underlying philosophy of that side. They all believe politics is about one big thing—an essence—that defines and divides left and right. In the following chapters we will show that this is a society-wide delusion.

The popularity of the "essentialist" view of ideology makes it no less mistaken. A false idea is false regardless of how many people believe in it. Most educated eighteenth-century Americans accepted the four humors theory of disease and most educated twenty-first-century Americans accept an essentialist view of the political spectrum, but both are equally erroneous. Societies can be misled into holding collective delusions, so it is necessary for people of common sense to point out the obvious and declare that the emperor has no clothes. As George Orwell put it, "We have now sunk to a depth at which restatement of the obvious is the first duty of intelligent men."[10] By stating the obvious fact that there is more than one issue in politics, we are simply doing our intellectual duty and, as radical as our thesis might seem, it is nonetheless where the evidence leads.

With the myth of left and right so widespread in American culture, is the so-lution simply a matter of educating the mass public in a reality that intellectual elites have long understood? Unfortunately, no. As we will show in the chapters that follow, the left–right framework was actually imported into America by academics and journalists, and it is intellectuals that are largely responsible for spreading the myth of left and right in our popular culture over the past century. As a result, most scholars in the academy today are more blinded by the myth than those outside the ivory tower.

For example, while most historical scholarship today is premised on the as-sumption that race, class, and gender are social constructs, historians who have written about ideology nonetheless assume that "left" and "right" are trans-historical essences that remain fixed across time and place.[11] Thus, they invoke "left" and "right" in ways that speak of individuals, political groups, and the country "moving to the left" or "moving to the right" on a spectrum.[12]

This approach is also widespread in political science, where an entire litera-ture has emerged around the analytical concept of "polarization"—the idea that in recent decades Democrats have moved "to the left" and Republicans have moved, even farther, "to the right." Thousands of academic books and articles have advanced this claim. It is, as political scientists Michael Barber and Nolan McCarty note, "a broad scholarly consensus."[13] What very few scholars stop to ask is what sense it can make to speak of individuals and groups moving "to the left" or "to the right" over time when the very meanings of left and right change during that same time period? Some scholars of American political develop-ment working at the intersection of political science and history have recently recognized the evolutionary character of ideologies[14] and resisted the myth of left–right polarization,[15] but these scholars are in the minority.[16] This book is an attempt to give a more accurate conception of ideology in America and thereby correct common misunderstandings of ideology among the general public and among the intellectuals who promote these confusions.[17]

This rethinking of ideology is needed today for the same reason that a rethinking of medicine was needed in the nineteenth century. Operating under a false "four humors" understanding of health, many doctors bled their patients to death in earlier centuries, and operating under a false "essentialist" under-standing of ideology, political actors are bleeding our republic to death today. It is time to move beyond this flawed model of politics and let our public discourse begin to heal.

The Myth of Left and Right

The myth of left and right is the false belief that there is an essence behind the political spectrum. While it is undeniable that many Americans hold their political views in packages that we call ideologies—those who support abortion rights, for instance, are also more likely to support income tax increases and affirmative action—the question is "why?" Why is there a noticeable correlation between these seemingly unrelated issues and why do we find them clustering in patterns that are predictable and binary instead of random and pluralistic? In this chapter, we present and evaluate two competing explanatory theories that we will use as the analytical framework for the rest of the book.

The Two Theories of Ideology

The first theory is what we call the *essentialist theory of ideology*. This theory says that distinct issues cluster together in ideological bundles because all political issues grow out of a single master issue (an essence).[1] For example, "John" believes in abortion restriction, tax cuts, and the war in Iraq because John is on the "conservative" side of the master issue, while "Jane" believes in abortion rights, tax hikes, and opposing the Iraq War because Jane is on the "liberal" side of the master issue. Being on one side of this issue leads to one set of positions while being on the opposite side leads to the opposite set of positions. Some essentialists[2] believe that this master issue exists in nature and is found in all political communities across time and space,[3] while other essentialists believe that this master issue is a product of history and dominates only among modern pluralistic democracies,[4] but in either case, essentialists believe there are two sides to the left–right political spectrum because there are just two sides to this one master issue.[5]

This master issue is commonly understood to be *change*.[6] The essentialist theory says that all left-wing positions promote change while all right-wing

The Myth of Left and Right. Hyrum Lewis and Verlan Lewis, Oxford University Press. © Oxford University Press 2023.
DOI: 10.1093/oso/9780197680216.003.0002

positions try to arrest or reverse change. Issues as diverse as abortion, taxes, and affirmative action may seem unrelated, but that's only on the surface—deep down, a person's stance on change (for or against) determines their stance on all of these other issues. Change is the one essential issue that binds together all the others and defines left and right across time and space.[7]

If the essentialist theory is correct, then the political spectrum is a useful and accurate way to model where people stand on that one essential issue. Extreme pro-change "radicals" will be at the far left, extreme anti-change "reactionaries" will be at the far right, pro-change "liberals" and "progressives" will be at the center left, anti-change "conservatives" will be at the center right, and moderates who want some change (but not too much) will be in the middle.[8]

As an alternative to this essentialist theory of ideology, we propose the *social theory of ideology*. While the essentialist theory says that distinct political positions correlate because they are bound by a unifying essence, the social theory says that issues correlate because they are bound by a unifying tribe. According to the essentialist theory, people start with an essential principle, use that principle to think themselves to hundreds of distinct political positions, and then join the tribe that just happens to agree with them on all of those positions. The social theory says this is backward: people first anchor into an ideological tribe (because of family, peers, or a single issue), adopt the positions of the tribe as a matter of socialization, and only then invent a story that ties all of those positions together. Ideologies, in other words, are reverse engineered to fit tribal actions and attachments. They are "*post hoc* constructions designed to justify what we've just done, or to support the groups we belong to."[9]

According to the social theory, we do not need an essence to explain why conservatives support both lower taxes and abortion restrictions for the same reason we do not need an essence to explain why San Francisco 49ers fans supported both Joe Montana and Jerry Rice.[10] In each case, the support is explained by social group attachments. The essentialist theory says the political spectrum *describes* a reality of binary principles, but the social theory says the political spectrum *creates* a reality of binary tribes.[11] Tribalism without an underlying philosophy has been strong enough to sustain nationalism for centuries, and tribalism without an underlying philosophy is strong enough to sustain ideological identities today.[12]

Testing the Essentialist Theory

Since theories are validated or falsified through testing, let's look at the predictions that each theory makes. The essentialist theory predicts that since core principles define the political spectrum, we should find people holding a consistent set of "left" or "right" positions independent of socialization. For example, if both wealth redistribution and abortion rights share a left-wing essence, we should find that these issues naturally correlate across time, space, and social conditioning. In fact, we find the opposite. Political psychologists have shown that people do not hold political views that fit current ideological molds *until after they are socialized into the left–right way of thinking.*[13] The less tribal and the more ignorant of the political spectrum someone is, the less their views will align with the regnant ideological configurations.[14]

Let's take a moment to consider the implications of these findings: since there is no correlation between belief in abortion rights and redistribution of wealth except among the segment of the population that has been most socialized into the left–right way of thinking, then this means the correlation is explained *entirely by social conformism.* Research by Donald Kinder and Nathan Kalmoe has shown that, contra the predictions of the essentialist theory, people first anchor into an ideological tribe—because of family, peers, or a single issue they feel strongly about—and only then adopt the full range of beliefs associated with that tribe. Ideological identification, in other words, is the cause, not the effect, of a person's political views. In general, tribal identity comes first and beliefs come second.[15]

The "Religious Right" provides a great example of belief following tribe. According to political scientists Eric Gould and Esteban Klor, "Voting for a given political party in 1996, due to the individual's initial views on abortion in 1982, has a substantial effect on a person's political, social, and economic attitudes in 1997. . . . As individuals realigned their party affiliation in accordance with their initial abortion views, their other political views followed suit."[16] Millions of religious Americans had no ideological identity until abortion became a political issue in the 1970s. At that point, they anchored into the right-wing tribe and adopted its other positions (e.g., supply-side economics) as a matter of social conformity. These members of the Religious Right have been among the most reliable supporters of the conservative tribe ever since. Anchoring and conformism, not essence, explain why most people hold views that fit left–right molds and the predictions of the essentialist theory are not borne out in the data.

Testing the Social Theory

The social theory, by contrast, predicts that since the positions associated with left and right are not natural, but social, we should expect to see those on the left and right changing their political views depending on what their team is doing. Political beliefs, it predicts, will be contingent on social cues. This is exactly what we find. Political scientists Michael Barber and Jeremy Pope showed that conservatives would strongly agree with a policy (such as raising the minimum wage) when told that Donald Trump supported it but would strongly disagree with that same policy when told that Trump opposed it.[17] There was no commitment to an essential principle (such as limited government or free markets) underlying their policy preferences, but only tribal solidarity.

Psychologist G. L. Cohen conducted a similar study in which he had students read of a generous welfare proposal but told some that it was endorsed by the Democratic Party and others that it was endorsed by the Republican Party.[18] As we would expect under the social theory, he found that "for both liberal and conservative participants, the effect of reference group information overrode that of policy content. If their party endorsed it, liberals supported even a harsh welfare program, and conservatives supported even a lavish one."[19]

Political scientist Lilliana Mason found that "right-wing ideology" strongly predicts support for Donald Trump, but not support for particular political issues. In other words, ideological measures tell us *who* people support (tribe), but not *what* they support (principles).[20] Similarly, Gabriel Lenz showed that committed ideologues are far more likely to change their positions to fit the politicians for whom they vote than they are to change their vote to politicians who fit their positions.[21] In general, the game is "follow the tribe" as the social theory says, not "follow the principles" as the essentialist theory says.

Not only do ideologues change their views to conform to tribal leadership, but they also change to conform to tribal peers. A team of psychologists divided volunteers into different experimental "worlds" and had early movers in the different worlds take different positions on a variety of political issues. Against all essentialist predictions, those of the same ideological identity took opposite positions in the different worlds depending upon what the early movers in their group were doing. These "opinion cascades" generated "unpredictable political alignments in which the advocates on an issue might have instead been the opposition but for the luck of the draw in the positions taken by early movers."[22] Liberals and conservatives were unpredictable in *how* they would change their opinions (what principles they would follow), but highly predictable in *who* they would change their opinions to follow (peers of the same ideological label). "Social influence causes substantively unrelated issues to align," the authors of the study concluded, and this, not an invisible essence, explains the correlation we find between left-wing and right-wing views on fiscal, social, and foreign policies.[23]

Just as the social theory predicts, most people first choose whom to identify with (tribe) and only then choose what to identify with (policy). In the words of psychologist Dan Kahan, they "endorse whichever position reinforces their connection to others with whom they share important ties."[24] Far from having a coherent, well-thought-out ideology based on essential principles, most ideologues of left and right cannot even provide a definition of their ideology. They strongly embrace a left- or right-wing identity, but what that means in terms of principle is a mystery to them. Ideological self-categorization "taps not what the respondent thinks about various issues but rather the ideological label he or she finds most suitable."[25] Ideology is a social, not a philosophical, phenomenon.

According to psychologists Philip Tetlock and Dan Gardner:

> Our judgments about risks—Does gun control make us safer or put us in danger?—are driven less by a careful weighing of evidence than by our identities, which is why people's views on gun control often correlate with their views on climate change, even though the two issues have no logical connection to each other. Psycho-logic trumps logic.[26]

Some might assume that this position-switching based on social cues only happens among the uncommitted—the "weak ideologues" on the margins—but the experiments show that the more committed someone is to their ideology the more likely they are to change their positions. The stronger one's ideological commitment, the more one's views are contingent upon social factors.[27] If ideologues were principled, rather than tribal, we would see the most committed ideologues holding most strongly to their principles in spite of social pressure. In fact, we see the opposite. As the social theory predicts, being more ideological for most people means being more tribal, not more principled, and "extreme" left or right wing does not mean a strong commitment to some essential left- or right-wing ideal but means a strong commitment to following the left- or right-wing tribe.[28] Although there are "sticky ideologues" who are less likely to change their views with priming (see chapter 4), this is because they are loyal to a previous iteration of an ideology rather than an ideological essence. Those willing to change parties or ideological groups as "left" and "right" evolve are the exceptions to the rule. Humans do not naturally fit molds of left and right, as the essentialist theory says, but they do conform to them, as the social theory says.

The Essentialist Theory and Storytelling

While this evidence is devastating to the essentialist theory of ideology, many of its advocates nevertheless try to save it from falsification through ex-post storytelling. Here is one example of a typical essentialist story:

> Since opposition to change is the essence of the right, those on the right naturally favor free markets and tax cuts because they want to preserve the laissez-faire traditions of American capitalism. They oppose

abortion because they want to preserve Christian pro-life values. They favored the Iraq War because they wanted to preserve the tradition of American exceptionalism and military strength. They oppose free trade because they want to preserve American manufacturing. They oppose immigration because they want to preserve America's current ethnic composition.[29]

This story sounds plausible enough until we realize that we can, through the same method of creative storytelling, *also make opposition to change the essence of the left*. Consider this story:

> Since opposition to change is the essence of the left, those on the left naturally want to conserve the environment and the American welfare state. They favor government anti-poverty programs because they want to conserve the traditional Christian value of helping the poor. They favor abortion rights because they want to conserve a woman's right to choose. Those on the left oppose radical attempts to change the world using military force and want more immigration because they believe in conserving the American tradition of welcoming the "tired, poor, huddled masses" to the country. Leftists believe in conserving longstanding American institutions such as Social Security, teachers' unions, and the FDA, while those on the right want to change or abolish them.

The second story is less familiar but no less plausible than the first and together they make it clear that storytelling can make opposition to change the essence of either the right or the left.

Indeed, creative storytelling can make any essence fit any set of political positions. For example, here is a set of randomly selected political positions:

- pro-life
- high tax
- tough on crime
- pro–gay marriage
- anti–redistribution of wealth

Now here's a story that shows how the randomly selected essence of "assertiveness" unites all these positions:

> Assertive people are not afraid to stand up for the rights of others, including homosexuals and the unborn, and that's why they are pro-life

and in favor of gay marriage. Assertive people have no problem asserting themselves into other people's lives and therefore favor the high taxation that others might consider intrusive. Assertive people are not afraid to stand up against criminals and are therefore in favor of tough laws and harsh sentencing. Assertive people are more likely to be self-reliant and therefore less willing to favor redistribution programs that cause people to rely on government.

You've never heard this story before (we just made it up), but it is as valid as any of the other stories you've heard that uphold the essentialist theory of ideology. Just as storytellers come up with creative ways to unify everything conservatives believe using the "opposition to change" essence, so we can come up with a creative way to unify these random positions using the "assertiveness" essence.

We challenge the reader to do the same: take a random set of political positions and a random characteristic and then make up a story showing how the characteristic unifies all those random positions. It is an entertaining exercise and shows the worthlessness of storytelling as a method for validating ideological essentialism (or any other theory). When we mistake such stories for evidence, we are falling victim to "the narrative fallacy," and it is largely the narrative fallacy that keeps people believing in the essentialist theory.

Essentialist stories also get stuck in self-contradiction. For example, if "right wing" essentially means opposition to change, then we would expect "right wing" extremist Adolf Hitler to have been extremely against change. In reality, Hitler was committed to radically transforming the world through military conquest. Similarly, it is hard to think of a system more productive of change than capitalism—it is, in the words of historian Joyce Applebee, a force of "relentless revolution"—and yet we often call advocates of capitalism "right wing."[30] To complicate matters further, Hitler, like his counterparts in militarist Japan, was opposed to capitalism (he was, after all, the leader of the National Socialist Party), so it is either the case that Hitler was "left wing," advocates of capitalism are "left wing," or there is no "change essence" behind ideology.[31]

Recent studies further refute these essentialist stories by showing that liberals and conservatives are equally opposed to or accepting of change, depending upon the issue. If the status quo is pro-choice, those on the left want to conserve it; if the status quo is low tax, those on the right want to conserve it.[32] And if conservation is the essence of the right, then why is conserving the environment a cause of the left? The reality is that "Both conservatives and liberals resist and accept societal changes, depending on the extent to which they approve or disapprove of the status quo on a given sociopolitical issue" and there is "no evidence for a one-directional association between political orientation and the tendency to accept or resist change."[33] Psychologists Jeff Greenberg and Eva Jonas correctly note that "political conservatives are constantly clamoring for change."[34] The terms "conservative" and "progressive," it turns out, are misnomers.

At this point, essentialists might counter that while those on the right often do pursue policies of change, it is always in the name of going back to a previous state of affairs or some old fashioned set of values. The right, in other words, is "backward looking" while the left is "forward looking."[35]

This claim also fails to stand up to scrutiny. When out of power, both progressives and conservatives promise to reverse the actions of their adversaries and thereby "go backward" to a previous state of affairs.[36] No value is more "old fashioned" than giving aid to the poor (it shows up in the most ancient religious and ethical texts), and yet those on the left pride themselves on favoring anti-poverty initiatives more than those on the right. Moreover, Yuval Levin, Brink Lindsey, and others have shown that both liberals and conservatives are backward-looking and nostalgic depending on the issue.[37] For every "conservative" Milton Friedman looking backward to the less regulated economy of the 1920s, there is a "liberal" Paul Krugman looking backward to the more regulated economy of the 1950s. "Right-wing" libertarians, such as Jimmy Wales, Peter Thiel, and George Gilder, look forward to a technological future unshackled from stifling government control,[38] while "left-wing" communitarians, such as Karl Marx and Jean Jacques Rousseau, looked backward to a happy time before private property corrupted humanity.[39]

In the past generation alone, both the left and the right have been pro-change at different times and on different issues. Ronald Reagan often quoted the radical revolutionary Thomas Paine, saying, "We have it in our power to begin the world over again"—pro-change sentiments indeed from the leading hero of the modern American right.[40] Two of the top futurologists of the late twentieth century, Herman Kahn and Alvin Toffler, were also leading lights in conservative circles. Right-wing congressman Newt Gingrich employed the rhetoric of "winning the future" more than any other national leader of his time and, as Speaker of the House, he assigned Toffler's books to members of Congress.[41] Few things could be more "future oriented" than the integration of the world economy, and yet self-described leftists have held anti-globalization protests at international economic summits, noting (correctly) that globalization radically changes societies and upsets local traditions.[42]

Declaring someone or something "forward looking" also assumes we know the future. We don't.[43] If we did, our track record of prediction as a species wouldn't be so poor. The "forward-backward" essence fails as completely as does the "change-preserve" essence.[44]

Despite the storytelling to the contrary, it should be clear that those in both the left- and right-wing tribes want to preserve what they like and change what they don't like. Nearly everyone, regardless of political persuasion, believes in changing things that are bad and preserving things that are good—they just disagree about what is bad and what is good. Stories about left-wingers being in favor of change are not evidence for the truth of the essentialist theory any more than stories about Leos being courageous are evidence for the truth of astrology.[45] We humans love to spin narratives—we are the storytelling species after all—but essentialist narratives are not evidence of much other than our desire to see signals where there is only noise.

An analogy can further illustrate the problems of the essentialist theory. Imagine someone claimed the following:

> There are two types of teenagers in America: Jocks and Nerds. Jocks are athletic, dumb, and attractive while Nerds are clumsy, smart, and ugly. Those of moderate looks, athleticism, and intelligence fall in the middle between the Jock–Nerd extremes. All high school students and groups can be placed somewhere on this "teenage spectrum."

Most people would immediately realize that this does not accurately describe high schoolers, most obviously because there is no necessary connection between these three characteristics. This teenage spectrum says that athleticism, good looks, and stupidity necessarily go together, but, in fact, they are completely independent of one another. Regardless of what the stereotypes say, someone can be both smart and athletic or smart and attractive. The idea that our intelligence will decline if we play sports or that we will get uglier if we study is manifestly absurd.

Likewise, there is no necessary connection between the fiscal, social, and foreign policy realms of politics.[46] Someone can be against both government intervention in the economy and military intervention in foreign countries.[47] There is no more a natural correlation between what someone thinks about abortion and what they think about wealth redistribution than there is between someone's ability to do math and run fast.[48] An essentialist view of the political spectrum, like an essentialist view of the teenage spectrum, erroneously bundles together matters that are distinct.[49]

If high school Jocks and Nerds sorted themselves into competing tribes, would the teenage spectrum be useful in describing those tribal affinities? Yes, but that's all it would indicate. It would say nothing about an "essence" tying together the unrelated characteristics of looks, athleticism, and intelligence. The same is true of the political spectrum: it effectively models commitments to tribes, but not commitments to an essence. People have sorted themselves into two tribes and a spectrum can measure their tribal commitment, but it tells us nothing about an essential connection between the social, foreign, and fiscal realms of politics—such a connection does not exist.

And it's not just that those three realms do not cohere with each other; they don't even cohere with themselves. Just as there are many ways to be smart, athletic, and attractive, so there are many ways to approach social, foreign, and economic policy. A teenager might be good at math but bad at writing, good at swimming but bad at basketball, attractive in appearance but unattractive in demeanor. Likewise, a voter might be against abortion but also against a border wall. in favor of a minimum wage but against higher taxes, against the Iraq War but also in favor of a strong military.

In the realm of social policy alone there are hundreds of distinct and unrelated issues, such as free speech, immigration, gay marriage, drug restriction, racial justice, abortion, law enforcement, and religious liberty, and yet we still use the term "socially conservative" or "socially liberal" as if all these disparate issues were one. Is someone who favors both gay marriage and stronger border enforcement socially "right wing" or "left wing"? The question itself, like the model that frames it, is meaningless. When we are dealing with an abundance of distinct political concepts, it is overly simplistic to speak about politics as if it is about just one essential issue.

As this analogy shows, the rise of a left–right spectrum has also meant the concomitant rise of an essentialist illusion. Americans have sorted themselves into left–right categories and convinced themselves that a philosophy underlies all of the unrelated issues they embrace. Although the tribes have coalesced around "left–right," "liberal–conservative" concepts, these concepts are as fictional as are Jock and Nerd. There is no essence uniting the Jocks or the Nerds; there is no essence uniting liberals or conservatives.

But isn't the essentialist view of ideology necessary to bring order to the complexity of politics? No more than an essentialist view of teenagers is necessary to bring order to the complexity of high school.[50] Real-life adolescents manage just fine with more than two categories of high-school students; doctors manage just fine with more than two categories of illness; workers manage just fine with more than two job types; and those getting dressed manage just fine with more than two outfits. Why, then, should we assume that citizens will freeze up with confusion if presented with more than two political categories? Few of us would entertain the idea that all medical issues can be reduced to just two sides—with all doctors, patients, and treatments sharing one of two essences—and yet most of us accept the equally strange idea that all political issues can be reduced to just two sides. In this, essentialism violates basic common sense and yet we rarely stop to consider the absurdity we perpetuate by using it as our guiding framework.

Not only is essentialism simplistic, it also leads to conformism and hostility. Since tribal stereotypes tend to become self-fulfilling, the rise of a teenage spectrum would lead athletic kids who identified as Jocks to band together, stop studying, and turn hostile toward the Nerds, and would lead smart kids who identified as Nerds to band together, stop playing sports, and turn hostile toward the Jocks. The traits attributed to each side—even though they do not have a *natural* connection—would begin to correlate for *social* reasons. Simply believing in Jock–Nerd essentialism would not only create hostility, it would also cause young people to conform to group expectations and waste their talents and efforts.

This is exactly what has happened in politics. Thanks to the essentialist way of thinking, Americans have coalesced into two opposing tribes with all of the conformism and rancor this entails. Unrelated issue positions have begun to correlate among the politically engaged, not because they naturally go together but because those identifying with left and right tend to fall in line with whatever their tribe favors at a given moment.[51] These tribal identities trigger the most atavistic of human impulses and lead ideologues to hate those on the "other side." Simply believing in left–right essentialism has fanned the flames of discord and wasted the talents and efforts of millions of Americans.[52] Policy disagreements can be real and divisive, but that animosity is amplified when the policy is bound up with a binary identity taken from an essentialist illusion. Sadly, millions of Americans organize their lives, their loves, their hates, and their very identities around this destructive fiction.[53]

This is of more than just incidental importance, since our paradigms exert a powerful influence on our thoughts and actions. Although everyone must rely on simplified models of reality in order to function, some models are misleading and do more harm than good.

The essentialist theory of ideology is simple and elegant, but also tragically wrong. It is not just an imperfect model but a positively harmful one that is responsible for much of the ignorance, confusion, and hostility that characterizes contemporary political discourse. Just as the four humors theory led doctors to bleed their patients to death in previous centuries, essentialism is bleeding our republic to death today. We are incapable of finding solutions to our most pressing social problems because an incorrect paradigm is preventing us from even asking the right questions.

This chapter has shown that, of the two theories that explain the uniting of distinct political positions into bundles ("ideologies"), the social theory is far more plausible than the essentialist theory.[54] There is plenty of evidence that tribalism is natural, but there is no evidence that left–right political categories are natural.[55] To be useful, terms must be predictive, but the terms "left," "liberal," "right," and "conservative" are only predictive in a social sense, not an essentialist sense. They indicate *who* we support across contexts (a tribe), but not *what* we support (principles). Ideological essentialism—no matter how attractive for its simplicity and pervasiveness—cannot stand up to scrutiny. We can either cling to a false essentialist paradigm by telling convoluted and contradictory *ex post* stories, or we can confront the reality that ideological terms are tribal rather than essential and that "left-wing," "right-wing," "liberal," and "conservative" are entirely social designations.[56]

|| 2 ||

The Origins of Left and Right

While the first chapter made clear that left–right ideology is a social construct, this chapter will show *how* it was constructed. We explain the origins and early evolution of the political spectrum in America and ultimately show that the radical changes in the meanings of left and right further validate the social theory of ideology.

The Rise of the Spectrum in Europe

Using the words "left" and "right" in a political context first emerged during the French Revolution when supporters of the revolution sat on the left-hand side of the National Assembly and opponents of the revolution sat on the right-hand side. This terminology became entrenched in French politics when the Chamber of Deputies continued to seat themselves in this way during the Bourbon Restoration. Eventually, the terms "left" and "right" became political identities among French citizens rather than simply labels applied to their representatives in the legislature.[1]

During the nineteenth century, this usage spread around continental Europe, but its most consequential adoption was by the Bolsheviks in early twentieth-century Russia. The Russian Revolutionaries saw themselves as pursuing the same cause as the French Revolutionaries 130 years earlier. They identified themselves with the cause of egalitarian revolution—what they believed to be an inevitable product of historical forces—and their opponents with hopeless reaction against the direction of history.[2]

The Myth of Left and Right. Hyrum Lewis and Verlan Lewis, Oxford University Press. © Oxford University Press 2023.
DOI: 10.1093/oso/9780197680216.003.0003

The Absence of the Spectrum in America

But even though the spectrum was present in Europe after the French Revolution, it did not migrate across the Atlantic to the United States until much later. Before the 1920s, Americans did not think in terms of a political spectrum. There were simply two parties which stood for different political principles at different historical moments. Any talk of earlier figures being on the left or right is the work of later historians anachronistically imposing the political spectrum on people who did not think in those categories.[3]

For example, at the time of the American Revolution, the revolutionary Whigs ("liberal" and "left wing" according to later historians) believed that God had endowed human beings with equal natural rights to life, liberty, and property. This natural rights philosophy led them to advocate for limited government, lower taxes, and free markets. They formed revolutionary militias to combat a powerful central government that they believed had acted tyrannically in regulating the colonial economies and levying burdensome taxes that did not respect their property rights. The loyalist Tories, on the other hand ("conservative" and "right wing" according to later historians), defended the virtues of centralized government and economic regulation.[4] Given the contemporary meanings of "left" and "right," these labels are misleading with respect to the political beliefs of the American revolutionary generation if we assume an essential left and right that makes them somehow analogous to contemporary Americans.[5]

After the ratification of the Constitution, political parties emerged and began an evolutionary process that went through four distinct phases or "party eras." During the First Party System—in the years of the early republic—the Jeffersonian Republicans believed in laissez-faire economics (as Jefferson put it in his first inaugural address, the government should leave individuals "free to regulate their own pursuits of industry and improvement"),[6] while the Hamiltonian Federalists believed in a more powerful national government that would increase taxes, increase federal spending, and control the American economy.[7] Historians who routinely refer to Jeffersonians as "on the left" and Hamiltonians as "on the right" are using current-day ideological categories to describe people of the past who did not use those terms and who embraced different principles. Too often, historians assume that those on the left throughout American history share an essence with Jeffersonian Republicans and those on the right share an essence with Hamiltonian Federalists, but this essence does not exist.[8]

In the Second Party System—during the antebellum period—the Jacksonian Democratic Party called for the forcible removal of Native Americans from their ancestral homelands, defended slavery, called for the military conquest of Mexico, and advocated laissez-faire economic policy. The Whig Party, on the other hand, called for a more conciliatory policy toward Native Americans and Mexico, more government control of the economy, limitations on human slavery, and increased federal spending. And yet, strangely, historians tell us that Jacksonian Democrats share a "left-wing" essence with today's Democrats and that the Whig Party shares a "right wing" essence with today's Republicans.[9]

During the Third Party System—at the time of the Civil War and its aftermath—both parties saw themselves as allies of democracy. Lincoln's party chose the name "Republican" to remind people of Jefferson's Republican Party and the Jeffersonian principle of the equality of all men. The opposing party continued to use the name "Democratic" to indicate their preference for majority rule on the state level (even if that meant tyrannizing the minority). Nonetheless, today's political scientists confusingly identify the Republican Party of the late nineteenth century as extremely "conservative" and the Democratic Party of the time as extremely "liberal."[10]

The crucial point here is that even though twentieth-century historians imposed the left–right framework on these figures of the past, the historical actors did not think of themselves in those terms. Pre-1900 Americans conceived of themselves as "Whigs," "Federalists," "Republicans," "Nationalists," "Democrats," and "Unionists"—indicating their opposition to monarchy, their support for a federal union, or their opposition to aristocracy—but not as "left-wing" or "right-wing." Americans back then simply did not think in terms of a political spectrum.

The Rise of the Spectrum in America

This would change in the twentieth century. The first hint of the emerging ideological approach to politics came in the Civil War years when the words "liberal" and "conservative" first entered the American political lexicon. Initially, they had no left–right connotations and "liberal" simply referred to those who, like the Liberals in England, advocated for free trade, limited government, and civil service reform, while "conservative" was synonymous with "moderate."[11]

But around the turn of the century, "liberal" evolved to take on more and more pro-government connotations, eventually becoming a synonym for "progressive."[12] Both major parties had insurgent progressive factions within them and both had nominated reformers to the presidency (William Jennings Bryan and Teddy Roosevelt). These progressive reformers tended to be more in favor of national government power, higher taxes, more spending on social welfare programs, and greater government regulation of the economy.[13] The leading self-proclaimed liberal of late nineteenth-century America, *Nation* editor E. L. Godkin, lamented this shift. He believed that the essence of liberalism was freeing the individual from the "vexatious meddling of government," but saw that many self-proclaimed liberals were making "common cause with the socialists."[14] He, like many essentialists since, had a hard time realizing that ideological labels will often evolve to mean the opposite of what they once did. But crucially, although "liberalism" was evolving to stand for opposite policies, the narrative of "progress" and "reform" remained constant. Then, as now, the "change" trope was capacious enough to encompass any policies that anyone wanted to christen "liberal" through *ex post* storytelling.

Even though the words "progressive," "liberal," and "conservative" were prevalent in American politics around the turn of the century, there was no concept of a political spectrum. People in the United States used the terms "left wing" and "right wing" in reference to sports, architecture, military formations, or aviation, but not politics.[15] The followers of Teddy Roosevelt, for instance, were routinely referred to as "progressives," but not "left wing." Henry George, William Jennings Bryan, and their followers were called "radicals" or "socialists" in their time, but only referred to as "left wing" by later writers.[16] The political spectrum was absent from the American collective consciousness for the first 140 years of the nation's history.

This changed in the decade 1916–1926 when the political spectrum crossed the Atlantic and became central to American political discourse. This happened in three phases that we call "reporting" (1916–1918), "importing" (1919), and "domesticating" (1920–1926). In the "reporting" phase, American journalists began using the terms "left" and "right" to describe the competing factions of socialists in the Russian Revolution.[17] Since Bolsheviks placed the different socialist schisms on a left–right spectrum, Americans reporting on the Russian revolution naturally used those same categories when writing about the revolution for their American audiences. Even so, from 1916 to 1918, the use of the political spectrum was confined to reporting on foreign affairs and had no application to American politicians, parties, policies, activists, or institutions.

During the "importing" phase in 1919, journalists began applying the left–right terms not only to the competing factions of Russian socialists but also to the competing factions of American socialists. This was particularly common among Marxists in the United States. As champions of the Soviet cause, writers such as Lincoln Steffens, Max Eastman, and John Reed began employing a left–right spectrum when describing the American socialist movement, hoping that importing the Russian political framework would also help import the Russian political system.[18] In June 1919, Eastman exulted that "at last, even in the United States, we have a Left Wing, with its own organization, and its own spokesmen, and its own press."[19] Although Marxists celebrated the importation of the spectrum to America, mainstream journalists remained uncomfortable referring to American politics using this European paradigm and, as a way to underscore its foreignness, generally used quotation marks or the phrase "so-called" when talking about "left" and "right."[20] But regardless of political persuasion, Americans in 1919 used the political spectrum exclusively as a way to refer to competing factions of socialists—it hadn't yet begun to have associations with mainstream ideologies or parties.[21]

That changed during the "domesticating" phase. In the early 1920s, the political spectrum went mainstream and began to be associated with the common American ideological terms ("progressive," "liberal," and "conservative"). This domestication began with various third-party movements that were said to have "left" and "right" wings, but by the early 1920s, the spectrum was being used to describe divisions within the two main parties themselves.[22] Senator Robert LaFollette was a major figure in this transition. Ever since Teddy Roosevelt stepped down from the presidency, LaFollette had been the leader of the "progressive" movement within the Republican Party. After a brief flirtation with a third party in 1920, LaFollette returned and created what he called a "left–right" split among Republicans that pitted "progressives" against "conservatives."[23] When a similar split developed in the Democratic Party, the process was complete: the political spectrum had migrated out of socialist discourse and into the two major parties and, more importantly, had been grafted onto the longstanding ideological terms to indicate more government intervention in the economy ("left wing" and "progressive") or less ("right wing" and "conservative").[24]

Even as progressive politicians were imposing the political spectrum on the American present, progressive historians began imposing the political spectrum on the American past. Historians Vernon Parrington, Charles Beard, and Carl Becker were instrumental in spreading the political spectrum to intellectual circles by applying the left–right and liberal–conservative labels to American historical figures. They began writing history that placed the revolutionary Whigs, Anti-Federalists, Jeffersonian Republicans, Democratic Republicans, and Democrats on the left and the loyalist Tories, Federalists, National Republicans, Whigs, and Lincoln Republicans on the right.[25] History is a major force for shaping identity, and by rewriting history using the political spectrum the progressive historians helped create a greater sense of left–right identification among Americans.

So, although the spectrum in America had originally been used exclusively to report on the divisions between European socialists, it was then imported to refer to competing American socialist factions, and finally, by the early 1920s, had been domesticated to apply to the question of more versus less government intervention—the issue that would dominate American political discourse and define "liberal" and "conservative" for a generation.

Ideological Parties

By the late 1920s, only one piece of today's ideological system was missing: ideological parties. There were ideological terms (progressive–conservative), there was a political spectrum (left–right), but the parties were not yet identified with one side of this spectrum or the other. There were politicians in both parties who accepted the "progressive" moniker and sought to increase income taxes, government spending on social programs, and the federal government's role in facilitating "cooperation" among industries.[26] Both candidates in the 1932 presidential election considered themselves "liberals," but the term "liberal" had not fully completed its transformation from the nineteenth-century meaning. The liberal Democrat Franklin D. Roosevelt criticized the incumbent progressive Herbert Hoover for believing "that we ought to center control of everything in Washington as rapidly as possible" and proposed instead a "reduction in Federal spending as . . . the most direct and effective contribution that Government can make to business."[27] In 1932, it was not just the presidency but liberalism itself that was up for grabs—which of the two parties would seize it?[28]

Franklin Roosevelt settled the matter during his first term. When Roosevelt rolled out the New Deal, despite his campaign rhetoric, the Democratic Party became the party of activist government and therefore the institutional home of "progressives," "the left," and the "new liberalism."[29] Roosevelt's New Deal was revolutionary not only in transforming the role of the federal government, but also in transforming American political discourse and introducing the Fourth Party System.[30] During the New Deal, the language of "liberal" and "conservative," "left" and "right," increasingly descended from the ivory tower into ordinary political discourse. The public had come to identify "liberal" with "the left" and the Democratic Party, and "conservative" with "the right" and the Republican Party.[31]

Even so, there were dissenters within each party. Many old-line "progressive" Republicans supported the New Deal while a number of Democrats opposed it.[32] An outraged Al Smith, the Democratic Party's 1928 presidential candidate and now its leading "conservative," spoke of what he saw as the New Deal's perfidy, saying, "It is all right with me if they want to disguise themselves as Norman Thomas or Karl Marx, or Lenin, or any of the rest of that bunch, but what I won't stand for is to let them march under the banner of Jefferson, Jackson, or Cleveland."[33] These dissenters notwithstanding, the party lines had been drawn: in the public mind, the Democratic Party was now "liberal," and relatively "left," while the Republican Party was "conservative" and relatively "right."[34]

While intellectual supporters of the New Deal had no problem calling themselves "liberal," many of its intellectual opponents were initially reluctant to embrace the label "conservative," preferring to call themselves either "individualists"—to set themselves apart from the "collectivists" in the Democratic Party—or "true liberals," indicating their belief that the New Dealers had apostatized from the "true liberal" Jeffersonian faith.[35] Throughout the thirties and forties, intellectual opponents of the New Deal held out against the labels "conservative" and "right-wing."[36] While they opposed statist policies, they did so using the narrative tropes of liberalism, arguing that, in fact, free markets were the drivers of progressive change in society.[37]

This began to change in the postwar years when a handful of political theorists began to wear the conservative label as a badge of honor and invented a narrative of preservation to match the liberal narrative of change. The first prominent figure to do so was Peter Viereck, a professor of history at Mt. Holyoke College who would later win a Pulitzer Prize for poetry. In his 1949 book, *Conservatism Revisited*, he argued that there was a long, venerable history of conservative thought in the European tradition that he was proud to identify with.[38] For Viereck, a conservative was someone who opposed revolutions, and if revolutions could be destructive, then conservatism was a respectable intellectual position and conservative was a respectable political identity.[39] For Viereck, conservation of what was good in Western civilization against the modern revolutions of both fascism and communism was the task of conservatives.[40]

Like Viereck, historian Russell Kirk also embraced the conservative identity and tried to give it a respectable pedigree by attaching the label "conservative" to intellectual heavyweights like Edmund Burke, Alexander Hamilton, John Adams, John Randolph, Samuel Taylor Coleridge, Sir Walter Scott, Nathaniel Hawthorne, and Walter Bagehot. But Kirk went further than Viereck by accepting the connection between conservatism and the anti–New Deal agenda of the Republican Party.[41] If the New Deal was left-wing and liberal, said Kirk, then those who opposed it could proudly identify as right-wing and conservative. Kirk had adopted the progressive historians' characterization of American party history as divided between a "liberal left" and a "conservative right," but, unlike them, he identified proudly with the right. In 1955, Kirk helped found the *National Review* magazine with another young author, William F. Buckley Jr., and started a "conservative" intellectual movement that accepted a position at the right side of a political spectrum from where its proponents would "stand athwart history yelling 'stop.'"[42]

Viereck, Kirk, and Buckley had birthed a conservative narrative of tradition and caution to match the liberal narrative of reform and progress. This narrative could have just as easily been attached to the policies of the opposite party (indeed, Viereck remained a Democrat and claimed that the New Deal was "conservative"), but it became the dominant framework for the *ex post* story-telling that has tied together all Republican policies up to the present. Politics at the time was unidimensional (more versus less government), but the narrative tropes of each side were sufficiently vague and capacious ("change" versus "conserve") to encompass any new dimensions of politics that would emerge over the subsequent decades. The policies associated with each side would evolve and even reverse over the decades, but the "languages of politics" would remain, thus giving the illusion of philosophical consistency to inconsistent political positions.[43]

Thus, by the early 1950s, the ideological system that persists to this day was in place: there were ideological labels ("liberal" and "conservative") bound up with an ideological political spectrum ("left" and "right") that was attached to ideological political parties (Democratic and Republican).[44] Although there were more dissenters from the party lines in those days (e.g., "conservative Democrats" and "liberal Republicans"), the party lines themselves had come to define what it meant to be "conservative" and "liberal."[45] A "liberal Republican," such as Dwight D. Eisenhower, was simply someone lukewarm to the party's smaller government stance, while a "conservative Democrat," such as Martin Dies, was simply someone lukewarm to the party's larger government stance.[46] Liberal-left had become synonymous with what the Democratic Party stood for, while conservative-right had become synonymous with what the Republican Party stood for.[47]

This has been the case ever since. Today, a liberal is someone committed fully (rather than moderately or selectively) to the Democratic agenda and a conservative is someone committed fully (rather than moderately or selectively) to the Republican agenda. While there are differences of degree—many conservatives wish the Republicans would go farther with their platform and many liberals wish the Democrats would go farther with theirs—there are no differences in kind. The Democratic Party largely stands for liberalism and the Republican Party largely stands for conservatism, and it has been that way since the New Deal.

But even though the parties had undergone ideological sorting during the New Deal era, there is an important difference between their time and ours: back then, the political spectrum modeled only a single dimension of politics. A uni-dimensional model can represent a unidimensional reality and, during the 1930s and 1940s, national politics was primarily about just one issue—the size of government. The New Deal so dominated national political discourse that all other issues were peripheral and debated non-ideologically at the local level.[48] In 1940, if someone was asked, "Do you think we should move to the left?" or "Do you think we should be more liberal?" they understood it to mean, "Do you believe we should expand the size of government?"[49] Issues such as abortion, gay marriage, affirmative action, environmentalism, McCarthyism, or the Vietnam War didn't cross their minds—those hadn't yet appeared on the national political landscape.[50] Not even civil rights were on the table, and describing southern segregationist Democrats of the 1930s as being "conservative" is anachronistic.[51] "Conservative" only referred to opponents of the New Deal, and inasmuch as southern Democrats supported Roosevelt's economic policies they were considered part of the "liberal" coalition.[52] Then, as now, liberals wrapped their political views in a heroic narrative—the forces of enlightened "progress" overcoming the forces of backwardness and "reaction"—but this story was put to work in the service of a single cause: advancing the economic reforms associated with the New Deal.[53]

Since the political spectrum simply modeled more versus less government, and since it provided a useful shorthand to indicate where someone stood on this one question, Americans used the terms "left" and "right" with ever-greater frequency throughout the 1930s and 1940s.[54] At that point, there was just one issue that bound together the people, ideas, and institutions of each side. For a brief moment in American history, the political spectrum effectively modeled a single dimension of politics. As we will see in the next chapter, it wouldn't stay that way.

The Development of Left and Right

In the years after World War II, new issues beyond "more versus less government" arose to complicate American political discourse and render the political spectrum obsolete. The addition of these new dimensions to American politics led directly to the myth of left and right that has been the source of so much confusion and hostility in contemporary public life.

Becoming Multidimensional

It began with the rise of conservative militarism. During the first half of the twentieth century, liberal/left/Democrats were typically more hawkish while conservative/right/Republicans were typically more dovish. Liberal Democrat Woodrow Wilson took America into World War I, liberal Democrat Franklin Roosevelt took America into World War II, and liberal Democrat Harry Truman took America into the Korean War.[1] In both rhetoric and practice, liberal Democrats were more interventionist in foreign policy while conservative Republicans were more isolationist. Conservatives even created pacifist organizations such as America First, and routinely criticized Democrats as "warmongers."[2]

At that point, the political spectrum still measured principle (size of government) and not just tribe, since foreign wars meant an expansion of government power. The military dimension mapped onto the left versus right framework, since both the New Deal and military buildup expanded the size of government.[3] Liberal foreign policy (more government) matched liberal domestic policy (more government), and conservative foreign policy (less government) matched conservative domestic policy (less government).[4] As late as 1952, the political spectrum was still accurately modeling the "one big issue" that divided Americans.

The Myth of Left and Right. Hyrum Lewis and Verlan Lewis, Oxford University Press. © Oxford University Press 2023.
DOI: 10.1093/oso/9780197680216.003.0004

During the 1950s it all began to unravel. Because the right/conservatives/ Republicans had defined themselves by a commitment to economic freedom, they had a special dislike for communism as the antithesis of their free-market ideology. Conservatives like Whittaker Chambers and William F. Buckley Jr. believed that the fight against communism was simply the fight against New Deal liberalism raised to another level.[5] Since, in their view, both the New Deal and communism threatened economic freedom, both had to be vigorously opposed. Accordingly, Buckley and other champions of the right began to break with their small government principles in the name of rooting out communist subversion. They supported government infringements on privacy, civil liberties, and free speech, believing that this sacrifice of freedom was necessary to preserve a free government from communist overthrow.[6] As they saw it, they had to violate individual rights in order to save them. In the words of Marxist-turned-conservative Max Eastman, "We are fighting this cold war for our life, and we must fight on all fronts and in every field of action."[7] At that moment, conservatives had crossed the Rubicon: they were now advocating, in one realm at least, an expansion of government power.

At first, this conservative anti-communism only played out domestically in the infamous "red hunts" conducted by Senator McCarthy and the House Un-American Activities Committee in the early 1950s, but over the next decade, it would evolve into an interventionist foreign policy stance. Conservative Republicans went from criticizing liberal Democrats for being too hawkish in the 1930s to criticizing them for not being hawkish enough in the 1960s.[8] Liberals steadily backed away from the militarism that had been central to their ideology during World War II, and, by the late 1960s (after the Vietnam War had gone sour), they had become more pacifist than conservatives. The same way economic interventionism was contested between the parties until FDR settled the issue with his New Deal, so hawkishness was contested between the two ideologies until the Vietnam War settled the issue.[9] In 1972, Democratic presidential nominee George McGovern ran on an explicitly anti-war platform, thus completing liberalism's transition from foreign policy interventionism to isolationism. "Neoconservatives" who began to identify with the right in the 1970s were "neo" for a reason: their foreign policy views had aligned them with the left until Democrats became more dovish than Republicans during the Vietnam War.[10]

Just at the moment Democrats were abandoning hawkishness, new social issues were emerging to further complicate the political landscape. In the early twentieth century, many social issues that would later be identified with the right had been more associated with the left. Progressives were more likely to favor Prohibition, censorship, and racist eugenic policies than those on the right, and, by the standard measures of congressional ideology, segregationist Southerners were the most reliably left-wing members of the Democratic Party.[11] Heroes of the "conservative" tradition, such as Alexander Hamilton, Henry Clay, and William Howard Taft, had far more enlightened racial views than their "liberal" rivals Thomas Jefferson, Andrew Jackson, and Woodrow Wilson—showing that not even racial equality is an "essential" liberal principle.[12] Issues considered "socially conservative" today were not associated with conservatism at all in the early twentieth century.[13]

This changed in the 1960s and 1970s when Republicans decided to capitalize on public anger at Supreme Court decisions (e.g., *Abington v. Schempp*, *Engel v. Vitale*, and *Roe v. Wade*) by adding a number of social positions to their platform as a way to draw southern and religious voters to their side.[14] Since the inception of the ideological-party system in the New Deal, highly religious voters had generally been allied with the left, and according to historian Doug Koopman, "The Social Gospel provided the philosophical basis for the New Deal and Democratic supremacy from the 1930s through the 1960s."[15]

Beginning in the sixties and seventies, Republicans increasingly tied the social issues associated with Christianity to their ideology. This alienated prominent secular libertarians such as Ayn Rand, Friedrich Hayek, and Max Eastman, but attracted evangelicals such as Jerry Falwell, Pat Robertson, Ralph Reed, and their millions of supporters. Thus, the Religious Right was borns.[16]

The conservative capture of militarism and Christian social issues meant that by the late 1970s, the "more versus less" government spectrum had become obsolete. Expansion of government was now context-dependent: the liberal/Democratic/left wanted more government when it came to fiscal policy, but the conservative/Republican/right wanted more government when it came to foreign policy and most aspects of social policy. There were now multiple dimensions to politics, and which party favored more or less government depended entirely upon the issue. Republicans continued to trot out the same attacks on "big government" they had used since the New Deal, but, by the early twenty-first century, this was all rhetorical posturing—they had become just as favorable to expanding government power as Democrats when it came to fiscal policy and more so when it came to foreign and social policy. There was no longer a single issue that defined politics but many distinct issues that could not be modeled on a single-issue spectrum.

But even as more dimensions were added to politics, *Americans retained their old unidimensional model.* The ideological landscape had changed, but the map of the landscape had not. The political reality outgrew the political framework in the late twentieth century when a proliferation of new political issues rendered a unidimensional approach to politics obsolete, and yet ideologues wouldn't face up to this reality: they wanted to believe that their side was right about everything and the other wrong about everything. Partisans of left and right began to invoke ad hoc narratives to save their essentialist understanding of the spectrum from falsification. Public intellectuals got ever more creative in making up stories about how this new pluralism was an illusion, insisting that there simply had to be a single philosophy uniting everything that each party stood for—a "liberal" philosophy to unite everything in the Democratic Party platform and a "conservative" philosophy to unite everything in the Republican Party platform.[17] Thus was born ideological essentialism and the self-contradictory, *ex post* storytelling that it entails. The self-deception to justify tribalism had begun.

The Essentialist Theory and Political Parties

The preceding account of the development of left and right not only substantiates the social theory of ideology, but it forces us to reconceptualize the relationship of our two political parties to left–right ideologies. In the essentialist theory, parties can move "leftward" or "rightward" on the spectrum as they change their relationship to the single essential issue, but under the social theory the parties largely *define* the ideologies. The social theory predicts that since left and right are tribal designations and the two parties are the central social organizations that unite the tribes, then left and right will often be defined by whatever their associated parties stand for at a given moment.

The essentialist theory, it turns out, is as mistaken about parties as it is about ideologies. Essentialists making the argument that the parties have moved "leftward" or "rightward" can only do so by redefining the essence of left and right to fit whatever the parties happen to be doing at a given moment. In the McCarthy era, for instance, essentialists insisted that free speech was an essential principle of the liberal left, and yet when Democrats later reversed course and turned against free speech, essentialists still called it a move "to the left."[18]

When the Republican Party moved in a small-government direction under Barry Goldwater, the essentialists called it a move "to the right,"[19] but when the Republican Party moved in a big-government direction under George W. Bush and Donald Trump, they also called it a move "to the right."[20] When the Republican Party moved to foreign interventionism under Bush, they said it was a move "to the right,"[21] but when the Republican Party moved to foreign isolationism under Trump, they also said it was a move "to the right."[22] When the Republican Party moved in a globalist direction under Reagan, they said it was a move "to the right," but when the Republican Party moved in a protectionist direction under Trump, they also said it was a move "to the right."[23] No matter what Republicans do—even when they pursue opposite policies—essentialists invariably tell us that it's a move "to the right."[24] Strangely, these scholars argue that the Republican Party has moved to the "extreme right" in the last decade even as Republicans have become much more favorable to gay marriage, minimum wages, free speech, government regulation of the economy, and social welfare spending, while also becoming more opposed to the Iraq War, big corporations, capital punishment, free trade, and laissez-faire capitalism.[25] So either there is an essential set of conservative principles—in which case the Republican party has moved unambiguously to the left on many (if not most) issues—or there is no consistent set of principles that defines the left and right—in which case it's meaningless to talk about the Republican Party moving leftward or rightward. Yes, the Republican Party is always changing, but, no, there is no set of fixed, essential, "right-wing principles" that it is changing toward.

The essentialist method amounts to this: "Tell me what the Republican Party is doing, and I will define this as 'the right' and then conclude that the Republican Party has moved to the right." This is not informative; it is tautological. It only tells us "The Democrat and Republican parties are doing what the Democrat and Republican parties are doing." Starting with a conclusion and then redefining terms until the conclusion becomes true is classic circular reasoning.

It's conventional wisdom that George W. Bush pulled the Republican Party "to the right" during his two terms as president,[26] but such a position requires a redefinition of "the right" to fit Bush's actions ("Bush is on the far right because Bush is acting like Bush").[27] From 2001 to 2009, the Republican president and Congress set records for expanding federal government power and spending but at the same time, according to the conventional wisdom, the Republican Party moved to the "extreme right." If, instead of engaging in circular reasoning, we use a fixed, measurable definition of the right, such as limited government, we find that Bush moved the Republican Party decisively and unambiguously to the extreme left. [28] Rather than face up to the implications of essentialism, too many of us escape into tautology.[29]

We find historians making the same error when covering earlier periods. Essentialists say that since "conservative" Goldwater lost in a landslide in 1964 while "conservative" Reagan won in a landslide in 1984, the country must have moved "to the right" during the intervening two decades.[30] The problem is that they are mistaking *tribal labels* for *substance*. Goldwater and Reagan belonged to the same tribe and carried the same ideological label ("conservative") but did not run on the same policies. Goldwater wanted to roll back the New Deal, opposed civil rights legislation, favored abortion rights, and opposed tax cuts while Reagan took the opposite approach to all of these issues.[31] The same ideological term was attached to different policies. It wasn't that the country or the Republican Party had moved "to the right" to elect Reagan, but that the Republican Party and its associated ideology—conservatism—had evolved to take on more mainstream positions.[32] In arguing that the country has undergone a "rightward shift," historians are mistaking tribal labels for essences.

The conservative divergence from Goldwater has only become more pronounced since Reagan's presidency. Goldwater opposed tax cuts, favored abortion rights and gay rights, and believed in cutting government spending, while George W. Bush favored tax cuts, opposed abortion rights and gay rights, and set records for increasing government spending (with the help of a Republican Congress). Where is the essential conservatism uniting these two politicians who pursued opposite policies? It does not exist.

How could Goldwater have been considered "far right" by holding the "left wing" position on abortion? Because being pro-choice was not considered a left-wing position in 1964. Once again, ideologies evolve. Reagan himself favored abortion rights until the Republican Party turned against it in the 1970s. Goldwater hadn't moved "leftward" and Reagan "rightward" on abortion; it's that abortion was not a left–right issue until *Roe v. Wade*.

In fact, George W. Bush had much more in common with Goldwater's liberal opponent in the 1964 election, Lyndon Johnson, who also pushed through large income tax cuts, vastly increased government spending, and started an unpopular overseas war. Those who argue that Bush moved the Republican Party to the "extreme right" can only do so by redefining "the right" to make it coterminous with what was considered "liberal" in 1964.[33]

This disconnect of the right from limited government became even more pronounced under Donald Trump. Cutting government spending was once seen as essentially "far right," but when Trump promised *not* to cut government spending he was also considered "far right." Donald Trump said during the 2016 campaign, "I'm not going to cut Social Security like every other Republican and I'm not going to cut Medicare or Medicaid. Every other Republican is going to cut."[34] And it wasn't just rhetorical: under Trump, the size of government and the national debt grew far more than under any Democrat in history up to that point.[35]

Furthermore, Republicans under Trump became significantly more favorable to gay rights, economic regulation, minimum wages, pacifism, and restriction of private transactions, so why do essentialists say that Trump moved the Republican Party "to the right"?[36] Because Trump is "right-wing."[37] Again, it's circular reasoning. If a study declared "bachelors are increasingly unmarried," we would all recognize the tautology, and yet we take seriously the studies which make the equally tautologous claim, "Republicans are increasingly right-wing."

We find the same circular reasoning among those who use congressional roll call votes to quantify ideology. In the mid-twentieth century, political scientists began following historians and journalists in analyzing politics in spatial terms like "left" and "right." Notably, in 1957, Anthony Downs adapted Harold Hotelling's spatial modeling of market preferences to the spatial modeling of political preferences running from the "extreme left" to the "extreme right."[38]

While Downs assumed a unidimensional ideological space mirroring the left–right spectrum, other political economists assumed multi-dimensional spaces.[39]

One of the big breakthroughs in this literature was Poole and Rosenthal's inductive approach to spatially modeling ideology. Poole and Rosenthal recorded every roll-call vote cast by every member of Congress in American history, and then used a nominal, three-step estimating scaling application (NOMINATE) to place each vote and each member of Congress in ideological space. They found that a unidimensional spatial spectrum, which they defined as running from liberal on the left to conservative on the right, accurately "predicted" the voting behavior of members of Congress for most of American history (a two-dimensional model was needed at times when racial policy became as important as economic policy).[40]

Of course, to place each member of Congress in ideological space requires choosing "anchor" members in each Congress to identify the "liberal" and "conservative" sides of the spectrum every two years. The choice of these anchors baked in the results because, unsurprisingly, Democrats tend to vote with Democrats and Republicans tend to vote with Republicans (the very definition of a legislative party). Thus, most of the anchor's co-partisans are identified as residing on their same side of the ideological spectrum and most of their cross-partisans are identified as residing on the opposite side. While a spatial model of ideology does not necessarily have to rely on the essentialist theory of ideology, unidimensional spatial models that cover more than one legislative session, like DW-NOMINATE, do exactly that because they make claims about individuals and groups moving "left" and "right" over time. The unexamined assumption here is that left and right have static meanings over time—otherwise, the claims would be nonsensical.[41]

These formal models of ideology stack the deck according to the assumptions posited by historians. When the roll-call vote data is processed (in which, obviously, Democrats tend to vote with Democrats and Republicans tend to vote with Republicans), we find that Democratic members of Congress are overwhelmingly found on the "liberal" side of the ideological spectrum and Republican members of Congress are overwhelmingly found on the "conservative" side. Too many scholars fail to realize that roll-call scaling applications like DW-NOMINATE define "left" and "right" in terms of whatever the Democratic and Republican parties happen to support at a given moment.

In other words, DW-NOMINATE does not measure how the parties fit an exogenous, essential definition of ideology; it only measures how united the members of each party are in their voting. For example, if Democrats vote for a tax cut, DW-NOMINATE codes those votes as "left wing" not because tax cutting is an eternal pillar of left-wing ideology, but simply because Democratic support for a bill defines it as "left wing" in DW-NOMINATE.[42]

Contrary to what the essentialists say, DW-NOMINATE scores actually support the social theory by showing that "liberal" is coterminous with whatever the Democratic Party is doing and "conservative" is coterminous with whatever the Republican Party is doing. Yes, the congressional representatives of each party have become more homogenous in their voting, but this has nothing to do with the parties moving leftward or rightward on a spectrum.[43] Scholars are mistaking party unity for ideological extremism.[44]

The Social Theory and Political Parties

While the essentialist theory makes circular arguments about parties and ideologies, the social theory makes falsifiable predictions. It says that since parties define ideologies, we should find the meaning of ideologies changing to fit party actions. This is exactly what we find. The historical record shows that ideologies are just as mutable as parties and, in recent years, the parties and ideologies have evolved in tandem.[45]

In the past decade alone we've seen self-described conservatives go from being decidedly anti-Russia to decidedly pro-Russia, strongly pro-trade to strongly anti-trade, believing that the personal character of a politician matters a great deal to believing that it matters hardly at all, highly concerned with the budget deficit to highly indifferent to the budget deficit (and back again), interventionist in foreign policy to isolationist, and strongly in favor of big business to strongly critical of big business.[46]

In 2004, at the height of the Iraq War, 54% of self-identified conservatives and 37% of self-identified liberals believed it was best for America to be active in world affairs. A decade later, those numbers had flipped.[47] By 2016, 63% of conservatives were saying they wanted to let other countries deal with their own problems while only 27% of liberals agreed. This right-wing reversal on foreign policy happened with remarkable suddenness. Almost as soon as Bush left office, conservatives came to believe (even more than liberals) that America intervenes too much in the affairs of other nations.[48] As tribal leadership on the right passed from interventionist George W. Bush to isolationist Donald Trump, the views of rank-and-file conservatives changed accordingly. Conservatives supported the War in Iraq in much higher numbers than liberals, not because the War aligned with conservative *principles* but because it aligned with conservative *people*.

We find similar sudden shifts in economic views. From 2015 to 2017 conservative support for free trade dropped by almost 50% while liberal support for free trade rose significantly.[49] For decades, Republicans were considered "far right" for espousing free-market trade policies, but in 2018 Republicans were considered "far right" for espousing anti-trade policies.[50] We could turn to essentialist stories to explain this shift—for example, "Free trade is a longstanding American tradition so naturally conservatives want to conserve free trade" or "Free trade destroys American jobs so naturally conservatives want to conserve jobs by opposing free trade"—but such "heads I win, tails you lose" storytelling has more in common with astrology than with social science. The better and simpler explanation is that conservatives turned away from free trade because they were following protectionist Donald Trump whose rise to leadership of the right coincided exactly with this reversal. We don't need unfalsifiable stories to explain how the essence of the right causes conservatives to favor free trade one minute and oppose it the next; we only need to accept the social theory which predicts that conservatives will conform to whatever the Republican Party happens to be doing.

Views of Russia also switched sides with the rise of Trump. Throughout the Cold War and up until 2016, conservatives had strongly negative views of Russia (and, according to some, a hardline approach to Russia was the defining issue of the right).[51] And yet once Donald Trump began to speak favorably of Putin and Russia, those on the right suddenly became far more pro-Russia than those on the left.[52]

Self-identified conservatives and liberals have also recently switched places on the importance of personal morality in public officials. During the Clinton years, conservatives were nearly unanimous in believing that the personal character of a politician was crucial to his or her performance in office—it was one of their central justifications for impeaching President Clinton—but as soon as Trump assumed leadership of the right, conservatives reversed course.[53] Before Trump, only 36% of Republicans believed that "public officials can behave ethically in their professional roles even if they acted immorally in their personal life," but after Trump's nomination, that number shot up to 70%.[54] More recently, Gallup found that:

> Six in ten Republicans say they would rather have a president who agrees with their political views but does not set a good moral example for the country, as opposed to one who sets a good moral example but does not agree with them politically. In contrast, 75% of Democrats prefer a president who sets a good moral example over one who agrees with their issue positions. In 1999, Republicans' and Democrats' opinions were reversed, with Republicans favoring a president who sets a good moral example and Democrats preferring one who agrees with them politically.[55]

The timing makes it clear that this reversal had nothing to do with an underlying essential principle and everything to do with changes in tribal leadership. When the leader of the right is low on moral character, those on the right will say character doesn't matter; when the leader of the left is low on moral character, those on the right will say it matters a great deal. Where is the "essential principle" behind all of this ideological flux on key issues? It does not exist.[56]

Lilliana Mason asks, "How could self-identified 'conservatives' find appeal in a candidate [Donald Trump] who did not hold consistently right-leaning policy positions?"[57] The answer is there are no "consistently right-leaning positions." The meaning of "the right" varies radically across time and space depending on tribal activity. Trump was not an apostate from "true conservatism"; rather, he was an agent of mutation who changed the meaning of conservatism on key issues, such as the size of government, the Iraq War, and free trade.[58] If the right were defined by unchanging principles, Trump's views on these issues would have put him on the "far left," but since the right is nothing more nor less than a tribe whose principles are constantly shifting, Trump's stances on various issues are irrelevant to his status as a right-winger.

And such redefinitions of liberal and conservative are not new with Trump. It has been going on for over a century. There is no principle so essential to "liberalism" that it hasn't at some point been identified with "conservatism," and vice versa.[59] If there were an essence (rather than a tribe) holding disparate ideological positions together, we would see issue positions cohering across time, but we don't. The positions associated with left and right are constantly evolving as the tribal coalition evolves.[60]

In their study of American political beliefs, Barber and Pope expected to find "principled" ideologues behaving differently from "tribal" partisans, but instead found that partisans and ideologues were equally tribal. Conservatives and liberals were just as likely to shift their views with social priming as were Republicans and Democrats. There was, they noticed, no difference between the views and behaviors of a "strong conservative" and a "strong Republican" or a "strong liberal" and a "strong Democrat." Democrat and liberal, Republican and conservative, they found, had become synonymous.[61] Likewise, Kahan and his co-authors have shown that partisanship and ideology are equal predictors of politically motivated reasoning.[62] If partisanship were tribal while ideology were principled, as the essentialist theory says, we would expect to see a divergence between the behavior of partisans and ideologues, but we do not.

Similarly, Christopher Johnston and Julie Wronski found that the social and economic views associated with each ideology do not tend to correlate in the absence of partisan cues.[63] That is, those who oppose abortion do not also tend to support tax cuts until they are told that the Republican Party supports tax cuts. Only then do they change their views to align with their party's platform. It's not that liberals join the Democratic Party because it stands for liberalism, but that self-identified liberals change their views to fit what the Democratic

Party is doing. Not only does this show that the glue binding distinct political dimensions together is social, not essential, but it also shows that the political parties have become the primary source of this social binding. Partisan cues determine ideological issue positions.

While the social theory recognizes that parties define ideologies, essentialists are in denial, claiming that they are making an empirical argument ("The Republican Party has moved to the right") when, in fact, they are making a tautological one ("Let's redefine the right to fit what Republicans are doing"). Once we accept the social theory, there's no need to redefine our terms until the Democratic Party moves "leftward"; we only need to recognize that parties don't evolve to fit ideologies, but ideologies evolve to fit parties, and the many party mutations over the years have yielded many distinct iterations of liberal and conservative.[64]

Not only have the ideologies evolved; so have the demographics associated with each ideology. During the New Deal era, educated and wealthy Americans in urban areas overwhelmingly identified as Republican and were considered "right-wing," while working-class Americans in rural areas overwhelmingly identified as Democratic and were considered "left-wing." In the twenty-first century, the demographic bases of the two parties have completely switched. Working-class whites in the Rust Belt and Appalachia, who had been part of the "left-wing" Democratic Party coalition during the mid-twentieth century, now vote for, and identify with, the "right-wing" Republican Party. This social divide between urban coastal elites and working-class whites in "flyover country" is a dominant dividing line in American politics. Despite this massive shift in the demographic bases of the two parties, the ideological labels remain the same: those demographic groups associated with the Democratic Party were previously considered "liberals," but now that they are associated with the Republican Party they are considered "conservatives." The people and their values haven't changed substantially, but the ideologies have.[65] Demographic groups who were standing still in their priorities and commitments now find themselves in the opposite tribe. It's not that urban America has shifted leftward and rural America has shifted rightward, but that the parties who define left and right have changed their issue positions to be more agreeable to opposite constituencies.

While it's true that a party can become more extreme in one or more of its positions, calling this a move "leftward" or "rightward" would suggest that left and right are fixed when they are not. The Republican Party can become more extreme in protectionism, but protectionism was considered "left-wing" a decade ago. Many say that the Democrats have moved "left" on immigration, and yet immigration restriction was long a cause advocated by left-wing figures (e.g., Bernie Sanders and Cezar Chavez) concerned about the wages of American workers. Since immigration restriction can be "right wing" one minute or "left wing" the next, it's incoherent to call a more extreme position on immigration a move to the left or the right. The Democratic Party can become more anti-interventionist in foreign policy, but anti-interventionism was considered "right wing" for much of the twentieth century.[66] The Republican Party can become more extreme in promoting tax cuts, but for most of American history, tax cuts have been promoted by those who historians have considered "left wing." At the time of the founding, "right-wing" Alexander Hamilton favored higher taxes while his nemesis, "left-wing" Thomas Jefferson, favored lower taxes. In the antebellum years, "right-wing" Henry Clay favored higher taxes while his nemesis, "left-wing" Andrew Jackson, favored lower taxes. In the Gilded Age, "right-wing" William McKinley favored higher taxes while his nemesis, "left-wing" Grover Cleveland, favored lower taxes, and so on.

If we are using the terms "far" or "extreme" in a descriptive, rather than pejorative sense, then someone on the "far," or "extreme," left is nothing more, nor less, than someone extremely committed to the policies of the Democratic Party at a given moment (as of 2022, this includes environmentalism, redistribution of wealth, abortion rights, anti-racism, etc.) and someone on the "far," or "extreme," right is nothing more, nor less, than someone extremely committed to the policies of the Republican Party at a given moment (as of 2022, this includes tax cuts, immigration restriction, abortion limitation, etc.).

Concessions

A few political analysts are finally coming around to accept the tribal nature of ideologies. After years of fighting it, journalist Jonah Goldberg recently conceded that, "For most Americans, conservatism basically means the stuff Republicans are for, and liberalism means whatever Democrats are for."[67] And *Vox* editor Ezra Klein, even though he has long identified as a liberal, now says:

> In theory, ideology comes first and party comes second. We decide whether we're for single-payer health care, or same-sex marriage, or abortion restriction, and then we choose the party that most closely fits our ideas. You're a liberal and so you become a Democrat; you're a conservative and so you become a Republican. The truth, it seems, is closer to the reverse: We choose our party for a variety of reasons— chief among them being the preferences of our family members, core groups, and community—and then we sign on to their platforms.[68]

Atlantic staff writer Andrew Ferguson correctly noted that:

If the last thirty years have taught us anything, it is that there is no ideological core around which the Republican party revolves. There is no real Republican. There's just Republicans, corralled together for reasons they're increasingly uncertain about. The chief thing that holds each party together is contempt for the opposite team.[69]

While Ferguson was correct in his observation, he would have been just as correct saying:

If the last thirty years have taught us anything, it is that there is no ideological core around which conservatism revolves. There is no real conservative. There's just conservatives, corralled together for reasons they're increasingly uncertain about. The chief thing that holds left and right together is contempt for the opposite team.

What we have today, then, is a strange ideological system of three parts—ideological terms (liberal and conservative), an ideological spectrum (left and right), and ideological parties (Democrat and Republican)—but each of these parts mean the same thing even as we pretend that they are distinct. Today there is no meaningful distinction (in kind if not degree) between Democrat, liberal, and left-wing, just as there is no meaningful distinction between Republican, conservative, and right-wing, and yet we talk as if they are different categories. We are in collective denial, convincing ourselves that principled ideologues hold fast to the eternal principles of liberalism or conservatism, when, in reality, they simply follow the party line and then invent stories *ex post* to explain how the party's actions (which are constantly changing) just happen to fit their political philosophy. The sooner we recognize this fact, the sooner we can disabuse ourselves of this harmful delusion and reduce the irrational tribalism that is undermining American democracy.

The "Authentic" Left and Right

Now that we've covered the myth of left and right, the origins of left and right, and the development of left and right, we turn to the main objection to the social theory of ideology: that it does not deal with the "authentic" left and right.

Authentic Ideologues

Many essentialists believe that although the evidence is clear that some people who call themselves "liberals" and "conservatives" follow tribe rather than principle, this only proves that those people aren't *true* liberals and conservatives. The essentialist theory holds, they say, for authentic ideologues.

This outlook is especially common among "Never Trump conservatives."[1] They claim that Donald Trump was an imposter—a pseudo-conservative who hijacked the movement and turned it away from the timeless principles it once stood for.[2] Even though the major conservative institutions in America supported Trump (e.g., the Republican Party, Fox News, right-wing talk radio, conservative think tanks, and the Conservative Political Action Conference), this just means those institutions had become conservative in name only.[3] The media called Trump supporters "conservatives"; the public called them "conservatives"; they called themselves "conservatives," but, in the Never Trump view, they nonetheless weren't true conservatives but apostates from the true principles of the right.[4]

This view is also prevalent among many scholars who study ideology. Kinder and Kalmoe, despite finding overwhelming evidence that tribe precedes principle for ideological Americans, still maintain that this only shows that Americans lack "genuine ideological identification."[5] In other words, Kinder and Kalmoe believe there are "true ideologies," but most Americans are not sophisticated enough to understand and align with them. Lilliana Mason, despite showing that there is no distinction between the views of ideologues and partisans, nonetheless

The Myth of Left and Right. Hyrum Lewis and Verlan Lewis, Oxford University Press. © Oxford University Press 2023.
DOI: 10.1093/oso/9780197680216.003.0005

argues that this is because the ideologues she studies aren't authentic "issue position" ideologues but only "identity" ideologues.[6]

The central problem with this "not true ideologue" charge is that it falls prey
to the private language fallacy—the erroneous belief that a *private* individual can
arbitrarily decide the meaning of *public* words.[7] Those who believe that Trump
supporters are fake conservatives assume that the term "conservative" has a
meaning independent of its public usage, but words are public by nature. We use
them to communicate with others and to use a private definition of a word that
is at variance with its public usage results in confusion.

For instance, Andrew Sullivan insists that Barack Obama is actually a *true*
conservative, Bruce Bartlett insists that George W. Bush is actually a *true* liberal,[8] Jonah Goldberg insists that Adolf Hitler was *truly* on the left, and Harry
Ausmus insists that Karl Marx was *truly* on the right.[9] Such attempts to assert
private definitions of ideology produce conceptual muddling. It's much better
to realize that, as the public uses the terms today, "liberal" and "conservative" are
tribal designations and therefore those who compose the liberal and conservative tribes are, by definition, authentic liberals and authentic conservatives.[10]

The tendency to declare the latest iteration of an ideology "inauthentic" has
been around for decades. Every time an ideology evolves, the cry goes up that
the advocates of the new iteration are "impostors." Taft conservatives called
Goldwater conservatives "impostors" for advocating military interventionism;
Goldwater conservatives called Reagan conservatives "impostors" for focusing
on religious issues; Reagan conservatives called George W. Bush conservatives
"impostors" for promoting big government; and Bush conservatives called
Trump conservatives "impostors" for rejecting military interventionism.[11]

Those making this "not true ideologue" charge are the "sticky ideologues"
mentioned before. They are often intellectuals of a particularly individualist bent,
who are so attached to a particular iteration of their ideology that they resist going
along with subsequent transformations. As the left or right "leaves them," they
declare independence from their former tribe and often switch over to the other.
They refuse to change their positions under social pressure, not out of loyalty to
an ideological essence but out of loyalty to a previous ideological iteration. They
are left clamoring about a "true" conservatism or liberalism that does not exist.

For example, the most prominent liberal at the turn of the century, E. L.
Godkin, lamented the rise of "so-called liberals" who advocated more government intervention in the economy.[12] Herbert Hoover kept insisting that he was
a "true liberal" long after he had become a hero of the right. Senator Robert Taft,
today a conservative icon, went to his grave clinging to the idea that he was actually a "true liberal" (while the New Dealers were liberals in name only).[13] And
Deirdre McCloskey is just one of the latest in a long line of free-market advocates
to say that, actually, "true liberals" support laissez-faire capitalism.[14]

Many American Liberty League Democrats (including the Democratic Party's previous national committee chairman and presidential candidate) switched from the Democratic Party to the Republican Party when liberalism evolved from a pro-market to an anti-market ideology in the early twentieth century.[15] This small fraction of liberals who refused to evolve with their tribe included future president Ronald Reagan. In 1984, the President reminded the Republican National Convention that he cast his first presidential vote for FDR in 1932 when:

> Democrats called for a twenty-five percent reduction in the cost of government by abolishing useless commissions and offices and consolidating departments and bureaus, and giving more authority to state governments. As the years went by and those promises were forgotten, did I leave the Democratic Party, or did the leadership of that party leave . . . me?[16]

In the 1960s and 1970s, some liberal Cold War foreign policy hawks switched from the Democratic Party to the Republican Party when liberalism evolved away from hawkishness. Although small in number, many of these "neo-conservatives" served in foreign policy positions in Republican presidential administrations. Likewise, many "Never Trump" conservatives switched from the Republican Party to the Democratic Party when conservatism evolved in the 2010s to accommodate Trumpism.[17] Although most ideologues are more attached to their tribe than an ideological iteration, sticky ideologues are more attached to an ideological iteration than their tribe.

Of course, just because E. L. Godkin, Al Smith, Herbert Hoover, and Robert Taft believed they were the "true liberals" fighting for individual liberty against big government tyranny does not mean they defined "liberalism" for all times and places.[18] Ideological labels like "conservative" and "liberal" only exist in linguistic communities with meanings that are determined by the community at large, and therefore these meanings evolve. It would be more accurate to say that their nineteenth-century definition of liberalism was replaced by a New Deal iteration. Hardly anyone today would call opponents of the New Deal, like Herbert Hoover and Robert Taft, "liberals"—the ideology has evolved. Yes, the term "liberal" was commonly associated with laissez-faire economics in earlier times, but that's no longer the case—it only confuses to claim otherwise.

Likewise, just because New Deal liberals like Norman Podhoretz, Irving Kristol, and Daniel Patrick Moynihan opposed the evolution of liberalism in the 1960s, with its embrace of the anti-war and counter-cultural movement, this does not mean they defined "liberalism" for all times and places. As the New Left turned against the Cold War and against traditional cultural values, many New

Deal liberals switched teams and had to call themselves "neo-conservatives" to distinguish themselves from the "old conservatives" who had opposed the New Deal.

More recently, we have witnessed dramatic transformations of the word "conservatism" during the Trump era. Some Reaganite conservatives have opposed conservatism's embrace of isolationism, protectionism, vulgarity, authoritarianism, economic nationalism, populism, personal cruelty, and deficit spending as an apostasy from the true conservative faith.[19] Despite protests that they are the "true conservatives," people like Jeff Flake are now considered RINOs, CINOs, centrists, or liberals because they hold on to the prior iteration of conservatism rather than go along with the new version. It's not uncommon for the highly educated to cling to the version of an ideology that they first fell in love with in their youth, but this does not mean they are faithful to an ideological essence—it only means they are faithful to a previous ideological iteration.[20]

Usually, the ideology that essentialists consider "authentic" is simply the one they grew up with. Kinder and Kalmoe note that high-education voters are far more likely to hold what they call "consistently conservative principles," but by "consistently conservative" they simply mean the principles of the Republican Party during the Reagan years.[21] However, there is nothing sacred about Reagan's conservatism that makes it more authentic than any other version before or since. By the standards of the Taft, Goldwater, George W. Bush, or Trump eras, Reagan conservatives were just as "inconsistently conservative" as anyone else. One may adhere to a previous version of an ideology, but that by no means makes it more genuine than any other version. Kinder and Kalmoe argue that ordinary Americans are just ignorant of true ideology, but we argue that it's not the American people who are ignorant of true ideology but essentialists who are ignorant of the fact that there is no true ideology. The usage community decides the meaning of words, not private individuals, and in present-day America, left and right are entirely tribal designations.[22]

We run into the same private language problem when it comes to labeling people "extremists" of the "far left" or "far right." Whereas essentialists generally use the terms "true liberalism" or "true conservatism" to denote an ideology they like, they generally use the terms "extreme" or "radical" left/right to denote an ideology they dislike.[23] Former White House Counsel John Dean, for instance, claims that Senator Goldwater was a moderate, responsible, and sensible conservative while George W. Bush and his followers were extremist, "far right" "conservatives without conscience."[24] But this is quite an odd charge considering that Goldwater was an opponent of both the Civil Rights Acts and the welfare state while Bush was in line with the American mainstream in supporting both of these causes (and, in the case of the welfare state, actively expanded it). What makes Bush an extremist then? The fact that Dean extremely dislikes him.

We find historian Nancy MacLean making the same error when she claims that economist James Buchanan was a member of the "radical right" in America.[25] Buchanan rejected the label "conservative," opposed American militarism, denounced racism, and believed that "persons are to be treated as natural equals, deserving of equal respect and individually responsible for their actions."[26] These sentiments could have come from Dr. Martin Luther King Jr., so why does MacLean label Buchanan "radical right"? Because MacLean dislikes his views. There is no objective definition of "radical right" that MacLean references in making her charge, only a high degree of her own subjective distaste for Buchanan's ideas.

Historian Anne Applebaum talks about those on the "moderate right" who moderately believe in free markets and those on the extreme right who oppose free markets.[27] But if those on the "extreme right" disagree with the defining issue of the right (free markets), in what sense are they right-wing at all? Applebaum doesn't say.

Andrew Sullivan calls Barack Obama a center-right "conservative" while Stanley Kurtz calls Obama a far-left "radical"—who is correct? Neither, because there is no essential definition of "far left" or "center-right" that we can appeal to. In using the terms "center" and "radical," Sullivan and Kurtz tell us nothing about Obama's ideology, but much about their personal feelings toward him.[28] Calling both Obama and Stalin "far left" doesn't make Obama like Stalin, it just expresses hatred for Obama, and hating both Obama and Stalin doesn't mean they share an essence any more than hating both country music and broccoli means that country music and broccoli share an essence. Let's not confuse our subjective dislike of something for an objective definition of an ideology.[29]

The essentialist theory and its associated private language approach to ideology is useful for smearing political opponents and creating false associations, but useless for understanding reality and engaging in constructive public discourse.[30] Instead of everyone creating their own private definitions of left and right, liberal and conservative, we should instead face up to the fact that, according to public usage, these terms designate tribes rather than essences.

Authentic Ideologies

While many essentialists reject the social theory on the grounds that it doesn't deal with authentic ideolog*ues*, other essentialists reject it on the grounds that it doesn't deal with authentic ideolog*ies*. In other words, they believe that although we may have falsified the "change versus preservation" essence, that's only because it's not the *true* essence that actually defines ideologies of left and right. Ideological essentialism will work, they say, if we identify the actual essence behind the political spectrum.

So, if "change versus preservation" is not the real essence, what is? Here are some of the popular ones we've encountered over the years:

- arrogance vs. humility
- autonomy vs. control
- barbarism vs. civilization
- big vs. small government
- big vs. small institutions
- chaos vs. order
- collectivism vs. individualism
- compassion vs. greed
- complex vs. simple
- courage vs. cowardice
- democracy vs. plutocracy
- dissent vs. conformity
- empathy vs. apathy
- entitled vs. grateful
- equality vs. hierarchy
- equality vs. liberty
- government vs. markets
- heart vs. head
- historicism vs. transcendence
- humility vs. hubris
- idealism vs. realism
- ignorance vs. intelligence
- intentions vs. outcomes
- internationalism vs. nationalism
- liberty vs. order
- man vs. God
- masses vs. elites
- naïve vs. realistic
- nominalism vs. ontological realism
- nurture vs. nature
- nurturing vs. strict
- open- vs. closed-minded
- oppressed vs. oppressor
- optimism vs. pessimism
- pluralism vs. monism
- poor vs. rich
- pragmatism vs. dogmatism
- reason vs. tradition

- relativism vs. absolutism
- risk vs. caution
- secularism vs. religiosity
- simple vs. complex
- thrive vs. survive
- unconstitutional vs. constitutional
- unconstrained vs. constrained vision
- virtue signaling vs. virtue
- weakness vs. strength

This list could be extended almost infinitely since almost everybody has their own idea of what the political spectrum is "truly" about. Although there is near-unanimous agreement that there is just one issue in politics (the unstated assumption of a unidimensional political spectrum), there is little agreement as to what that one issue is. Ask a hundred different people to define the political spectrum and you may get a hundred different answers.

Although this fundamental lack of agreement about the true essence is itself prima facie evidence against any essence at all, it turns out that none of these proposed essences works any better than the "change versus preservation" essence we addressed earlier. Going through and falsifying them one-by-one would be a never-ending game of whack-a-mole, since new essences pop up every day, but we can address some of the most prominent of them and, in so doing, expose the problems common to all proposed left–right essences.

Compassion versus Greed

Let's start with one that is especially popular among liberals: compassion versus greed. In this view, liberals are defined by their concern for the poor while conservatives are defined by their concern for the rich. The political spectrum, then, ranges from compassion on the left to greed on the right.[31]

The problems with this essence are obvious and myriad. Like most proposed essences, "compassion versus greed" ignores all dimensions of politics that would falsify it. Even if we stipulate that (1) liberals are more likely to support government programs for the poor,[32] and (2) "greed" is the only possible reason to oppose such programs, we are still stuck with the fact that this essence sidesteps most of the political issues that are so hotly debated today, such as abortion, drug legalization, military interventionism, trade policy, surveillance, policing, free speech, diplomacy, criminal sentencing, and nationalism. The "compassion versus greed" essence posits a unidimensional view of politics by ignoring all dimensions except for welfare policy.

And notice how both sides of a current-day debate, such as cancellation of student loans, can be justified using the same poor versus rich narrative. If Democrats were against student loan cancellation, liberals could talk about how it's unfair to give financial relief to the highest earners in society—college graduates—but since Democrats currently favor cancelling student loans, liberals talk about how college education helps promote greater economic equality. The same "compassion versus greed" narrative can justify opposite policy positions.

This essence also sets up a straw-man characterization of conservatives. Most conservatives and liberals believe in helping the poor, but they have different views about how best to go about it: liberals are currently more in favor of government programs while conservatives are currently more in favor of private giving. Holding a different view about *how* to do something does not make someone against that something. For example, opposing the invasion of Iraq did not necessarily make someone against democracy in the Middle East.[33] Those who say the political spectrum is about "compassion versus greed" mistake a practical disagreement about *means* (government or private) for an essential disagreement about *ends* (help for the disadvantaged). A conservative opposing a government education program is no more against education than a liberal opposing the government's "Operation Iraqi Freedom" program is against Iraqi freedom.

Now, at this point liberal essentialists might claim that the conservative anti-poverty approach does not count as "concern for the poor" because it doesn't work, but isn't that exactly what conservatives say about liberal anti-poverty initiatives?[34] And if liberals then want to question the motives of conservatives (e.g., "They are lying about their concern for the poor"), couldn't conservatives do the same with liberals?

Big versus Small Government

Recognizing the above, many essentialists will then say that this fundamental disagreement about means—government versus private—is itself the essence of ideology. That is, the political spectrum is all about size of government: moving leftward means more government, while moving rightward means less government. Since conservatives generally default to market solutions and liberals generally default to government solutions, then this must be what really divides left and right.[35]

Belief in this essence is remarkably widespread (possibly because, as we showed earlier, it used to be accurate). Economist Bryan Caplan tells us that the essence of the left is an "anti-market" philosophy while journalist Kevin Williamson tells us that the essence of the right is an "anti-government" philosophy.[36] According to literary critic Adam Kirsch, "Whether you think the greatest threat to liberty comes from the state or the market [is] the point on which conservatives and liberals have traditionally divided."[37] Talk show host Mark Levin has claimed that "government versus market" is the essence of left versus right,[38] as have political scientists Philip Converse, Lloyd A. Free, Hadley Cantril, John R. Zaller, and James A. Stimson, and historians Robert Crunden, Kim Phillips-Fein, and Kenneth Whyte.[39] Even William F. Buckley Jr. and Senator Barry Goldwater sometimes said that limited government was the essential political philosophy behind their conservative movement.[40]

It turns out that the "more versus less government" essence is as mistaken as it is popular. As we saw previously, which side wants more government is both domain-specific and time-specific: it depends on both which issue and which historical era is being examined because the issues on which liberals and conservatives want more or less government are constantly changing. Over the past decade conservatives have at various times advocated for more government in the realms of military, domestic surveillance, immigration restriction, law enforcement, trade restriction, and programs supporting "traditional values," while liberals have advocated for less government in each of those realms (sometimes simplified as: "Conservatives want government out of the boardroom; liberals want government out of the bedroom").[41]

Nonetheless, when Donald Trump ran for president in 2016, and broke with the Paul Ryan iteration of conservatism by promising not to cut longstanding entitlement benefits (and keeping that promise), he was routinely referred to as "far right." If the left were essentially pro-government, rather than a social group tied to the Democratic Party, then Trump should have been considered "far left" for his vast expansions of government power.

George W. Bush pushed through the most dramatic expansions in the size and scope of government since World War II while Bill Clinton oversaw the most dramatic cuts, but Bush is considered the more "right wing" of the two.[42] This is exactly what we would expect under the social theory—liberals opposed Bush and conservatives opposed Clinton because of their tribal affiliations—but the opposite of what we would expect under the essentialist theory. Either Bush and Trump were the most "far left" presidents since FDR, or size of government has nothing to do with ideological essence.

The evidence makes clear that which side wants to limit government is entirely domain specific. Liberals generally want to limit government power (and emphasize the Constitution and the rule of law) when Republicans are in office whereas conservatives generally want to limit government power (and emphasize the Constitution and the rule of law) when Democrats are in office.

And if the right is anti-government, then we should find those on the extreme right being extremely anti-government, but, in fact, we find the opposite. The credo of far-right Italian fascists was, "Everything in the State, nothing outside the State, nothing against the State." Far-right Nazis in Germany held to "a philosophy animated by extreme nationalism that called for government control of virtually all aspects of political and economic life."[43] The reality is that Hitler and Mussolini were extremely pro-government and extremely right-wing—an impossibility under the "more versus less government" essence. And if size of government is the essence of the spectrum, then why are anarchists who want no government at all considered extremely left-wing and why is it that left-wingers, not right-wingers, want to "defund the police" when police forces are part of the government?[44] There is no essence that unites "big government" liberal FDR with "small government" liberal Thomas Jefferson, and only ex post storytelling can make it seem otherwise.

Intelligence versus Ignorance

We find the same problem when one side or the other tries to make the spectrum all about intelligence.[45] Those who say that their political opponents are defined by stupidity must confront the fact that there is no linear relationship between intelligence (or education) and one ideology or the other. Those on the left congratulate themselves for their superior brains when they see the political leanings of college professors (generally Democrats) but ignore the political leanings of high-school dropouts (also Democrats). Liberals pride themselves on having higher average IQ's than conservatives but ignore the fact that they have lower average IQ's than "right-wing" libertarians.[46] And if one side is more intelligent than the other, why do we find combined groups of liberals and conservatives outperforming politically monolithic groups on cognitive tasks?[47] If intelligence defined one ideology or the other, wouldn't including "idiots from the other side" bring down the collective cognitive ability of a group rather than raise it?

Accusing the other side of bad faith or stupidity simply takes us away from the objective definitions that essentialists claim are at the heart of left and right, and back to "them bad, us good" tribalism, which, we maintain, is really what left and right are about. Going *ad hominem* to save an essence ultimately concedes that the social theory of ideology is correct.

Idealism versus Realism

Many conservatives tout "idealism versus realism" as the essential issue behind the political spectrum. In this view, those on the left are more utopian (they see things as they would like them to be), while those on the right are more realist (they see things as they really are). According to economist Thomas Sowell and psychologist Steven Pinker, liberals have an "unconstrained" vision of grand hopes and aspirations while conservatives have a "constrained" vision that recognizes tradeoffs and limitations.[48] Senator Ben Sasse claims that a conservative is someone who takes the realist view that "corruption originates inside of us" while idealist liberals believe corruption is external and therefore can be fixed by changing external conditions.[49] Historian John Diggins believed that conservatives throughout history have had a "tragic" view of reality while liberals have been fundamentally hopeful.[50] Yuval Levin claims that the left sees humans as infinitely perfectible, while the right sees humans as flawed and needing correction by mediating institutions.[51] Phrase it how you will—unconstrained versus constrained, hopeful versus tragic, optimistic versus pessimistic, arrogant versus humble[52]—it boils down to left-wing positions being idealistic and right-wing positions being realistic.[53]

This essence is as much a caricature of the left as "compassion versus greed" is a caricature of the right. We have yet to meet a liberal who claims their political views emerge from an inability to confront reality. In fact, liberal heroes such as John Dewey and Arthur Schlesinger Jr. have defined their ideology as a commitment to pragmatic realism.[54] Like most proposed essences, idealism versus realism tells us more about those asserting it than it does about actual liberals and conservatives.

The Iraq War also soundly refutes this essence. Skeptical realists were those most likely to oppose the invasion of Iraq, while Bush and his idealist advisors believed that they could democratize the Middle East through military force.[55] Perhaps no presidential inaugural has carried more idealist overtones than Bush's 2005 address, which said the United States would pursue "the ultimate goal of ending tyranny in our world."[56] If the right were defined by a constrained vision, as Sowell maintains, then conservatives, not liberals, should have been the ones opposing the Iraq War.[57] (Did "extreme-right-wing" Adolf Hitler have an "extremely constrained vision" when trying to remake all of Europe and establish a Thousand Year Reich?)

Just as conservatives often sound optimistic notes, liberals often sound pessimistic ones. Perhaps the most convincing justification for expanding the welfare state is the liberal view that selfish humans will not share unless compelled by governments.[58] Conservatives, by contrast, often claim that government welfare programs are not necessary since decent, ordinary people would voluntarily share their resources if un-coerced by the state. Which view is more idealistic in assuming innate human goodness?

Consonant with the social theory of ideology, studies have shown that optimism versus pessimism is domain specific. Conservatives are more optimistic on some political dimensions and liberals more optimistic on others, but nei-ther is more optimistic in general.[59] As with all other essences, idealism versus realism is both time specific and domain specific: which side has the more "constrained vision" depends entirely on the issue and the historical era. Many of the arguments those on the right make against socialist intervention in domestic markets (there are negative unanticipated consequences, government force isn't the answer, etc.) are the same ones those on the left make against intervention in foreign countries, intervention in abortion choices, and intervention in the drug trade. The "idealist versus realist" essence simply cannot stand up to scrutiny.

Equality versus Hierarchy

Another popular essence is that of "equality versus hierarchy" or "oppressed versus oppressor." The left, according to this view, wants to bring about greater human equality by fighting oppression while the right believes in upholding hierarchies. A conservative, says journalist David Ropeik, "believes in and feels safe in a structured world of order and hierarchy in which positions and power and social stratification are based on fixed and unchanging characteristics like race, gender, ancestry, and wealth."[60] The policies of the left, in other words, help the powerless masses while the policies of the right uphold the power of elites.[61]

Not only is this essence another straw man, but Kurzban and Weeden have shown that much of the evidence for it comes from circular reasoning. For instance, many liberals (1) define opposition to affirmative action as "hierarchical and racist," (2) show that conservatives are more likely to oppose affirmative action, and then (3) conclude that conservatives are more hierarchical and racist.[62] In fact, all these liberals have done is redefined conservatism to be synonymous with racism to con-clude that conservatives are racist. Conservatives could just as easily prove liberals are racist using the same method: (1) define support for affirmative action as racist (treating races differently), (2) gather data showing that, indeed, self-identified liberals are much more likely to favor affirmative action, and then (3) conclude that liberals are racist. Saying conservatives are racist because they oppose affirmative action is like saying liberals are unpatriotic because they opposed the Iraq War—it's just redefining terms to make the other side guilty by definition.

The fact is, there is plenty of commitment to equality on the right as well as the left. Right-wing economists claim that market reforms will bring greater equality of opportunity to the oppressed peoples of the developing world; right-wing advocates of school vouchers talk of bringing equal opportunity to racial minorities by improving the education system; right-wing neoconservatives believed in bringing democratic equality to the Middle East; and "right-wing" libertarians are committed to equality before the law.[63]

Progressives often tell the story that those on the right stand with the powerful against the powerless ("might makes right") while those on the left stand with the powerless against the powerful ("might makes wrong"), but why, then, do progressives stand with the United States government—objectively the most powerful entity in the history of the world—when it comes to public health restrictions, regulating private companies, taxing wealth, and, increasingly, controlling speech?[64] Progressives also currently stand with powerful organizations and interest groups, such as the major tech companies, lawyers' guilds, teachers' unions, major media outlets, the film industry, and the world's wealthiest universities. They might claim that their alliance with these powerful groups works ultimately in favor of the powerless through some kind of "trickle down" effect, but isn't that what conservatives have often claimed in the past to justify their support of the rich and powerful?

And if those on the left are uniquely concerned with the oppressed of the world, why were conservatives more likely to speak out against Stalin's Gulags, Mao's cultural revolution, and Pol Pot's killing fields?[65] The essentialist theory has no answer, but the social theory tells us that it's simply because both sides are selectively against oppression depending on which tribe is doing the oppressing. Since these dictators were "on the left," many in the left-wing tribe were reluctant to condemn their "fellow leftists."

Furthermore, oppression itself is multi-dimensional. Someone more concerned about one kind of oppression may be less concerned about another. Those who believe with Karl Marx that class oppression is the key to politics may be more likely to oppose racial identity politics on the grounds that it divides the working class against itself and prevents the collective, class-based political action that could bring about economic reform.[66]

The same holds when we frame this essence in terms of "elitism." Conservatives tend to rail against cultural elites (e.g., Hollywood, the media, and academia), liberals tend to rail against economic elites (e.g., plutocrats, the rich, and corporations), and both tend to rail against political elites when the other tribe controls government, but neither side is more "anti-elitist" in general. Liberals might disagree with conservative approaches to equality, and vice versa, but that does not make either side inherently opposed to equality.[67]

The prevalence of conservative populism also makes it clear that anti-elitism is alive and well in both political tribes. Right-wing Senator Joseph McCarthy's "red-hunts" were aimed against elites of the "establishment," and historian Richard Hofstadter famously explained support for McCarthy as an ugly manifestation of mass resentment toward those of higher status.[68] The Obama era saw a widespread revival of conservative populism in the form of Tea Parties that protested elitist spendthrift politicians and elitist corporate leaders receiving government bailouts.

This anti-elitist tendency on the right only became more pronounced in the Trump era when many conservatives came to see themselves as working-class middle-Americans under assault from global and coastal elites. If Trump was "far right" and the right is defined by elitism, then we would expect Trump to have been extremely anti-populist. Instead, he was widely considered one of the most populist politicians in American history.

Right-wing discourse is filled with denunciations of "unelected judges" who overturn democratically implemented measures, and conservatives have used plebiscitary measures, such as the initiative and recall, to greater effect in recent years than have liberals.[69] Liberals are more likely to favor abortion being decided by unelected judges, rather than by elected officials, while conservatives are more likely to believe that "Ending unjust discrimination on the basis of race, sex, and sexual orientation could have been achieved by electoral coalitions to enact democratic legislation, without the imposition by elite judges."[70]

Throughout American history, both sides have grounded their arguments in appeals to equality and popular rule—whether it was William Jennings Bryan decrying "the encroachments of organized wealth," Theodore Roosevelt speaking of "conflict between the men who possess more than they have earned and the men who have earned more than they possess," Franklin D. Roosevelt calling for an overthrow of the power of "economic royalists," Ronald Reagan criticizing "the intellectual elite" and "the government planners" for trying to control the lives of ordinary Americans, or Donald Trump telling his audiences that "the system is rigged" against them.[71] There is a reason that the names of the two major parties are "Democratic" and "Republican": they both see themselves on the side of "the many" fighting against "the few" elites who control American politics, economics, or culture. The idea that either side is more democratic and anti-elitist than the other is just more self-congratulation.

Secularism versus Religiosity

Since today's conservatives are more likely to be religious than liberals, some see religiosity itself as the essence dividing left from right.[72] Whether phrased in terms of man versus God, profane versus sacred, or irreligious versus religious, the idea is that the positions of the left grow out of a secular worldview, while the positions of the right grow out of a religious worldview.

A quick look at history soundly falsifies this essence. Before the 1960s in America, the left was far more religious than the right. Historians generally view the 1896 William Jennings Bryan presidential campaign as one of the most "far-left" campaigns in American history, but it was also the most religiously charged. Bryan believed that his proposals—nationalization of industry, regulation of railroads, free coinage of silver, and aid to American farmers—were the natural political expressions of his evangelical Christianity. Perhaps no major presidential campaign address has ever been more laden with Christian themes than Bryan's "Cross of Gold" speech.[73]

Teddy Roosevelt's Progressive "Bull Moose" Party campaign in 1912 was also saturated with religious imagery. "We stand at Armageddon, and we battle for the Lord," cried Roosevelt in speeches to his progressive supporters, and his party adopted the hymns "Onward Christian Soldiers" and "Praise God from Whom All Blessings Flow" as their theme songs. The 1912 Progressive Party convention in Chicago "was not a convention at all," wrote a contemporary *New York Times* reporter, but "an assemblage of religious enthusiasts."[74] Roosevelt also called his philosophy of government "the New Nationalism," showing that even nationalism itself had once been more a cause of progressives than conservatives (and it has continued to be in certain contexts, such as when indigenous peoples have resisted Western conquest in India, Vietnam, and Iraq).[75]

Courage versus Fear

Social scientists frequently try to argue for psychological essences that divide left from right by invoking statistical correlations. They often present data showing a correlation between a certain trait and an ideological identification and then assume that the trait is the essence that *causes* people to hold all the views associated with the ideology. For instance, some scholars claim to have shown that liberals and conservatives differ in their levels of "threat sensitivity." They say that conservatives, when confronted with stimulating images, tend to show higher levels of fear, disgust, and negativity response at both the conscious and neurological levels than do liberals.[76] In this view, the political spectrum simply indicates where someone is on the threat sensitivity scale: it ranges from extreme courage on the left to extreme fear on the right. If there is a correlation between identifying as conservative and being fearful, they assume, then fear must be what causes conservatives to call for lower income taxes, more military spending, less abortion, less immigration, more nationalism, more tariffs, and so forth.

It's easy to spin explanatory stories around this essence. Here's one example:

> After 9/11, conservatives were so fearful of Islamic terrorism that they worried themselves into two wars, numerous domestic-surveillance programs, a Department of Homeland Security, and the Patriot Act. Courageous liberals, by contrast, opposed these measures believing that our overreaction to the threat was worse than the threat itself and

that a large sacrifice in freedom was not worth a marginal increase in safety.

Now substitute the word "Covid-19" for "Islamic terrorism" and we find the two sides completely reversed on threat sensitivity.[77] In 2020, it was conservatives, not liberals, saying that our overreaction to the threat was worse than the threat itself and that a large sacrifice in freedom was not worth an increase in safety.[78] During the Bush years, it was liberals complaining about government infringements on private liberty in the name of security; during Covid-19 it was conservatives making those same arguments.[79] The "lower threat sensitivity" that was supposedly the defining characteristic of the left in 2003 was, in 2020, a central characteristic of the right.[80] Of course, these contradictory responses have nothing to do with a "threat sensitivity" essence and everything to do with tribe: in 2003, a right-wing president took extreme anti-terror measures while in 2020 a right-wing president took a lax approach to Covid-19 suppression. If Donald Trump had ordered everyone confined in their homes to prevent disease transmission, it would have been liberals, not conservatives, protesting lockdowns.

But what about those studies? Didn't they show scientifically that conservatives are generally more fearful and threat-sensitive than liberals? They did not. It turns out that those studies failed to replicate for the simple reason that those who conducted them chose questions and images specifically designed to elicit fearful responses in conservatives, but not liberals. For instance, they asked about family breakdown, which they knew would draw a fearful response from conservatives, but did not ask about gun violence since they knew that would draw a fearful response from liberals. A team that attempted to replicate one of the threat sensitivity studies reported,

> About a decade ago, a study documented that conservatives have stronger physiological responses to threatening stimuli than liberals. This work launched an approach aimed at uncovering the biological roots of ideology. Despite wide-ranging scientific and popular impact, independent laboratories have not replicated the study.... Our analyses do not support the conclusions of the original study, nor do we find evidence for broader claims regarding the effect of disgust and the existence of a physiological trait.[81]

Biased elicitors produced biased results and the "conservatives are more fearful than liberals" study was one of the prominent examples of scientific malpractice chronicled by psychologist Stuart Ritchie in his book, *Science Fictions*.[82]

Follow-up experiments that used an equal number of right and left elicitors found that neither side has a higher fear response in general—it depends entirely on the issue (as the social theory predicts).[83] Conservatives are more afraid of some things (e.g., Islamic terrorism, abortion, illegal immigration, and same-sex marriage) and liberals are more afraid of others (e.g., white nationalist terrorism, climate change, war, nuclear energy, gun violence, and Covid-19), but neither side is more fearful in general.[84] As psychologist Dane Wendell put it, "Liberals and conservatives do not have persistent differences in avoidance sensitivity or negativity bias."[85] What each side fears is a function of tribe, not underlying disposition.

Other studies making the "conservatives are fearful" claim were guilty of cherry picking or using an inadequate sample size.[86] A team led by psychologist John Bargh, for instance, claimed to have found that all conservative positions are driven by a "fear of things going wrong," and yet, predictably, their study did not look at *all* conservative positions, but only those where they knew, a priori, conservatives would show more fear than liberals, such as "gay rights, abortion, feminism and immigration."[87] They cherry-picked only the issues that would substantiate their thesis and ignored all those that would falsify it (e.g., war, economic deregulation, safe spaces, trigger warnings, government safety nets, climate change—all issues where conservatives tend to show less fear than liberals). A study that ignores all falsifying evidence is not a valid study at all.

The question that should concern us here is not "Which side of the spectrum is more threat sensitive?" but "How could such poorly designed studies have been produced, approved, circulated, and widely accepted?" Why is it that social science professors, normally so careful and rigorous in their research, are so careless and tendentious when it comes to researching their ideological opponents? The probable answer is that academic monoculture creates a "myside bias"— one of the most pervasive of cognitive biases, but the one that intelligent people (like academics) are the least likely to recognize in themselves.[88] This is just one more reason that the world (including academia) would be a better place if we all stopped conforming to ideological tribes.[89]

Tolerance versus Authoritarianism

Another correlation progressive essentialists like to invoke is that between the left and tolerance. According to this view, those on the left side of the spectrum are fundamentally tolerant and flexible in their thinking while those on the right side of the spectrum are fundamentally intolerant and authoritarian in their thinking.[90] One group of scholars summarized it thus:

> A constellation of psychological attributes and evocable states—
> including dogmatism, closed-mindedness, intolerance of ambiguity,
> preference for order and structure, aversion to novelty and stimulation,
> valuing of conformity and obedience, and relatively strong concern
> with threat—leads to a preference for right-wing over left-wing polit-
> ical ideology.[91]

This essence gained traction in the 1950s when the critical theorists of the
Frankfurt School gathered survey data showing that conservative Americans
demonstrated the same rigid and dogmatic "authoritarian personality" traits as
proto-fascist Germans in the 1930s.[92] A number of later studies claimed to have
reinforced those initial findings.[93]

But once again, these studies suffered from the same design flaw as those
that looked at "threat sensitivity": they stacked the deck by using elicitors specifically designed to draw out intolerant responses from conservatives, but not
from liberals (e.g., asking about toleration of atheists, but not toleration of religious fundamentalists).[94] Once the questionnaires asked a more inclusive set
of questions, evenly drawn from issues important to both the left and right, it
turned out that neither side showed more intolerance, closed-mindedness, dogmatism, or authoritarianism than the other.[95] Political scientist Michael Lind
further notes that the authoritarian personality test

> was supposed to measure latent fascist propensities along mul-
> tiple vague dimensions, many of which were connected with fascism
> only in the minds of mid-twentieth century Marxists. . . . Those who
> prefer old-fashioned values to fads and nudist camps are defined as
> "authoritarians."[96]

Sociologist John Levi Martin has even gone so far as to say that "the Authoritarian
Personality is probably the most deeply flawed work of prominence in political
psychology."[97] A replication crisis in the social sciences has revealed many prominent findings to be nonsense, and these studies about inherent conservative authoritarianism are among them.[98]

While the essentialist prediction about one side being more authoritarian
has not been borne out, the social theory prediction that authoritarianism is
context-dependent has. Liberals are more intolerant about policies their tribe
favors; conservatives are more intolerant about policies their tribe favors; and,
naturally, both are intolerant toward the other tribe. But neither tribe is more
intolerant in general.[99] It depends entirely on context. In some places and on
some issues, an authoritarian attitude is associated with left-wing ideology, and
in other places and on other issues, it is associated with right-wing ideology.[100]

The debate over free speech only further underscores the context-dependence of left–right authoritarianism. In the 1950s, many of those on the anti-communist right wanted to restrict speech on the grounds that certain ideas were dangerous, harmful, and oppressive.[101] In the 2020s, many of those on the anti-racist left want to restrict speech on the grounds that certain ideas are dangerous, harmful, and oppressive.[102] Tribalism, again, explains this reversal in ways that essentialism cannot: in the 1950s, the targets of speech suppression were on the left and today they are on the right. "Left-wing" campus activists are more likely to silence views they disagree with simply because campus is where they dominate—if the right-wing tribe controlled college campuses, the roles would be reversed. It's not that either the left or right is defined by an essential commitment to free speech, but that liberals tend to defend left-wing speech and conservatives tend to defend right-wing speech. Authoritarianism is not characteristic of one side or the other but is a function of which tribe finds itself in the majority in a given context. This is unsurprising from a group psychology or social theory perspective, but it directly contravenes the essentialist theory of ideology.

Sometimes the "openness vs. authoritarian" divide is framed as "relativist vs. absolutist," and yet, at different times, conservatives have claimed both values as the essence of their worldview. In the latter half of the twentieth century, leading conservative intellectuals such as William F. Buckley Jr. and Frank Meyer claimed that belief in absolutist conceptions of truth (ontological realism) was the essence of conservatism, while today Jonah Goldberg claims that a relativist "comfort with ambiguity" is the essence of conservatism.[103]

Irrelevant Correlations

But even if openness and threat sensitivity don't correlate with ideology, aren't there other traits that do? Isn't it true that liberals tend to manifest certain characteristics while conservatives tend to manifest others?

Yes, indeed. Here are some of the traits and behaviors that correlate with identifying as conservative:

1. Being a NASCAR fan
2. Enjoying country music
3. Living in a rural area
4. Owning a gun
5. Being white
6. Being male
7. Being married

8. Having kids
9. Going to church
10. Living in a nursing home

Here are some traits and behaviors that correlate with identifying as liberal:

1. Being a fan of Broadway plays
2. Enjoying rap music
3. Living in a city
4. Being a racial minority
5. Being female
6. Being LGBTQ+
7. Having a doctoral degree
8. Belonging to a labor union
9. Donating to NPR
10. Being vegetarian

But these examples should make clear that a trait correlation does nothing to establish an essence. All these correlations tell us is that certain demographic groups tend to belong to the Republican Party (and therefore the right-wing tribe), and other demographic groups tend to belong to the Democratic Party (and therefore the left-wing tribe). What they do not tell us is that these correlations somehow *cause* people to adopt the entire range of views associated with left and right. These correlations describe ideological tribes, not ideological essences.

Those who say otherwise are falling into one of the most basic statistical fallacies: mistaking correlation for causation.[104] All too often, essentialists identify a correlation between a trait and an ideology and then assume that the trait is the essence that causes people to hold all the positions of one side of the spectrum or the other. This is an error.

To jump from correlation to causation without rigorous causal analysis is dangerous. Skin color and ethnicity correlate with ideology, but it would be foolish to claim that skin color or ethnicity *cause* an individual's issue positions or ideological self-identification. Instead, people of certain ethnicities are born into, and socialized into, certain social, cultural, and economic contexts based upon certain social structures that exist in society. People who are socialized into certain social, cultural, and economic ways of living are also socialized into certain ideologies, but it is not the color of someone's skin, their ethnicity, or their psychological traits that cause them to adopt the whole range of left or right issue positions.

Some scientists claim to have discovered neurological differences between liberals and conservatives, but that's only because different demographics tend to have different brain patterns and different demographics tend toward different political parties.[105] Trait correlations do not establish ideological causation.[106]

Who would claim that being a NASCAR fan somehow causes someone to favor tax cuts, invading Iraq, restricting immigration, raising tariffs, and deregulating the economy? The correlation simply tells us that NASCAR is currently popular among rural, southern whites and so is the Republican Party (in the 1930s that same demographic was associated with the Democratic Party and "the left").[107] Committing crime correlates with identifying as liberal not because a criminal disposition somehow causes someone to hold the whole range of liberal views, but because crime is committed disproportionately by those with low income and those with low income also tend to vote Democratic.[108] Women are more likely to identify as liberal, but that does not make womanhood the essence of the left; attractive people are more likely to identify as conservative, but that does not make attractiveness the essence of the right.[109]

Studies which show differing characteristics (moral, psychological, or otherwise) between those on the left and right only tell us what we already know: there is a different demographic profile associated with each tribe, and the people who tend to become Democrats are different from the people who tend to become Republicans. Just knowing that someone lives in New York City, for example, allows us to predict their politics as "on the left" with 70% accuracy, but few of us would conclude that residing in the Big Apple is the essence of the left, so why do we assume that other such correlations are essential (e.g., religiosity, education level, amygdala size, etc.)?[110]

A century ago, religious Americans were more likely to identify with the left than the right, but it would have been just as much a mistake to assume that religiosity was the essence of the left in the 1930s as it is to assume that it is the essence of the right today.[111] We can find relationships between any number of characteristics and an ideology, but this only describes tribal demography. We can predict which tribe someone is likely to anchor into once we know something about them, but this has nothing to do with the existence of an ideological essence.

Some argue that conservatives have a militaristic disposition, but liberals were far more likely to support American military interventions in the twentieth century until the Vietnam War.[112] Others claim that empathy defines the political spectrum (empathy on the left, apathy on the right),[113] but why would empathy lead someone to opposite policy views at different times (e.g., oppose free trade in 2015 but support it in 2017; oppose eugenics in 2020 but support it in 1920; oppose the welfare state in 1880, but support it in 1980)?[114] And, if conservatives are so lacking in empathy, why do they understand liberals better than liberals understand conservatives, and why would empathy lead someone to oppose the minimum wage if they thought their tribe opposed it, but support the minimum wage if they thought their tribe supported it?[115] But aren't liberals essentially more concerned with due process and leniency for criminals than conservatives? It depends on who the defendant is.

In the Clinton years, some psychologists noticed a correlation between outrage at the immoral behavior of politicians and conservatism. They assumed that this correlation was essential until Trump became the leader of the right and conservatives began manifesting much less outrage than liberals on this metric.[116] Once again, the outrage was simply a function of tribe. As we would expect under the social theory, conservatives were furious about Clinton's history of adultery because he was in the left-wing tribe, but indifferent to Trump's history of adultery because he was in the right-wing tribe—it wasn't about immorality per se, but about who was guilty of the immorality. Correlation is not causation, and correlated traits are not ideological essences.

Causative Correlations

But even if the correlations mentioned above do not have a causative relationship to political beliefs, aren't there others that do? For instance, high income correlates with opposition to higher income taxes (currently a right-wing cause), so doesn't it stand to reason that this relationship is causative? A strong sense of religiosity correlates with supporting school prayer (also currently a right-wing cause), so doesn't it stand to reason that this relationship is causative?

Yes, but notice that each of these variables has a causative relationship to a *single* issue position, not to the whole bundle of positions that we call ideologies. They have a *one-to-one* causal relationship to a *particular* political position, not the *one-to-many* relationship to *all* political positions that is required by ideological essentialism.[117] It's true that having high income will have a causative relationship to opposing higher income taxes, but it will have no causative relationship to opposing abortion, opposing immigration, and opposing affirmative action—those are separate issues. There are, in other words, specific orientations (inborn or otherwise) toward specific political positions, but not general orientations toward entire ideologies.[118] So while there are "one to one" causative relationships between a single trait and a single political issue, there are not "one to many" causative relationships between a single trait and an entire ideology as ideological essentialism says.

We see this "one to many" error popping up in much of the "moral foundations" literature. Some psychologists have noticed that there are correlations between certain moral foundations and an ideological identification and have then assumed that these moral foundations cause someone to hold the entire set of issue positions of an ideology.[119] But if there were an essential set of moral foundations that bound all political dimensions into one, we would expect to see the foundations correlating equally across dimensions. In fact, different moral foundations correlate differently with the different parts of an ideology. Moral foundations that have a positive correlation with certain social positions considered "conservative," for instance, have a negative correlation with certain economic positions considered "conservative," showing, once again, that there is no intrinsic connection between these distinct political domains and that the relationship between moral foundations and political views is issue-dependent.[120]

Jonathan Haidt, one of the pioneers of moral foundations theory, has now conceded that there is not a simple relationship between a given moral foundation and an ideology; rather, the moral foundations are applied differently by liberals and conservatives depending on the issue.[121] Conservatives are currently more concerned about the "purity" foundation when it comes to sex, but liberals are currently more concerned about purity when it comes to food or the environment.[122] Today, liberals believe more in autonomy when it comes to abortion rights, but conservatives believe more in autonomy when it comes to running a business.[123] Conservatives are more likely to believe in genetic determinism when it comes to intelligence, but liberals are more likely to believe in genetic determinism when it comes to homosexuality.[124] We find both sides manifesting different commitments to the moral foundations depending upon the context. In other words, there are moral foundations underlying individual issues in politics, but none underlying ideologies as a whole—a finding consonant with the social theory but contradicting the essentialist theory.[125] The research makes clear that the different parts of an ideology are only united by tribe, not by a common commitment to a set of moral foundations, and the psychological "foundations" of ideology are not foundations at all but just manifestations of party demography and tribal solidarity.

The same holds for the correlation between liberalism and "open-mindedness." Although there is a (slight) correlation between identifying as liberal and being more "open to experience," this correlation disappears once we break liberalism down into its constituent parts. It turns out that openness to experience only predicts current liberal social views, not current liberal economic views, suggesting not only that the social and economic domains are independent (i.e., not bound by an essence) but that "openness" extends only to certain parts of the ideological package.[126] As the social theory predicts, and as many studies have borne out, the social and economic domains of politics are completely independent of one another and have distinct, unrelated, and sometimes opposite psychological correlates. Studies about "open-mindedness" and ideology only serve to reinforce the fundamental insight of the social theory: that the various parts of an ideology do not cohere naturally, but only by social happenstance. There is no essence connecting these different dimensions of politics.

Genetic Correlates

The "one-to-many" error is also particularly visible among those who claim to have identified a genetic basis for ideologies. Some geneticists say that since we can use genetic data to predict with a high degree of accuracy who will become liberal or conservative, the political binary must be natural and biologically hardwired.[127] In this view, just about everyone emerges from the womb with one of two political dispositions which then inclines them to the hundreds of distinct positions of one side of the spectrum or the other. These geneticists believe that people are born liberal or conservative just like they are born female or male (with occasional exceptions, such as libertarian or intersex people).[128]

But, actually, these studies do not show that people are biologically predisposed to *all* positions of left or right, only to *particular* positions of left or right.[129] Those trying to attribute ideological disposition to genetics are confusing individual issue-positions for an entire ideology. It's not that a genetic predisposition causes someone to hold *every* left- or right-wing position, but that a genetic predisposition causes someone to hold a *single* political position, which then leads them to anchor into an ideological tribe and adopt its other positions. Psychologists Ariel Malka and Christopher Soto found that individuals with certain predispositions tend to first adopt an ideological identity and only later "adopt issue stances described as ideologically appropriate in order to bolster and protect their political identities." Furthermore, these underlying predispositions "predict substantively unrelated political views merely because political elites have bundled these views with others into an ideological package."[130] There are genetic predispositions to pacifism, secularism, environmentalism, feminism, or communalism, but these inborn predispositions do not come packaged together.[131] Biology can explain propensities to *individual* political positions, but not to *collections* of positions (ideologies)—socialization explains that.

For instance, if we can use biology to predict that John has a relatively higher probability of identifying as gay than the general population, we can also predict that John has a higher probability of identifying as liberal—no surprise—but this does not mean that this same biological predisposition also predisposes him to favor abortion rights, higher income taxes, and lower import taxes.[132] It's simply that, as a gay man, John is more likely to be committed to gay rights and therefore to anchor into the tribe that currently has the reputation of championing this cause (left/liberal/Democrat). John is then likely to adopt the other positions of that tribe as a matter of socialization.[133] Biology does not naturally package people into two distinct political categories, but political tribes do, and we confuse the kinds of people that gravitate to each party for genetic types.[134] Even though political tribes are binary, the genetics of politics are not, and since political positions do not come in one of two packages, neither do the genetic dispositions that underlie them.

Furthermore, if the political spectrum were biologically hardwired into humans, we would expect to find it everywhere, instead of only in particular times (after the French Revolution) and particular places (European nations and their colonies). Western powers not only imperialized Chinese politics in the late nineteenth century, they also spread ideological conceptions among them such that, by the 1960s, Chinese Red Guards were persecuting and killing their fellow citizens for being "rightists."[135] There was no talk of "left-wing" or "right-wing" in China before Western imperialism, and yet by 1960 it had become the predominant model of politics. Left and right are not natural psychological types; they are socially constructed types that, sadly, have spread like a virus by way of Western imperialism.

And just as ideologies vary in meaning according to time, they also vary in meaning according to place. China's "left-wing" communist government cracks down on pornography, homosexuality, and drug use, as did the Soviet government in Russia, while Romania's "left-wing" communist government restricted abortion—these, of course, are "right-wing" causes in America today.[136] Socialism is considered "extreme left-wing" in early twenty-first-century America, and yet the most notorious socialist in German history was considered "extreme right wing" in the early twentieth century. The meaning of left and right will differ depending on both when we look and where we look.

As should be clear from the above, the search for the Holy Grail, the "one big issue" behind the political spectrum, is a futile quest, and the rivers of ink spilled in trying to define the true essence of left and right have been wasted. We need to give up the quest for this fantasy and realize that, like every other complex realm of human activity, politics is about many distinct issues, not just one. The most prominent attempts to save the essentialist theory from falsification have all come up short, and the social theory remains the better explanation of ideology despite the unfounded claims that it doesn't account for authentic ideologues or ideologies.

The Persistence of Left and Right

Now that we've traced the rise of left and right and addressed the failed defenses of the essentialist understanding of the spectrum, we turn to the question of why it persists. Why do so many Americans, including most intellectual elites, cling to ideological essentialism when it defies common sense, social science, and everyday experience?

Simplicity

The first and most obvious answer is simplicity. A model which says that all politics is about just one big issue is tidy and elegant. It satisfies our need to feel like we have everything figured out. Two-and-a-half centuries ago, philosopher Thomas Reid pointed out that "there is a disposition in human nature to reduce things to as few principles as possible . . . this love of simplicity, and of reducing things to few principles, hath produced many a false system."[1] The essentialist theory of ideology is just such a false system. Sadly, given the choice between a simple lie or a complex truth, we humans will often prefer the simple lie.

For millennia, intellectuals have indulged this tendency for simplicity by searching for "monist" explanations of reality that try to reduce all of a given domain to just one big thing. The pre-Socratic philosophers tried to reduce all of physical reality to a single substance—for Thales it was water, for Heraclitus it was fire, for Anaximenes it was air, and for Anaximander it was "apeiron"— but they were intelligent people on a fool's quest. Material reality isn't just one substance but many, as the periodic table of elements makes clear. Pluralism obviously describes physical reality better than does monism, but too many intellectuals throughout history have wanted the beautiful simplicity of an all-encompassing monistic theory and have been willing to go to great storytelling lengths to have it.[2]

The Myth of Left and Right. Hyrum Lewis and Verlan Lewis, Oxford University Press. © Oxford University Press 2023.
DOI: 10.1093/oso/9780197680216.003.0006

Ideological essentialism is simply one recent manifestation of this misguide. quest for monism. It is a psychological shortcut that people use to reduce uncertainty and avoid complex thinking. The desire for simplicity has misled some of the brightest minds throughout history and it continues to mislead some of the brightest minds today. Tragically, the more complex politics becomes, the more intense the desire to retreat from that complexity with this simplifying model. There are new issues that were not even on the table in previous generations, such as Covid, gay marriage, climate change, driverless cars, mandatory vaccination, and transgender bathrooms. The world is more populated, technological, and globally integrated than ever before, but instead of engaging the politics of this complexity in more productive ways, we have increasingly retreated into the comforting monist illusion of essentialism.[3] With each new issue that emerges, left–right essentialism becomes ever more obsolete, but ever more entrenched.

The tendency to simplify the world into two sides is a mental error called "splitting"—"a defense mechanism by which people unconsciously frame ideas, individuals or groups of people in all-or-nothing terms."[4] Because splitting distorts reality by simplifying it, mental health professionals have to help cure their patients of this malady.[5] What is ideological essentialism, then, if not a society-wide case of splitting, in which we simplify politics by making it about two sides arguing over one big issue? And if essentialism is a collective mental illness, then aren't we in need of a collective cure?

But why does monist thinking persist in politics and not in other complex realms of life, such as science, business, recreation, technology, entertainment, or medicine? One popular answer is that it's because politics is democratic: experts who can handle multidimensional complexity make the decisions in most realms, but in a democratic society the masses make the political decisions and they lack the sophistication to deal with anything more complex than a single dimension. Doctors receive over twelve years of training before diagnosing and treating medical problems, but the average citizen receives almost no training before diagnosing and treating political problems. Since the uneducated masses are the primary political actors, don't we need the simplistic essentialist theory to help them out?

Unfortunately, this "simplicity for simpletons" view can't stand up to scrutiny. It turns out that there is a *positive* correlation between education and acceptance of essentialism: the more educated someone is, the more likely they are to think about politics in unidimensional terms, while the less education someone has, the more multidimensional their approach to politics is.[6] College professors are much more likely to embrace essentialism than the average person, and university campuses are at once the most educated and the most ideological places in America.[7] In most other domains of life, cognitive elites have the ability to see through false, simplistic models, but in politics the cognitive elites are far

more likely than the masses to accept a simplistic, essentialist view of the political spectrum.

Some essentialists try to use this education differential to bolster their theory,
saying that the more educated are more ideological because they, unlike the
masses, understand the essential philosophy behind left–right ideologies and are
therefore more likely to arrive at the philosophically consistent set of "left" or
"right" principles.[8] But more educated people who have not been socialized into
ideological thinking are just as likely to have positions that do not fit left–right
molds as are the uneducated.[9] The educated are only more ideological because
they are also more socialized into the left–right way of thinking.

In a sense, this shouldn't be too surprising. Health statistician Hans Rosling
has pointed out that the highly educated are more given to the "gap instinct"—
the tendency to make reality conform to exciting narratives with blockbuster plot
lines, in which there is a clear gap between good and evil, heroes and villains, us
and them.[10] Ideological essentialism clearly offers this, and those with high education levels are more likely to accept such gap-affirming narratives. The complex, multidimensional, "shades of gray" political narrative, although more based
in reality, is not as satisfying to the educated Americans who are more adept at
spinning stories and given to fitting their experiences and findings into the dramatic essentialist narrative of "our side all good; their side all bad."

But is such simplification necessarily bad? Isn't that one of the main functions
of scholars and intellectuals—to give us simplified models of the world that help
us navigate complexity more effectively?[11] While it is true that all models are
simplifications of reality, this does not mean that all models should be accepted—
a bad model is worse than no model at all (as the four humors theory of medicine makes clear). For us to accept a model, it must be accurate and useful rather
than inaccurate and harmful. Since "the illusion of knowledge is more insidious
than a lack of knowledge, and harder to overcome," we should only use models
that bear enough relationship to reality to help us navigate it more successfully.[12]

Ideological essentialism does not pass this test. It is not a simplification of
reality; it is a distortion of reality. Good models are simple without being simplistic, but essentialism is just simplistic.[13] Many argue that ideological essentialism is a "useful heuristic,"[14] but abundant research shows that essentialists are
less rational, more given to cognitive error, and less able to solve problems than
those who are not, meaning that essentialism is not "useful" (nor is it a truth
hidden from the masses and "discovered" by the elites).[15]

The idea that the essentialist theory is necessary for the masses who are not
sophisticated enough to deal with political complexity is as unjustified as the
idea that the four humors theory was necessary for the masses to deal with
medical complexity. Moving beyond the essentialist theory would not leave us
without guidance any more than moving beyond the four humors theory left

medicine without guidance. Medical doctors today, using an issue-by-issue approach, are far more effective than those in previous eras who used the totalizing four humors approach. It was only when doctors gave up their simple framework that medicine finally began to save more lives than it took. Physicians exchanged a less accurate model of reality for a more accurate one and it has been all to the good. There is no reason the same would not be true of politics: giving up the simplistic essentialist framework would be liberating, not confusing.

Elite physicians no longer espouse the four humors theory, elite scientists no longer espouse alchemy, but elite political thinkers do continue to espouse the essentialist theory. This is a tragic waste of talent. Instead of leading the way in developing more adequate political paradigms, educated elites are doubling down on an incorrect one and are primarily to blame for the persistence of our monistic political thinking. This indicates that simplicity cannot be the full explanation for the prevalence of ideological essentialism. There must be more.

Disguise Tribalism

A second explanation for the persistence of the essentialist theory is the need to disguise our tribalism. The literature on the power of tribalism is vast. Numerous recent studies have shown that coalitional instincts are a dominant, fundamental part of our psychology.[16] We earn membership in a group by sending signals that affirm belief in certain propositions, and the content of these propositions matters much less than our willingness to affirm them.[17]
In fact, the more outlandish the belief, the stronger the signal of our coalitional commitment since only the truly committed are willing to sign on to a far-fetched proposition. Ideologies, like religions, require members to accept articles of faith not because they tap into fundamental philosophies but because they signal coalitional membership. "We tend to adopt positions on issues that confirm the thinking of the members of our group, both to strengthen the group and to increase our acceptance within the group."[18] As Barber and Pope showed, ideological extremists are simply extreme in following tribal leadership—not in articulating a coherent set of beliefs. What is important to ideologues is affirmation of a belief that signals tribal commitment, not the belief itself.[19]

Although most people understand that the tribal impulse is real and powerful, what has been much less understood is the degree to which humans feel the need to deny their tribalism. Recent studies in psychology have found that humans are inclined not only to tribalism but also to cloaking their tribal instincts behind high-sounding, rational language. In the words of Jonathan Haidt, the emotions are the elephant, and reason is the rider. The elephant, much larger and more powerful than the rider, often will go where it wants, but the rider will tell himself that he is actually in charge.[20] So it is with tribe and principle: we tend to follow our tribes but fool ourselves and others (through creative storytelling) into believing that we are following principles. We go with our tribal emotions and then, *ex post*, explain how our actions were actually motivated by philosophical principle. The elephant carries us to a destination and then we make up a story about how it was where we wanted to go all along.

This is particularly true of our tribal commitment to political parties. Since colonial times, Americans have denounced partisanship as an ignoble indulgence of emotion over reason. In 1753, political journalist (and future New Jersey governor) William Livingston wrote:

> From the moment that Men give themselves wholly up to a party, they abandon their reason, and are led captive by their passions. The cause they espouse, presents such bewitching charms, as dazzle the judgment; and the side they oppose, such imaginary deformity, that no opposition appears too violent; nor any arts to blacken and ruin it, incapable of a specious varnish. They follow their leaders with an implicit faith, and, like a company of dragoons, obey the word of command without hesitation. Though perhaps they originally embarked in the cause with a view to the public welfare; the calm deliberation of reason are imperceptibly fermented into passion; and their zeal for the common good, gradually extinguished by the predominant fervor of faction. A disinterested love for their country, is succeeded by an intemperate ardor; which naturally swells into a political enthusiasm; and from that, easy is the transition to perfect frenzy.[21]

Livingston sounds like he is describing the frenzied politics of 2020s America just as well as 1750s New York, and few people today, as then, want to admit that their "judgment" and "reason" are corrupted by the "fervor of faction" or an "intemperate ardor" for their party.

Three decades later, James Madison observed that parties are the product of human frailty:

> As long as the reason of man continues fallible, and he is at liberty to exercise it, different opinions will be formed. As long as the connection subsists between his reason and his self-love, his opinions and his passions will have a reciprocal influence on each other . . . [thus] ensues a division of the society into different interests and parties.[22]

George Washington even condemned partisanship in his Farewell Address:

Let me now . . . warn you in the most solemn manner against the baneful effects of the spirit of party generally. This spirit, unfortunately, is inseparable from our nature, having its root in the strongest passions of the human mind. . . . The common and continual mischiefs of the spirit of party are sufficient to make it the interest and duty of a wise people to discourage and restrain it. It serves always to distract the public councils and enfeeble the public administration. It agitates the community with ill-founded jealousies and false alarms, kindles the animosity of one part against another, foments occasionally riot and insurrection. It opens the door to foreign influence and corruption, which finds facilitated access to the government itself through channels of party passions.[23]

Once again, Washington's description of "false alarms," "animosity," "riot and insurrection," and "foreign influence and corruption" seems just as applicable to recent presidential elections as the 1796 election. Washington warned his fellow citizens to guard against the worst excesses of partisanship in his farewell address because he understood that it enflamed emotion at the expense of reason.[24]

Many Americans of the nineteenth century took this advice to heart and kept parties at a distance, even abandoning them in the name of being true to political and religious principles. When Protestant abolitionist reformers could find no hearing for their abolitionist views in the Democratic or Whig Parties, they formed a variety of anti-slavery societies and third parties (including the Republican Party). When Republican civil service reformers and free traders were appalled at the corruption and protectionism of the Grant administration, they created the Mugwump movement and helped elect Democratic president Grover Cleveland in 1884. When the Democratic Party adopted the populism of William Jennings Bryan in 1896, Bourbon Democrats bolted from the party, held their own convention with their own platform under the name of the "National Democratic Party," and received the support of intellectuals and reformers like E. L. Godkin, Charles Francis Adams Jr., Henry Adams, Woodrow Wilson, and Louis Brandeis. When Social Gospel reformers could not get Theodore Roosevelt nominated by the Republican Party in 1912, they left the GOP to form the Progressive Party. They subordinated the tribal emotions generated by party affiliation to deeply held principles.

With the rise of the essentialist illusion, such principled oppositions to tribe began to decline. Since the 1950s, the idea that there are essences behind all left-wing and right-wing positions has allowed Americans to fall in line with everything their party does, while claiming that they are following a philosophy of "liberalism" or "conservatism."[25] Partisans conform to their party (giving in to the elephant of emotion) and then invent stories after the fact to explain how their party's actions—even when they are completely opposite from what they were shortly before—align with "liberal" or "conservative" philosophy (the rider of reason). By convincing ourselves that there are "two philosophies" in politics, we can indulge our partisan tribalism while deluding ourselves that it's actually high-minded commitment to a fundamental principle. The social science evidence shows that most people, including elites, are more willing to abandon their principles than abandon their tribe, and yet those same people maintain that they are following the eternal principles of liberalism or conservatism.[26]

Survey data finds that Americans are far more likely to identify with an ideology ("liberal" or "conservative") than a party ("Democrat" and "Republican"), meaning they see ideologies as noble and parties as ignoble, even though they are now one and the same.[27] Liberal has become synonymous with Democrat and conservative has become synonymous with Republican, but people typically prefer the principled-sounding ideological labels to the tribal-sounding partisan labels. Being a philosopher is noble, but being a tribal lemming is not and so, naturally, tribal lemmings like to tell the philosophical stories of ideological essentialism to justify their herd-following actions.

Why does left–right essentialism persist then? Because *it hides our partisan sins*. It allows us to *be tribal* without *feeling tribal*. It allows us to indulge our emotions while telling ourselves we are being rational. It allows us to conform to everything our team does without admitting that this is what we are doing. It allows the rider to be carried along by the elephant while feeling like he is in charge. The statement "I follow the philosophy of conservatism" sounds much better than, "I go along with whatever the Republican Party happens to be doing." The latter is the case, but the former is the story ideologues tell themselves.

The problem for American politics, then, is not tribalism per se—after all, tribalism is a fundamental part of human nature and an inevitable part of politics—the problem is that we don't *acknowledge* the tribalism. Instead of confronting the reality that we are conforming to tribes, we tell ourselves reassuring stories about how everything our party believes just happens to grow out of a principled ideological essence. The spectrum makes us feel like Churchill rather than Quisling—one who stands strong, not one who capitulates to expediency.

This means that self-deception is the primary reason ideological essentialism is so attractive. In our politicized age, everyone wants to see themselves as principled political combatants rather than as fickle partisans, so they invent stories to try to make their ideologies cohere. By spinning narratives about how all their various positions are bound together by some grand principle, they create false signals where there is only noise. Astrologers do the same when attempting to tie together all the actions of someone born in August behind the "essential traits" of Leo, but stories do not make astrology correct and stories do not make the essentialist view of politics correct either. It is our propensity to mistake stories for evidence that gives the essentialist theory so much of its staying power.

Self-deception also explains why the educated are more ideological. It's counterintuitive that more intelligent people would be more likely to accept a simplistic model in politics when they don't in other realms, but once we realize that intellectuals are more skilled in using "system two" thinking to rationalize "system one" impulses, it makes sense that they would be more likely to construct stories that make their partisanship sound principled.[28] Psychologist Tali Sharot notes that "the greater your cognitive capacity, the greater your ability to rationalize and interpret information at will, and to creatively twist data to fit your opinions."[29] If we accept the social theory and see left and right as groups, not essences, then it makes sense that the politically active (who are generally more educated) are more likely to be socialized into left–right categories than the politically inactive. Educated elites are far more ideological and far more likely to think in terms of left–right than Americans at large because they are much better at self-deceptive rationalization—the primary function of ideological essentialism.

Not only does ideology satisfy our need to hide our tribalism, it also satisfies our need for scapegoats. Human beings are uncomfortable with randomness. We don't like to believe that bad things just happen, so we seek identifiable villains to blame.[30] Historically, political groups have blamed those of other races, nations, or religions, but today, most Americans blame those in the other ideological tribe. They believe in ideological essentialism for the same reason many believe in conspiracy theories: both provide simplicity, moral certainty, and a scapegoat to explain the source of our problems. This is an attractive alternative to a reality that is complex, morally ambiguous, and often random. Conspiracy theories and the essentialist theory ultimately have many of the same psychological roots—the desire to see signals and purpose where there is only randomness and noise.[31]

Scapegoating is also an outgrowth of what Aristotle identified as "thymos"— the desire for recognition and status superiority over others—and one way to fulfill this desire is by aligning oneself with a "superior" group, such as a race, nation, ethnicity, or religion.[32] Political tribes are only one of the recent groups through which our desire to feel more righteous and advanced than the outgroup finds expression. Splitting the world into heroes and villains not only fills simplifying and self-deceptive functions, it also fills a thymotic function. Alongside our intrinsic need to belong to a tribe is an intrinsic need to assert that tribe's superiority.[33] Since politics is inherently binary and since we humans are inherently tribal, then it's inevitable that we will form binary political tribes or parties, but it's not inevitable to fool ourselves with essentialist stories that justify and magnify tribal antagonisms.[34]

The Party Incentive

A third reason for the persistence of the political spectrum is the institutional incentive. While individuals have a psychological need to create illusions of ideological purity, parties and their leaders have an incentive to stoke those illusions to gain popular support. Politics is the pursuit of power, and the parties themselves, in order to achieve power, manipulate the essentialist tendency among their constituents.

The essentialist myth is especially effective in creating party loyalty in the face of party evolution. Without the essentialist illusion, changes in party principles would mean a loss of membership (as happened in the nineteenth century); but with the essentialist illusion, partisans can remain in the party and justify reversing their own issue positions by appealing to a deep-seated ideological essence. Without the essentialist illusion, advocates of small government would have fled the Republican Party in droves during the George W. Bush presidency, but the essentialist illusion told them that Bush shared their "conservative" philosophy and therefore deserved their support. Without the essentialist illusion, moralists who demanded high character from their public officials would have fled the Republican Party in droves after Donald Trump's nomination, but the essentialist illusion told them that Trump shared their essential "right-wing" outlook and therefore deserved their support. How could Reagan's Secretary of Education, William J. Bennett, who wrote an entire book denouncing Clinton for his adultery and lack of character, support Donald Trump?[35] Essentialism allowed Bennett and his many fans to follow their tribal tendencies and support the Republican Party even when it meant going against their earlier beliefs. Before the rise of left and right, Americans were much more likely to defy their parties and create new organizations when they felt the party wasn't following their principles, but since the rise of left and right, Americans have been much more likely to stick with their party and justify its actions with essentialist stories.

In fact, ideological essentialism may be the best explanation for the lack of viable third-party challenges to our two-party system over the past century, since third party challenges have declined in step with the rise of left and right.[36] Before the essentialist illusion emerged in the mid-twentieth century, discontent partisans were more likely to rise up and form new or splinter parties, such as the National Republican (1824), Whig (1834), Republican (1856), People's (1890), or Progressive "Bull Moose" (1912) parties. But with the rise of left and right, major third-party challenges have become increasingly rare. This is not a coincidence—essentialist illusions keep Democrats and Republicans content with their parties even as those parties depart from previously held principles.

Notice that during the mid-twentieth century, when Republicans were shut out of power, they turned their back on Theodore Roosevelt's "New Nationalism" and became the party opposed to national government power, in general, and executive power in particular. Using the new language of left and right, Republicans argued that their new anti-government stance was actually required by "conservatism." The foremost Republican critic of national government power in the 1960s, Barry Goldwater, wrote that "the heart of the Conservative philosophy" was limiting government power—in particular the power of the executive and judicial branches of government that "roamed far outside their constitutional boundary lines."[37]

During the Vietnam War, and especially during the presidency of Richard Nixon, Democrats retreated from the internationalist and militarist interventionism articulated by Wilson, Franklin D. Roosevelt, Truman, Kennedy, and Johnson. Confusingly, those on the left began arguing that liberalism no longer required a military policy that fought totalitarianism abroad; it now required American troops to "come home." Some hawkish Democrats did switch parties during the 1970s as a result (calling themselves "neoconservative" in opposition to the "new left"), but this was mostly confined to a few intellectuals and national security professionals. The redefinition of liberalism allowed most self-identified "liberals" to stay in the Democratic Party and claim philosophical consistency.

After Republicans controlled the presidency for twenty of twenty-four years, between 1969 and 1993, the Republican Party changed its stance on presidential power once again, and revived Teddy Roosevelt's ideas about executive power. At the turn of the twenty-first century, Republican constitutional scholars justified an imperial presidency and a powerful executive on the grounds that a "conservative" interpretation of the Constitution necessarily implied giving presidents tremendous political power.[38] Virtually no Republicans left the GOP over this drastic change in party ideology: only a tiny minority became Libertarians, and even fewer became Democrats. Rather than switching parties, Republican partisans were content to tell themselves they were being principled by spinning essentialist stories. The contrast to the principled departures from parties that had happened before the rise of left and right is striking. The essentialist illusions that developed in the mid-twentieth century kept people on board with parties and their platforms despite radical changes in what those parties stood for.

Most recently, as Trump has changed the Republican Party's positions on fiscal policy, foreign policy, and trade policy—among others—individual Republicans have convinced themselves that they are not blindly following their party leader but following eternal conservative principles. In each case, Republicans made up stories to justify increased federal spending, increased federal deficits, isolationist foreign policy, and protectionist trade policy as "conservative." Comparatively few Republicans left the GOP over the Trumpification of the party. In all of these examples (and there are countless more we could relate), tribal partisans justified party change by appealing to the supposedly eternal and unchanging principles of "liberalism" or "conservatism."

Claiming that the party stands for an essential philosophy keeps partisans in the fold even when there are reverses in the party platform. As a result, those who profit from the persistence and power of our two major parties have an incentive to hide low-sounding partisanship behind high-sounding ideology. This allows them to repeatedly contradict themselves in an effort to justify what their party leaders are doing in office, because they can always claim consistent adherence to a set of ideological "principles" through *ex post* stories. The parties have used the essentialist myth to justify switching to the opposite sides of virtually every issue in the history of American politics. This is bad for the public interest, but great for party interests.

As James Madison pointed out, the "difference of interests," which divides political parties, can be "real or supposed." America's parties today really are divided on a variety of issues (which are always changing), but the claim that our two parties are divided by an underlying philosophy is simply a "supposed" difference that does not hold up under scrutiny.[39]

In summary, ideological thinking endures because it satisfies our desire for simplicity, satisfies our need to disguise our tribalism, and furthers the institutional incentives of our two parties. These factors explain the persistence of an essentialist theory of ideology that has been soundly falsified. Not only is essentialism false, but as we will show in the next chapter, it is also incredibly damaging.

The Consequences of Left and Right

We have spent the preceding chapters tracing the rise of left and right and showing that the essentialist view of the political spectrum is a myth, but some readers might at this point be asking themselves, "So what?" Yes, essentialism is false, but people have always believed a lot of harmless nonsense, so why all the fuss? The answer is that essentialism is far from harmless. It is taking a terrible toll on our collective well-being by causing severe intellectual, moral, and political damage.

Intellectual Consequences

Let's start with the intellectual damage. Simply put, essentialism reduces our cognitive ability. By giving the illusion that ideology is about principle instead of tribes, essentialism turns people into ideologues and ideologues are generally more dogmatic, less fact-based, less able to solve problems, more given to confirmation bias, more simplistic, less able to think critically, less able to develop creative solutions to problems, more likely to misinterpret data, quicker to jump to conclusions, less given to carefully weighing evidence, and less willing to update beliefs in the face of new evidence than others.[1] Ideologues are more easily driven to extremes, are more likely to base their opinions on fantasy rather than fact, and are more given to self-justifying, self-righteous, and self-aggrandizing beliefs.[2] In general, the more strongly someone buys into essentialism, the more strongly they identify with an ideology, and the worse their thinking becomes.

In his studies of successful forecasting, Philip Tetlock found that the most accurate political thinkers defied ideological categories. They were "political deviants." By contrast, poor forecasters were "united by the fact that their thinking was so ideological."[3] The primary driver of irrationality in politics today is not left-wing ideology (as conservatives would have us believe) or right-wing

The Myth of Left and Right. Hyrum Lewis and Verlan Lewis, Oxford University Press. © Oxford University Press 2023.
DOI: 10.1093/oso/9780197680216.003.0007

ideology (as liberals would have us believe), but any ideology at all. Ideologues often declare, "Truth has a left-wing [or right-wing] bias," but the reality is that truth has a "non-wing" bias.

The main reason ideology hinders thinking is that the ideological mind is a dogmatic mind.[4] The more ideological someone is, the more they are given to unjustified certainty, rigidity, and imperviousness to evidence.[5] "Adherence to *any* political ideology, and particularly extremism, is associated with dogmatism, intellectual simplicity, and needs for certainty and security."[6] Since the views of ideologues are bound up with their identity and status, they see it as dishonorable to admit error and will go to great lengths to hide any evidence that does not confirm their prejudices (which helps explain the rising prevalence of shout-down culture on university campuses).[7]

Humility—the willingness to change our minds and falsify our views—is the soul of rationality, but ideology makes us less humble and therefore less rational.[8] While humble thinkers subordinate status to truth and are more concerned about what is right than who is right, ideologues cling to their beliefs despite contrary evidence, seeing them not as propositions to be tested but as sacred doctrines to be protected. When we adopt an ideology under the essentialist illusion, we switch from discovery mode to defense mode and treat an attack on any of our political beliefs as an attack on our identity—such a mindset is antithetical to the pursuit of truth by its very nature. As Bavel and Pereira noted, "The tribal nature of the human mind leads people to value party dogma over truth."[9] Liberals accuse conservatives of being closed-minded and conservatives accuse liberals of being closed-minded, but it turns out they are both correct.[10] Ideology is a humility killer. It turns us into soldiers instead of scouts.[11]

It's easy to see why ideology produces dogmatism. The essentialist theory tells us that if we are correct about the *one* essential issue of politics, then we are correct about *all* political issues. By giving the illusion of monism, essentialism also gives the illusion of omniscience: once we have chosen the "correct side" of the master issue, then the thinking is done and all that remains is to silence any disagreement (no wonder cancel culture has taken such firm hold in both political tribes). Many argue that we should consider alternative viewpoints because "we might be wrong," but, actually, we should consider alternative viewpoints because we are *certainly wrong* and the only way to be less wrong is through open dialogue.[12] Ideological thinking stifles this open-mindedness that would help eliminate error in our views. Only the omniscient need no correction and yet ideologues, under the essentialist illusion of omniscience, believe they are correct about everything political. The point of politics should be the improvement of society, but ideological tribalism puts the quest for victory above the quest for truth. It leads us to assert our ideological dogmas with more force, hatred, and vehemence, which only retrenches us in our errors.[13]

While it is possible to test and discard policies that just happen to be associated with a party, we cannot test and discard policies that we believe are outgrowths of a deeply held worldview. Under the essentialist illusion, one part of an ideology cannot be wrong without the whole thing being wrong and therefore admitting error on any point falsifies one's entire ideology—this is intolerable to someone whose identity, morality, and sense of meaning are bound up with a political label. If an ideologue agrees with the "other side" on even a single issue, the entire edifice of their ideology will crumble.[14] By making politics about one issue instead of many, essentialism makes compromise and correction impossible.

The essentialist theory also promotes political extremism. If the political spectrum were about principle rather than tribe, then being an extremist would mean being extremely committed to one's principles. By telling us that ideology is about moral principle, rather than tribe, essentialism incentivizes us to be "extremely moral and principled" by taking all of the positions of our side to an extreme.

The social theory, by contrast, shows that ideological extremism is not extreme commitment to principle but extreme commitment to tribe—including the many irrationalities and errors of that tribe. Although ideologues conceive of themselves as stalwarts holding fast to transcendent values, the social theory reveals that they are far *less* principled than non-ideologues.[15] Under the essentialist illusion, ideologues today have come to believe they are moral heroes like Thomas More, Abraham Lincoln, Elizabeth Cady Stanton, Martin Luther King Jr., or Rosa Parks, fighting for eternal justice, but the reality is that they are moral chameleons fighting for whatever is currently popular in their tribe.[16]

Since the essentialist theory leads to the delusion that ideological extremism means greater commitment to truth and justice, recognizing the social nature of ideology makes us much more likely to moderate our views and be willing to change our minds. Mellers, Tetlock, and Arkes showed that when ideologues are forced to "translate their beliefs into nuanced probability judgments and track accuracy over time and questions" they become "more moderate in their own political attitudes and those they attribute to the other side."[17] If truth had a left- or right-wing bias, as ideologues claim, then we would expect to see prediction and testing leading people to the "correct side" of the spectrum; instead we find that such scientific thinking tends to lead people away from ideology altogether.

Beyond promoting dogmatism and extremism, essentialism also creates a mental prison by telling us there are only two ways to approach political issues. The reality is that there are infinite ways to think about political problems. We need creative "third way" solutions now more than ever, but essentialism makes this impossible by telling us there is no third (or fourth, or fifth . . .) way—there is only left and right. We cannot think "outside the box" about politics when we are stuck inside the box of essentialism that says there are just two options. Political pundits are notoriously bad at analysis and prediction, and the prison of ideological essentialism is a major reason for this.[18] Foxes (eclectic thinkers) outperform hedgehogs (monistic thinkers) when it comes to cognitive tasks, but by giving the illusion that there is only one issue in politics, essentialism turns us into hedgehogs.[19]

Essentialism also magnifies the "most pervasive obstacle to good thinking"— confirmation bias.[20] Ideological tribalists are more likely to ignore evidence that counters their beliefs, are more selective in their media use, are less consistent in their intellectual standards, are more likely to believe nonsense, and will even deny empirical facts that make "their side" look worse.[21] Rather than update beliefs in the face of new evidence, ideologues deny evidence that does not accord with their pre-established narrative.[22] They are far more likely to engage in misreporting and self-deception, even to the point of conjuring up non-existent memories of those on the "other side" doing evil things.[23]

For most people, receiving more information reduces misperception, but this is generally not the case for left–right ideologues. Psychologists Brendan Nyhar and Jason Reifler gave participants in their study false news that confirmed ideological prejudices and then later revealed that the news was not true. Incredibly, ideologues tended to become even more entrenched in the falsehood after hearing it was false, preferring to believe a blatant lie rather than consider that one of their views might be incorrect. "People who were ideologically inclined to believe a given falsehood worked so hard to come up with reasons that the correction was wrong that they came to believe the falsehood even more strongly."[24] Although the tendency to confirm pre-existing beliefs is a universal human flaw, ideological essentialism compounds it to an astonishing degree.[25] Scientists alter models to fit data while ideologues alter data to fit models, and since essentialism turns us into ideologues, it is fundamentally anti-science.[26]

Ideological essentialism not only reduces our intelligence; it actually turns our intelligence against us. In general, education is an antidote to bias and dogmatism, but this is not true of ideologues for whom more education just means more capacity for self-deception. Kahan, Dawson, Peters, and Slovic found that numeracy can be an asset in helping people think more clearly unless it is combined with a strong ideological disposition. At that point, it becomes a liability. "More numerate subjects would use their quantitative-reasoning capacity selectively to conform their interpretation of the data to the result most consistent with their political outlooks."[27] For an ideologue, intelligence simply gives greater ability to rationalize the falsehoods they want to believe. It makes them better at doubling down on errors and spinning narratives to justify tribal myths.

Because of the essentialist fallacy, high cognitive ability in politics is a double-edged sword: it can lead to better political understanding, but if wielded by an ideologue, it "makes it easier for citizens to defend their political attitudes through motivated bias."[28] Ideology turns intellectual firepower to the destructive task of justifying tribal prejudices. Quality political judgment is less dependent on the intelligence of citizens and more on their ability to follow evidence independent of ideological thinking. Since disinformation is worse than a simple lack of information, ideology, which creates disinformation, is a bigger problem for our democracy today than mere ignorance. Because ideology increases our capacity for self-deception, a non-ideological "partisan ambivalence" is a much better predictor of sound political thinking than is intelligence.[29]

But doesn't tribalism of any kind produce these negative cognitive effects? Don't we get motivated reasoning and dogmatism any time questions of group identity are involved? Yes, but it is worse with ideological essentialism because of the self-deception involved. It is true that identifying with a political party, nation, service organization, or even a sports team causes people to irrationally exaggerate the good and minimize the bad of the groups to which they belong. But when people identify with these tribes, they are conscious of their tribal nature; when they identify with a political ideology, by contrast, they fool themselves into thinking that they are identifying with an enduring and coherent transhistorical belief system. Essentialism makes them believe that all of the issue positions of their ideology are bound together by principle, which blinds them to the tribal reality at work. As a result, ideological tribalists are less likely to keep a critical distance from their tribe and challenge its beliefs and actions. Ideology binds and blinds.

For example, when a nation takes particular actions, its citizens naturally justify these actions to some extent because of their tribal attachment to the national community. But they will also recognize that their nation and its leaders are fallible—their government can make mistakes and recognizing this gives the citizens a degree of critical distance. They are not forced to bend the facts to justify national actions because they recognize that their national tribe—even though it is their own—can be wrong. Ideological tribes, by contrast, allow no such critical distance since the essentialist illusion says that everything done by one's side grows out of a true philosophy, and therefore is correct a priori. Notice that Americans in general could criticize the decision to invade Iraq since they understood that their national tribe's leaders were fallible, but tribal conservatives were far more constrained since they believed the invasion of Iraq was demanded by their deeply held "conservative principles." Ideology combines the pull of tribal solidarity with the illusion of infallibility, making adherents of the ideology feel compelled to agree with everything their group does. A social group like a party or nation can contain a diversity of opinions, viewpoints, and beliefs, but an ideology cannot since essentialism says that all the views associated with it emerge from the correct worldview.

Think of it this way: if grocery stores required us to buy one of two baskets of randomly selected products, we would all choose the basket containing more of the products we preferred, but would do so without the illusion that *all* the products in our basket were better than *all* the products in the other basket. Unfortunately, when it comes to the "baskets" of politics (parties), we have invented ideological essentialism to delude ourselves into believing that *everything* in our political basket (party platform) is superior to *everything* in the other party's basket. Just as it would be foolish for someone selecting one of two grocery baskets to make up a story explaining how all the groceries in their chosen basket were bound by an essential characteristic, so it is foolish of us to make up stories about how all the positions of our parties are bound by an essential characteristic.

Beyond making us more dogmatic, more given to confirmation bias, more extremist, and more willing to deny objective facts, the essentialist model of ideology also creates needless confusion, even among those who are not ideological. For example, under George W. Bush, government spending increased far more than it did under Barack Obama, but since Bush is considered "conservative" and Obama is considered "liberal," many believe the opposite.[30] Psychologist Jean Twenge recently noted that, "iGen is more likely to support abortion rights, same-sex marriage and legalizing marijuana and less likely to support the death penalty—usually considered liberal beliefs. But they are also less likely to support gun control, national health care and government environmental regulation. . . . How can iGen hold these seemingly contradictory beliefs?"[31] The confusion here is entirely the result of the essentialist illusion. The social theory of ideology shows that since there is no essence connecting all of these unrelated positions, then there is nothing "contradictory" about taking distinct positions on distinct issues (any more than there is something "contradictory" about buying granola, eggs, and canned soup). There is only a "contradiction" if we invent a non-existent essence to bind these unrelated issues together.

In a similarly sad example of ideology causing needless confusion, Glenn Kessler of the *Washington Post* makes the argument that the Nazis were not socialists because they were "right wing" and supported by "conservatives."[32] Notice that Kessler does not address the question of whether the Nazi party actually supported socialist policies, but instead diverts attention from the policies to talk about meaningless labels. A conservative could just as easily say, "The Nazis did not commit genocide because right-wingers do not believe in genocide." The label "right wing" does not tell us anything about whether Nazis pursued socialism or genocide; only the historical facts do, and when we examine those facts, we find that the Nazis were committed to nationalization of industry and radical increases in the redistribution of wealth (generally considered "socialist" policies), as well as the extermination of the Jewish race (generally considered "genocidal" policies). An essentialist view does not illuminate reality, it distracts from reality, causing us to engage in pseudo debates instead of real debates. Countless people have needlessly confused themselves with the essentialist fallacy. Ideology not only hurts the thinking of ideologues, but it hurts the thinking of society generally and makes even non-ideological citizens less informed about the objective facts of public life.

Moral Consequences

But it gets worse. Even as essentialism does considerable intellectual damage, it does moral damage as well. Ideological thinking generates unnecessary prejudice and hostility. It "makes us dislike each other and mistreat each other. It causes mutual distrust and diffidence."[33] Ultimately, essentialism makes us evil as well as stupid.

By telling us that there are two (and only two) ways to approach politics, the essentialist theory inherently pits a heroic, enlightened side against a villainous, foolish side. Those who disagree are "others" we can demean, belittle, and feel superior to. As Webster and Motta put it, "Americans have come to dislike members of the other political team . . . deeply enough to believe that others should suffer physical harm as suitable retribution for holding differing opinions about contentious issues."[34]

In previous eras, when there was greater understanding that parties were tribes (and only tribes), it was much easier to find common ground with someone of the other party. Without the essentialist illusion, contending partisans could engage those of the other party without believing they were wrong about *everything*. But with the rise of left and right, partisans came to believe that those on the other side adhered to a fundamentally evil philosophy. They were no longer people who happened to disagree on a few issues, but people with a diametrically opposed worldview. This mistaken, totalizing approach to politics has had a destructive effect on families, neighborhoods, workplaces, churches, communities, sports leagues, and civic cohesion.[35]

The standard explanation for why American politics has become so heated is that each party has been captured by an extremist ideology, but actually American politics is so heated because we are in thrall to a false paradigm. In practice, the parties are no farther apart on most key issues than they were in previous eras (for instance, most Democrats and Republicans currently favor gay marriage, believe in restricting trade, want to retain entitlement spending, oppose high taxes, and believe in foreign policy isolationism), but we are led to think otherwise because of essentialist illusions.[36] Increasing ideological tribalism in American society is contributing to what political scientists call increasing "affective polarization": the tendency for individuals to have more hostility and antipathy toward their political opponents independent of substantive disagreement.[37] This has resulted in a new and socially acceptable form of bigotry that we call "ideologism."

As other kinds of prejudice have declined in America, ideologism has risen to fill the void.[38] Fortunately, Americans are discarding the racial essentialism associated with racism, but, unfortunately, we are adopting the ideological essentialism associated with ideologism.[39] Race is a social construct, but believing that there are "essential" differences between races leads to hatred, discrimination, and prejudice;[40] likewise, ideology is a social construct, but believing there are "essential" differences between ideologies of left and right leads to hatred, discrimination, and prejudice. When those in the left-wing tribe, for instance, say that conservatives are essentially superstitious, unintelligent, and lazy at the biological level, they are echoing unfounded white supremacist myths about racial minorities. Racism leads people to judge and hate based on ancestry; "ideologism" leads people to judge and hate based on political labels.[41]

Even as America has become less racially segregated, it has become more ideologically segregated. Thanks to the essentialist illusion, which says the parties have been "captured" by ideologies,

> Republicans and Democrats are increasingly unwilling to get married, be friends, or live beside one another. In 1960, only 5% of Republicans and 4% of Democrats disapproved of their child marrying outside their party. In 2014, 30% of Republicans and 23% of Democrats disapproved of inter-party marriage. Compare this to interracial marriage, a former taboo. According to Gallup, 87% of Americans now favor interracial marriage, up from 4% in 1958."[42]

While fewer Americans now openly discriminate on the basis of race in the workplace and in hiring practices, more Americans now openly discriminate on the basis of ideological labels.[43] The result of this growing ideological hostility is a rise in conspiracy theorizing, ideologically motivated acts of terrorism, threats of secession, and domestic insurrection.[44]

Americans who would not discriminate against someone for having a different racial label are nonetheless willing to discriminate against someone for having a different political label.[45] Many who would not hate other people for their sexual preferences, nonetheless actively hate other people for their political preferences.[46] While education is effective at reducing racial and ethnic prejudice, education actually increases ideological prejudice since schools generally inculcate the essentialist error in students.[47] If bigotry means "formulating opinions about others not based on their individual merits, but rather based on their membership in a group with assumed characteristics," then ideologism is indeed a widespread form of bigotry.[48]

Claiming that there is an essential connection between unrelated traits leads to confusion and false stereotyping. We might call someone a "dumb jock" on the mistaken assumption that their level of athleticism tells us something about their intelligence, just as we might call someone a "warmongering right-winger" on the mistaken assumption that their belief in lower taxes tells us something about their views on the military.[49] A smart, athletic person could be labeled a "nerd" for being smart or a "jock" for being athletic just as a pro-life pacifist could be called "right wing" for being pro-life or "left wing" for being a pacifist. When we lump together characteristics that are unrelated, we create confusion by using the same term to refer to things that are opposites, and opposite terms to refer to things that are the same.[50]

Ideologism also leads to hatred by creating guilt by false association. By labeling someone "left" or "right," we can make them guilty of crimes they did not commit and ascribe to them beliefs they do not hold.[51] Senator Joseph McCarthy, for instance, was a master ideologist who labeled any opponent of his agenda "left-wing," and thereby made them guilty of the crimes of all communists everywhere. Many "conservatives" today similarly argue that "progressives" are guilty of eugenicist crimes because certain "progressives" of the past advocated eugenics.[52] Sadly, but predictably, many progressives themselves are not above this tactic. They often smear conservatives as "racists" simply because some people labeled "conservative" in the past supported segregation, or "fascists" because both "conservatism" and "fascism" are "on the right." Under the essentialist illusion, anyone opposed to abortion is guilty of Nazi crimes by right-wing association, and anyone opposed to the Iraq War is guilty of Communist crimes by left-wing association. The indeterminacy of political labels means that we can apply the terms "left" or "right" to nearly anyone for any reason. If someone is in favor of tariffs, we can call them a "fascist" for being "right wing"; if someone opposes tariffs, we can also call them a "fascist" for being "right wing." It's "heads you are a Nazi, tails you are a Nazi" reasoning. Religious zealotry in 1690s Salem meant that dozens of people were falsely accused of being witches, and ideological zealotry today means that millions are falsely accused of being "commies" and "fascists." It's a cliché that understanding is superior to hatred in human affairs, and yet far too few of us work to understand others when it comes to politics. With the exception of those who gain fame and fortune by stoking the flames of political anger (e.g., Rachel Maddow and Sean Hannity), most of us would like to see more civility in our public discourse. The essentialist view of ideology makes this difficult. We cannot have reasoned political debates when we consider those "on the other side" guilty of humanity's greatest sins. Far better to stop thinking in terms of ideological essences at all.

Political Consequences

A discussion of the political harm caused by the myth of left and right brings us back to where we started in the introduction to this book. Ideological tribalism may be the single greatest threat to the continuation of our constitutional democracy at present. In order for our republic to survive, we must have citizens who embrace pluralism, concede to the outcomes of free and fair elections, respect the rule of law, protect the separation of powers, and respect the individual rights of their fellow citizens. Unfortunately, ideologism undermines all of these important bulwarks of our constitutional order.

When a citizen views politics as a Manichean struggle between left and right, between good and evil, then there is no reason to embrace pluralism and tolerate differences of political opinions. Partisan opponents are not people who you disagree with on just a few things, but on *everything*—including the most basic ideas about human nature and morality. To defeat the other party is not just to advance a particular coalition of social groups, interest groups, politicians, and issue positions (some of which you agree with and some of which you disagree with) but to vanquish the forces of evil and advance the forces of righteousness. Given the implications of the left–right way of thinking about politics, it is no wonder that millions of Americans believed incorrect stories about election fraud and that thousands of them assaulted the Capitol Building on January 6, 2021, to try to stop Congress from counting the Electoral College votes cast in each state. In their minds (thanks to the essentialist illusion) Biden's election did not represent the triumph of a party with a pluralistic agenda, but the triumph of an evil worldview ("left wing") that would destroy the country.

If politics is divided between an essentially good side, with all of the correct political positions on one side of a left–right spectrum, and an essentially bad side with all of the wrong political positions on the other side, then it is justifiable to discard any constitutional niceties about the separation of powers between legislative, executive, and judicial authorities, or a division of powers between national and state and local governments. When your side is perfectly good and the other side is irredeemably evil, then of course your side should seek to maximize its power by any means necessary such that good can triumph over evil. After all, an authoritarian dictator is much more effective in achieving political goals than a slow, deliberative, constitutionally constrained democracy. Certainly, this kind of thinking had much appeal for voters who supported President Trump's claim that "I alone can fix it."[53]

It is also not a coincidence that the rise of left and right has gone hand in hand with the growth of presidential power in American politics. In the early twentieth century, when Americans understood that party platforms were heterogeneous grab-bags of political positions, they were rightfully fearful of conceding too much power to a president of either party. But *pari passu* with the rise of the essentialist illusion, Americans have been increasingly willing to invest presidents with more and more power to carry out an ideological vision.[54] It's not that Americans are worse than they were a century ago, but they have deluded themselves into thinking that philosopher (ideologue)-kings should rule to implement the correct vision of "their side."

Former Niskanen Center president Jerry Taylor recently summarized the sad situation of contemporary American politics:

> Ideology corrupts caring, idealistic, educated, and intelligent people. . . . Ideologies breed dogmatic thinking and lazy, decoder-ring policy analysis. They encourage motivated cognition. They give birth to excessive certainty, crowding out healthy intellectual skepticism. They moralize political conflict in an unhealthy fashion, yielding incivility, extremism, and social discord. They ignore the complexities of the modern world. They threaten the pluralism that a (small-l) liberal society is obligated to respect and defend.[55]

Political scientist Samuel Huntington famously predicted that in a post–Cold War world, identity and conflict would largely come from civilizations—transnational cultural units based on underlying values.[56] Huntington was right that culture would be central to identity in the twenty-first century, but wrong about the scale of these identities: they are not trans-national, but intra-national. The clash is not between civilizations, but between team red and team blue, and the hatred of cultural "others" is playing out domestically rather than internationally.

The thymotic desire to assert one's tribe as superior has been pervasive and destructive throughout human history—the seventeenth century had its wars of religion, the nineteenth century had its wars of empire, and the twentieth century had its wars of nation-states—and ideology has the potential to fulfill this destructive role in the twenty-first century. A blind commitment to national and racial tribes in the first half of the twentieth century led to extreme violence, and a blind commitment to ideological tribes could have a similar effect in the first half of the twenty-first century.

So, what have we learned about the effects of ideology in this chapter? We have learned that although ideologues of left and right constantly tell themselves that their ideological opponents are "stupid and evil," the reality is that the essentialist paradigm itself is making everyone stupid and evil. It shuts down thinking and stirs up anger and prejudice. While there are plenty of good and smart people who embrace ideological labels, those people would be better and smarter if they left their ideological thinking behind. Unfortunately for all of us, essentialism is as pervasive as it is destructive.

We have also learned that the primary function of essentialism is self-delusion. Ideologues delude themselves with the idea that all the positions of their side (left or right) grow out of a correct philosophy or principle, and then throw epithets ("commie" "fascist") at anyone who disagrees with them, hoping to discredit alternative beliefs, *ad hominem*, through guilt by association. Essentialism allows people to conform to everything their party does while convincing themselves that they are being rational, principled, and philosophical instead of emotional, tribal, and conformist. Americans socialized into "team left" or "team right" take the issue positions they do because they are falling in line with their party, but essentialism lets them believe they take these particular positions because they are following a philosophy.

Sadly, humans are naturally inclined to make politics about *who* is right, not *what* is right, and giving up essentialism would force everyone to concede that one side is not right about everything and the other side wrong about everything. It would force everyone to admit that there are many issues in politics and neither one of the two tribes has a monopoly on truth or goodness. This is an admission that few Americans want to make, and essentialism gives them an excuse not to.

The Future of Left and Right

We want to conclude this book on a hopeful note. While it is true that the essentialist paradigm currently has a firm grip on society, there is the possibility that we can break free. In the previous chapters, we charted the destructive rise of left and right, but we end by arguing that there can be a constructive fall of left and right. In this final chapter, we propose some specific steps to minimize the influence of essentialism and the irrationalism and hostility it has introduced into American politics.

Some political psychologists believe this is a fool's quest. They see irrational tribal bias as an ineradicable feature of human life, particularly when it comes to politics, and therefore believe it's futile to try to do anything about it.[1] We reject this fatalism on the grounds that it arises from one of the cognitive errors that these psychologists themselves have identified: the tendency to all-or-nothing thinking. Contra both positivism and relativism, we are not stuck with either perfect rationality or complete irrationality; we can instead achieve *greater* rationality. Our goal should not be to eliminate bias (impossible), but to *reduce* bias (possible); not to reach perfect objectivity (a "noble dream"), but to have *more* objectivity (a worthy goal).[2] The fact of human irrationalism is not an excuse to indulge irrationality any more than the fact of human dishonesty is an excuse to lie. As science writers Gordon Pennycook and David Rand put it, "The solution to politically charged misinformation should involve devoting resources to the spread of accurate information and to training or encouraging people to think more critically. You aren't doomed to be unreasonable, even in highly politicized times."[3] Perfection is impossible, but improvement is not, and improvement of American political discourse is all we are asking for. Shedding the essentialist illusion would take us in that direction.

Most would agree that political discourse has become more hostile and unreasonable over the past generation—that's the bad news—but the good news is that if it can get worse, it can also get better. If society has become more

The Myth of Left and Right. Hyrum Lewis and Verlan Lewis, Oxford University Press. © Oxford University Press 2023.
DOI: 10.1093/oso/9780197680216.003.0008

ideological, then it can also become less ideological. We believe that taking the
five steps we outline in this chapter can minimize the scourge of ideological essentialism and thereby make our political discourse more rational, charitable,
and productive than it would otherwise be.

Recognize the Myth

The first step is recognition. Simply being aware of cognitive biases can make
us less susceptible to them, so being aware that essentialism is a myth can make
us less prone to its distortions.[4] Keeping in mind that the set of political views
considered "left" or "right" are bound only by tribe, not by essence, makes us
more likely to treat political opinions as propositions to be tested, not dogmas
to be defended. Just recognizing the essentialist fallacy allows us to update our
beliefs without feeling like a traitor to a righteous cause. It can help change politics from a zero-sum war of "left" vs. "right" to a positive-sum, post-ideological
pursuit of truth. Yes, gaining a sense of identity from politics is inevitable, but we
are more likely to hold an identity lightly if we recognize it as tribal rather than
philosophical.[5]

Go Granular

The second step is to go granular. One of the most common questions we are
asked is, "If you want to get rid of ideology, what do you suggest we replace it
with?" Our response is simple: *granularity*. Since political positions do not come
naturally packaged together, we should stop pretending they do. Instead of
thinking in terms of left and right, we should think in terms of specific policies
and ideas, such as "income tax increase," "abortion rights," "deficit reduction,"
"affirmative action," or "free trade." We should replace meaningless ideological
categories, such as "liberal" or "conservative," with substantive categories, such
as "deficit hawk," "tax cut advocate," "immigration restrictionist," or "abortion
rights activist."

While ideology creates confusion by lumping opposites together, granularity
dispels confusion by distinguishing between diverse policies and people. With
granularity, we simply identify where someone stands in relation to a particular
position (e.g., "pro-choice") instead of trying to pin down their ideological label
(e.g., "far left"). Instead of considering how people or parties have changed their
relationship to an essence ("He moved to the left"), we should just consider how
they have changed on individual positions ("He turned against the Iraq War").
Although it usually takes more words to be granular, a little more speech is a

small price to pay for a lot more accuracy. (If teenagers can say, "She is on the tennis team" instead of "She is a jock," why can't adults say, "She is against free trade," instead of "She is right-wing"?)

Psychologists have found that we disagree more productively when we decouple unrelated positions from one another. This entire book has been a call for doing exactly that. Treating tax cuts and abortion as a single issue is confusing and inflammatory, while treating each issue as distinct is enlightening and informative. "Cognitive decoupling is simply the idea of removing extraneous context from a given claim and debating that claim on its own, rather than the fog of associations, ideologies, and potentials swirling around it,"[6] and this is precisely what political granularity can do for us.

The evidence for the benefits of granularity over ideology is abundant. One of the defining features of those who make accurate political judgment is the capacity to make fine distinctions.[7] Instead of conceptualizing politics ideologically or identifying as left or right, accurate thinkers tend to use specificity. They avoid forecasting in vague, ideological terms such as, "The Republican Party will move to the right next year" (an unfalsifiable statement since the meaning of "the right" is indeterminate), but instead make more specific predictions, such as, "Republicans will submit a balanced budget next year" (a well-defined statement that can be falsified). Granularity allows us to determine if we are correct or incorrect and update our beliefs accordingly; essentialism makes this impossible. There are millions of Americans who do not use an essentialist model of politics and they are more evidence-based than those who do. They are not "confused" or "chaotic" in their thinking, but generally more principled, rational, open-minded, and charitable than ideologues.[8] All of us can, by jettisoning essentialism, be more like them.

As neuroscientist Robert Sapolsky has argued, "individuation"—breaking out of all-encompassing categories that divides people into "us" or "them"—is a powerful way to reduce hostility and cognitive bias. Thinking of someone "as an *individual*" is "the surest way to weaken automatic categorization of someone as a Them." He urges us to "replace essentialism with individuation," and this advice applies as well to ideological divisions as it does to racial, ethnic, religious, and national divisions.[9] Granularity in politics, both in terms of thinking about issues *and* people, is perhaps the single best way to improve political discourse.

Lest anyone think this is unworkable, note that granularity was a core characteristic of the greatest political thinkers of the past century. Martin Luther King Jr.'s "Letter from a Birmingham Jail" contains no mention of "left-wing" or "right-wing," "liberal" or "conservative," but instead references specific goals, strategies, policies, and actions. Hannah Arendt understood totalitarianism better than her contemporaries because she analyzed it in terms of specific, meaningful categories (e.g., social isolation, anti-Semitism, mass society, and imperialism) rather than vague, essentialist categories. George Orwell was among the most persuasive and insightful political writers of his time not because he had the "correct" ideology, but because he eschewed ideology altogether. As an anti-fascist, culturally traditional, anti-communist socialist, he defied category; and because of this, not despite it, he became one of the clearest political thinkers of the twentieth century. George Kennan had a more lasting and positive impact on Cold War thinking than his contemporaries because he did not filter his ideas through an ideological lens. Had his pro-market views led him to identify as "right wing," he might have supported the Vietnam War in the name of tribal solidarity. The trenchant, granular analysis of King, Arendt, Orwell, and Kennan stands in sharp contrast to the sloppy sloganeering of those mired in essentialist categories.

Those who say we cannot be granular in politics because we need an over-arching model to bring order to a complex domain overlook the fact that we do without such an overarching model in all other complex realms of life. Few of us think in unidimensional terms when it comes to business, recreation, or medicine, and yet discourse in those domains is far more rational and civil than it is in politics. Instead of saying, "The company moved to the left" we say, "The company reduced its range of products"; instead of saying, "She's on the recreational right," we say, "She likes mountain biking"; instead of saying, "The patient has a left-wing illness," we say, "The patient has a fever." There is no reason we couldn't just bring that same granularity to politics with the same effect.

Granularity is also our response to the "probability" argument for ideology. Many of those who cling to essentialism do so on the grounds that even though left–right terms are not perfectly predictive, they are predictive with a high degree of probability. For example, if someone carries the label "conservative" we can be fairly certain that they are also against abortion. Our response to this is simple: why settle for the "high probability" of ideology when we can have the certainty of granularity? Instead of saying, "She's a liberal," and leaving us to wonder if she believes in abortion rights, why not just say, "She's pro-choice" and settle the issue? Instead of saying, "He has conservative economic views" and then leaving us to puzzle over what that means and with what degree of probability (Higher tariffs or lower tariffs? Reducing income taxes for "supply side" stimulus or increasing income taxes for fiscal responsibility?), why not just say, "He believes in higher tariffs" and end the confusion? The certainty we get with granularity is far preferable to whatever probability we get with ideology.

Granularity improves civility as well as accuracy. Since essentialist categories are as inflammatory as they are vague, using them has the effect of generating more heat than light in political interactions. For instance, notice how often opponents of the Affordable Care Act would throw around the term "far left" in an attempt to tarnish Obama and his signature policy by conjuring up associations with Stalinism (meanwhile supporters of the ACA would apply the term "far right" to their opponents, hoping to tarnish them by association with Nazism).[10] Instead of wasting countless hours fighting over where Obama and his policies fit on a line (He's "far left" according to Sean Hannity, "moderate" according to Fareed Zakaria, "conservative" according to Andrew Sullivan), it's better to just state Obama's policies and discuss them on their merits. If we say, "Obama supports the ACA," we state an accurate fact; if we say, "Obama is left wing" then essentialist assumptions lead to Stalinist associations that stir up anger and hostility. Ideological essentialism is great for self-deception and motive-mongering but terrible for helping us understand the actual substance of political debate.

The choice between ideological thinking and granular thinking is an important one: with ideology we sign up for a tribe, accept the orthodoxies of that tribe, declare we have the correct answer to all political questions, and then demonize those who disagree with us; with granularity we think through individual political issues, come to reasoned conclusions about each one, keep our minds open to the possibility that we could be wrong, and then engage in corrective dialogue on the assumption that there are good, intelligent people who disagree. Perhaps the single best way to improve American politics immediately is to give up ideological categories and simply go granular.

Change Our Speech

The third step is to change the way we speak about ideology. One doesn't have to be a deconstructionist to realize that language has a powerful influence on the way we think, and one of the reasons that thinking about politics has become so clouded is that misleading language has entrenched inaccurate political concepts. Since ideological terms refer to nothing more nor less than tribes, we should get our language to reflect that reality. We can refuse to reinscribe the essentialist theory by refusing to speak in the terms associated with it. Linguistic accuracy can be a powerful weapon against the essentialist illusion.

One easy way to make our language more accurate is to use words that correctly indicate social unity, rather than incorrectly indicate essential unity, when referring to political groups. When we talk about "the left" or "the right," we are falsely implying that there is some philosophical essence that divides these two political groups across time and place. If someone says, "Mary is a right-wing anti-abortion activist," what does the ideological prefix "right-wing" add? What informational value is there to calling Mary a "right wing anti-abortion activist" instead of just an "anti-abortion activist"? Using the ideological prefix is either redundant or an attempt to sneak an inflammatory term into the description by creating an association between the pro-life position and fascism. Accuracy, decency, and economy of expression suggest that we would be better off dropping all ideological terms.

While most commentators tend to add ideological prefixes to substantive terms ("right wing school voucher advocates"), we propose adding substantive prefixes to ideological terms. Instead of saying "the left" as if we are talking about people who share a philosophy, we can say "tribe left" (or, better yet, "team blue") to indicate that we are talking about people who belong to the same team. Prefacing ideological terms with the word "tribe" or "team" is a subtle but important verbal protest against ideological essentialism and we can make this protest every time we must refer to political collectives.

While the political spectrum can be a useful heuristic for scholars and analysts to understand where someone is in their tribal attachments and what this means for their policy views in a specific context, the meaning of ideological terms shifts so rapidly and the spectrum is so bound up with the essentialist myth that it would be better to stop thinking in terms of a political spectrum altogether, especially since there is a natural tendency to want to make cross-contextual comparisons. It's nearly impossible for us to say, "Hamilton was on the right" and "Goldwater was on the right" without jumping to the conclusion that somehow Hamilton and Goldwater had an essential political agreement, even though Hamilton's preference for expanded government was exactly opposite Goldwater's preference for shrinking government. The spectrum is so associated with essentialism that it's difficult to keep the spectrum without essentialist connotations. And while it might be beneficial for scholars to use the spectrum to understand tribal loyalties, voting patterns, and context-specific issue bundling, the costs for the public likely outweigh the benefits. This book has shown that there was a rise of left and right, but it's now time for the fall of left and right. The political spectrum came to America exactly a century ago, but a hundred years is enough: it's now time for us to move on.

Some believe we can dispense with the left–right talk but still continue to use the "liberal" and "conservative" labels, especially if we use them in ways that emphasize multidimensionality (e.g., "economically conservative" or "socially liberal"), but these terms are so deeply bound up with ideological essentialism that continuing to use them will, whether we intend it or not, only help perpetuate the myth of left and right. And since those spectrum-adjacent terms also lack sufficient granularity, it is far better to just replace ideological language with granular language whenever possible. Instead of saying, "economically conservative" and leaving us to wonder if that means "tax cuts" or "balanced budgets," just say, "deficit hawk" and settle the issue. Avoiding essentialist terms such as "liberal" and "conservative" in favor of specific terms, such as "environmentalist" or "deficit hawk" is more linguistically and conceptually accurate.

Another easy way to help bring political speech in line with reality is to re-place ideological terms with party labels. Many believe that getting rid of left–right essentialism necessitates getting rid of the two-party system, but this is incorrect. It is possible to have two political parties without the illusion that all the various positions of each party have an essential connection. Binary political coalitions (manifest in the U.S. in our two-party system) are probably inevitable and have many benefits—such as channeling factional energies in construc-tive directions, creating stability in the political order, branding candidates, and increasing the possibility of majority rule in elections—but we can have all the benefits of a two-party system without the illusion of fixed, enduring ideologies behind them.[11]

The problem with politics today is not our two-party system but the essen-tialist illusion that there is philosophical coherence in what each party stands for. As ideological illusions have entrenched, those who belong to political parties have become more dogmatic and lockstep. This is not coincidental: it is harder to keep a tribe at arm's length when we are convinced that everything it believes is part of a philosophical package.[12]

Since the reality is that there is no essence behind ideology and therefore no essence behind what each party stands for, then it follows that neither party (nor its associated ideology) has a monopoly on truth. We should keep the parties but kill left–right essentialism. There are many advantages to a binary political party system, but there are no advantages to a binary ideological system. Shedding es-sentialism and its concomitant myth of party infallibility would mean less dog-matism, more healthy skepticism, and more willingness to depart from the party line.[13]

When it comes to speaking, this means replacing the language of ideology (left–right) with the language of party (Democratic–Republican). Ideological terms communicate an essentialist illusion, but party terms communicate the re-ality that there are political teams. Instead of saying, "He's on the left," we can just say, "He's a Democrat"; instead of saying, "She's a conservative" we can just say, "She's a Republican." Using the terms "Democrats" and "Republicans" correctly implies that we are referring to political parties that are coalitions of groups that share a party platform, but whose ideas and issue positions are subject to change (with plenty of dissension in the ranks). Party labels have all the advantages of communicating tribal affiliation but none of the baggage of essentialism. Replacing ideology talk with party talk obviously would not solve the problem of political tribalism, but it would help diminish it. A partisan without the essen-tialist delusion is far preferable to a partisan with the essentialist delusion.

Many protest that using party labels rather than ideological labels will not work since there are many who belong to the parties who nonetheless do not subscribe to everything the party believes. But how, we wonder, is using party labels worse than using ideological labels when ideological labels are even less accurate? If the term "Republican" is imprecise in what it communicates, the term "conservative" is even less precise. Since the parties now define the ideologies, party and ideological labels each communicate affiliation with the same tribe, but at least party labels do not perpetuate the essentialist illusion. If someone says, "I'm a Republican," it conveys the fact that they belong to a party that has a specific platform, but if they say, "I'm a conservative," it conveys the falsehood that all of their beliefs are unified by a philosophical worldview. Ideological labels do not provide any more information than do party labels, but they do provide more *mis*information.

But doesn't an ideological label indicate a degree of commitment to the party that the party label alone does not? For example, doesn't the term "conservative Republican" sometimes refer to a Republican deeply committed to what the party stands for? Yes, so why not just call them a "committed," "staunch," or "lockstep" Republican instead of conjuring up essentialist illusions with the term "conservative." What if someone belongs to one of the two ideological tribes, but does not have a formal party membership? Then we have the options of granularity or tribal prefixes mentioned above, as well as the terms "Democratic leaning" and "Republican leaning" to indicate their sympathies. Although we generally have to *vote* in binary terms (Democratic or Republican), that does not mean we have to *think* in binary terms. Getting rid of the ideological language binary would go a long way toward helping us think more pluralistically and, by extension, more accurately.

Find Healthier Tribes

The fourth step is to find healthier tribes. Yes, human beings are inevitably tribal—we are naturally inclined to seek out communities of meaning and belonging—but there are better and worse tribes, and ideological tribes are among the bad ones. While ideological communities reduce social capital and well-being, other communities, such as families, service organizations, churches, and local associations have been shown to increase social capital and well-being.[14] It would improve life for all of us, collectively and individually, if we spent less time strengthening the bonds of ideological tribes built around an essentialist illusion and more time strengthening the bonds of healthy tribes built around interpersonal connection. We should all spend less time watching cable news, engaging in political argument on Twitter, listening to talk radio, or interacting with the politically like-minded on social media, and spend more time volunteering, interacting with family, forming connections with neighbors, and participating in churches or other intermediate associations.[15] Since ideological tribalism is destructive, we should funnel our tribal inclinations in more constructive directions. If America has moved from healthy tribalism to ideological tribalism to our detriment, there is no reason we cannot move from ideological tribalism to healthy tribalism to our benefit.[16]

With the decline in religious participation in the U.S. has come the need to fill that void with something else—ideological tribalism has proven a destructive substitute religion.[17] Mixing church and state has always been dangerous, so when political tribes become religions, we all suffer.

Engage in Adversarial Collaboration

The fifth and final step we can take to minimize the scourge of ideology is to engage in "adversarial collaboration." This means consciously and systematically incorporating constructive political disagreement into our lives. If there were a left–right essence, then arriving at political truth would be as simple as choosing the correct side, but since there is no essence, we can only hope to improve our political understanding by hearing arguments for and against individual positions and evaluating them accordingly.

The more we associate only with the like-minded, the more we take our views for granted and the more inflexible and dogmatic we become in those views. Perhaps the best way to check this tendency is to seek out and listen to those who see things differently. Once we have shed the "one side is right about everything" mentality facilitated by ideological essentialism, then someone who holds a different view on something is not an enemy to be defeated but a partner to be learned from. Such adversarial collaboration has been shown to reduce ideological identification and political error.

For instance, in her extensive studies of group cognition, psychologist Charlan Nemeth has found that the single best way to make a group more open-minded, accurate, and effective is to include authentic voices of disagreement in the group (and there is still a cognitive bonus to dissent even when the dissenters are wrong).[18] Other studies have shown that politically diverse teams are less biased, more careful, more able to spot cognitive blind spots, better at correcting error, more creative, and more informed than politically monolithic ones.[19] Social progress comes by error elimination, and we are much more likely to identify and jettison errors in our thinking when we engage those who disagree.[20] Journalist Steven Johnson reports that "homogeneous groups—whether they are united by ethnic background, gender or some other commonality like politics—tend to come to decisions too quickly. They settle early on a most-likely scenario and don't question their assumptions, since everyone at the table seems to agree with the broad outline of the interpretation."[21]

We are all given to confirmation bias, but we can reduce this tendency by working with those who disagree.[22] Simply put, adversarial collaboration is a powerful tool for helping us to correct cognitive error, especially the confirmation bias associated with essentialist thinking. Those who engage a diversity of viewpoints tend to become less ideological, less extreme, and less likely to view the world through the distorting essentialist lens. Adversarial collaboration necessarily leads to a healthier, more post-ideological outlook.[23]

At this point we need to correct a couple of misconceptions about adversarial collaboration. It does not mean that all views are equally valid—there are better and worse ideas out there—it only means that we are more likely to arrive at better ideas when we engage disagreement. Even if truth is not plural, our tools for seeking the truth should be.[24] Nor does adversarial collaboration mean that we must compromise or discard deeply held moral beliefs (our desires for freedom, social justice, and racial equality are and ought to be non-negotiable)—it only means being open to alternative views about how best to achieve these goals. We may have strong moral commitments, but that does not mean we know exactly which approach to every issue will best further them. Considering multiple points of view helps us find out.

While adversarial collaboration does not entail relativism or lack of moral commitment, it does entail a strong commitment to freedom of speech. We believe that the disturbing rise in hostility to open expression is largely a function of essentialist thinking. By telling us that we can instantly have all the right answers to every political question simply by choosing a side, essentialism gives the illusion of infallibility and if the infallible have nothing to learn, then there is no need for them to consider or even allow alternative viewpoints. They know those views are wrong a priori. According to essentialism, promoting truth is a matter of silencing the errors of others rather than correcting our own. Anyone silencing disagreement through force is implicitly assuming omniscience—such is the hubris that ideological essentialism creates.[25]

The social theory, by contrast, promotes the humility that is a necessary precondition of scientific rationality. Understanding that ideologies are tribes helps us see that the positions associated with those tribes can be wrong. In science as in politics, we eliminate error and get closer to the truth by subjecting our views to open criticism. Since social progress comes by falsifying incorrect policies and procedures, it also requires an open society that accepts and institutionalizes constructive disagreement.[26] Being non-ideological would make us more willing to change our minds in the face of new evidence, which is the key to rationality and, by extension, the key to human progress.[27]

Adversarial collaboration is particularly important in the realm of scholarship. Critics of higher education are correct to point out the problem that universities have become ideologically homogeneous: as universities become ever more uniform in viewpoint, the destructive effect this has on truth-seeking becomes ever more apparent. The problem with higher education today is not that the professors are "all a bunch of liberals"; the problem is that they lack the dissenting voices necessary for self-correction. Ideological homogeneity reduces the critical rationalism that would improve the teaching and research that is the primary function of colleges and universities.[28]

Some want to achieve a greater diversity of thought in academia with an affirmative action program for "conservatives," but this is misguided. As this book has shown, "conservative" has no essence, so any set of policies can wear the label "conservative" with enough storytelling. If there were affirmative action to hire "conservatives," those seeking coveted academic appointments would simply apply the label "conservative" to political outlooks that reinforced rather than challenged campus orthodoxies. For example, a socialist historian looking for a job could spin stories about how he believes in "conserving" traditions from predatory capitalism, a pro-choice historian could spin stories about "conserving" a woman's right to choose, a pacifist historian could spin stories about "conserving" America's tradition of anti-militarism, and so forth. Since "liberal" and "conservative" identities are upheld by fairytales, any affirmative action program to hire one or the other would just result in the telling of more fairytales. Demanding that universities hire "conservatives" would not result in a greater diversity of viewpoints but only in a greater rebranding of viewpoints.

Instead of promoting useless ideological affirmative action programs, we propose a much better way to improve academic research: institutionalizing adversarial collaboration by using the courtroom as a model. Courts of law are generally more objective than other realms of society, not because the *participants* are more objective but because the *process* is more objective. Our legal system has institutionalized disagreement by requiring a strong pro and con viewpoint for every question that comes into court. Instead of assigning just one attorney to a case and trusting them to be "fair and objective," our legal process ensures there are multiple attorneys who are literally invested in providing the strongest possible argument for the opposite sides in each dispute.

There's no reason we couldn't bring this same approach to scholarship. Currently, we simply trust scholars to be fair-minded without any checks or opposition—this is like paying a prosecuting attorney to find a guilty verdict while also expecting her to represent the defendant fairly. To fix this, we propose that scholars research controversial policy questions in teams that have representatives of both the pro and con side of that particular issue (e.g., research on the effects of minimum wage would be done by a team composed of advocates and opponents of the minimum wage).[29] Working together, these disagreeing scholars would design the study, determine falsifying evidence ahead of time, and then carry out their research accordingly. There is right and wrong in scholarship just as there is guilt and innocence in a courtroom, and scholars would be better able to determine what is right or wrong by considering both sides of any contested political issue.[30]

Not only would adversarial collaboration improve scholarship, but it would also improve public trust in scholarship. Currently, a large proportion of the country is coming to see academic research as ideologically biased to the point of worthlessness. But if we assigned multiple, disagreeing scholars to research political questions, the answers they came up with would not only be more correct, they would also be more likely to find acceptance among the public at large.[31] Just as jurors in a courtroom can be far more confident in their judgments if they have heard arguments from both the prosecution and the defense, so the public would be more confident in the findings of academic research if they knew the studies were informed by those of opposite perspectives rather than agenda-driven ideologues trying to get a "win" for "their side."

In summary, recognition, granularity, linguistic accuracy, redirection of tribal tendencies, and adversarial collaboration could work wonders in helping us overcome the left–right essentialism that is so pervasive and destructive in America today. A non-ideological America would be far preferable to our current America in which we are stuck thinking in the binary terms of scapegoats and saviors (an Obama to bring "change we can believe in" or a Trump to "make America great again"). Currently, we blame politicians for our problems because it's easy—it outsources responsibility and leaves us to simply check the boxes of "our side" in the voting booth and spout the clichés of "our side" in the public square. The reality is that political dysfunction is a capillary-level problem that we can only solve through bottom-up remedies. Ideological essentialism is a stubborn fiction, but one that millions of us can overcome by refusing to submit to it any longer.

Conclusion

The widespread reluctance to give up the essentialist theory of ideology today reminds us of the widespread reluctance to give up the geocentric theory of the universe in the Middle Ages. Early Greek astronomers created a simple, elegant astronomical model in which the earth sat at the center of the universe and all celestial objects orbited around it in perfect circles. When evidence poured in showing that this model had major problems, many of the greatest astronomers clung more tightly to the old paradigm by adding "epicycles" to save the theory from falsification.[1] Instead of abandoning the model in favor of a better, more complex one, they doubled down through creative storytelling. It took the Copernican revolution to finally break them away.

Today we are at a similar point in politics. Ideological essentialism does not describe reality any better than the geocentric model does, but current-day political actors are like medieval astronomers adding epicycle-like stories to save it from falsification. They should take the "Copernican leap" and move on from the false model. Just as human understanding of astronomy was limited until the geocentric model was overthrown, so our political understanding will be limited until the essentialist model is overthrown. Although educated elites believe in ideological essentialism today, educated elites also believed in the geocentric universe in the Middle Ages. In both cases the intellectuals were mistaken: the sun does not orbit the earth, and politics is not unidimensional. We all need to stop searching for the Holy Grail "essence" of left and right and start looking for the correct answers to individual political issues based on their merit.

Ever since the terms "left-wing" and "right-wing" emerged during the French Revolution, we have been asking the wrong question. Instead of asking, "What is the essential characteristic that binds ideologues together?" we should have been asking, "Why do people share the same views on so many distinct political positions when there is no essential characteristic binding them together?" This book has shown that social conformism is the best answer. Social ties, not

The Myth of Left and Right. Hyrum Lewis and Verlan Lewis, Oxford University Press. © Oxford University Press 2023.
DOI: 10.1093/oso/9780197680216.003.0009

philosophical ties, hold together the dominant ideologies in America today. While it's true that humans are unquestionably tribal, storytelling beings who live by tribes and stories, it's also true that some tribes are harmful and some stories false. The essentialist story is false, and the tribes that have formed around it are harmful.

The choice before us, then, is a stark one: we can either continue to be socially divided into warring political tribes based on the myth that we are fighting about fundamental worldviews, or we can discard the essentialist fiction and begin the constructive work of coming up with political solutions independent of the ideological framework. There is much talk these days about being on the "right side of history," but if our descendants have made any progress in political thinking, they will have moved well beyond ideological essentialism. It will look as bizarre, simplistic, antiquated, and risible to them as the geocentric theory looks to us today. It was not easy for astronomers to give up the geocentric theory in the Middle Ages, and it's not easy for us to give up ideological essentialism today, but we must discard it if we want to see the same progress in politics that we have seen in astronomy. Moving on from the essentialist illusion will not solve all our problems or completely eliminate irrational tribalism from public life, but it will move us in the right direction, and this is all we are asking for.

NOTES

Introduction

1. Larry Diamond et al., "Americans Increasingly Believe Violence Is Justified if the Other Side Wins," *Politico*, October 9, 2020, https://www.politico.com/news/magazine/2020/10/01/political-violence-424157; Marist Institute, "PBS NewsHour/Marist Poll Results: Insurrection at the Capitol," Marist Poll, January 8, 2021, http://maristpoll.marist.edu/wp-content/uploads/2021/01/PBS-NewsHour_Marist-Poll_USA-NOS-and-Tables_202101081001.pdf#page=3.
2. Although "ideology" in a broader sense can refer to any belief system, we use "ideology" in this book only to refer to ideologies associated with the left–right political spectrum (i.e., "progressive," "liberal," "conservative," "reactionary," "left-wing," "right-wing").
3. William Anthony Hay, "The Great Divide," *Wall Street Journal*, December 5, 2020, https://www.wsj.com/articles/conservatism-and-liberalism-two-books-on-the-great-divide-11607099696.
4. Arthur M. Schlesinger Jr., *The Vital Center: The Politics of Freedom* (Boston: Houghton-Mifflin, 1949); Edmund Fawcett, *Liberalism: The Life of an Idea* (Princeton: Princeton University Press, 2014); Edmund Fawcett, *Conservatism: The Fight for a Tradition* (Princeton: Princeton University Press, 2020). For examples of works that define left and right more specifically in terms of fiscal, social, and foreign policy, see Yuval Levin, *The Great Debate: Edmund Burke, Thomas Paine, and the Birth of Right and Left* (New York: Basic Books, 2014) and George Nash, *The Conservative Intellectual Movement in America since 1945* (New York: Basic Books, 1976).
5. Peter Berkowitz, "The Liberal Spirit in America and Its Paradoxes," in *Liberalism for a New Century*, ed. Neil Jumonville and Kevin Mattson (Berkeley: University of California Press, 2007), 14.
6. Abraham Lincoln, "Inaugural Address," ed. Gerhard Peters and John T. Wooley, The American Presidency Project, https://www.presidency.ucsb.edu/node/202167; Matthew S. Holland, *Bonds of Affection* (Washington, DC: Georgetown University Press, 2007).
7. Over the last generation, social scientists have been showing that categories of identity previously thought to be essential—e.g., race and nation—are, in fact, social constructs. See, e.g., Benedict Anderson, *Imagined Communities* (New York: Verso, 2006) and Matthew Jacobson, *Whiteness of a Different Color* (Cambridge, MA: Harvard University Press, 1998). This book does the same with the political spectrum, showing that it is a social construct with meaning that varies according to time and place. See Christopher M. Federico and Paul Goren, "Motivated Social Cognition and Ideology: Is Attention to Elite Discourse a Prerequisite for Epistemically Motivated Political Affinities?" in *Social and Psychological Bases of Ideology and System Justification*, ed. John T. Jost, Aaron C. Kay, and Hulda Thorisdottir (New York: Oxford University Press, 2009), 267–291.

8. Some find our thesis unbelievable on its face, but with each passing day more research emerges showing that tribalism and conformity are far more powerful influences on our beliefs than previously thought possible. If conformity can lead people to believe short lines are long and long lines are short (as demonstrated in the Asch Conformity Experiments), it can also lead people to believe that there is only one issue in politics. See Charlan Nemeth, *In Defense of Troublemakers: The Power of Dissent in Life and Business* (New York: Basic Books, 2018) and Cory J. Clark et al., "Tribalism Is Human Nature," *Current Directions in Psychological Science* 28, no. 6 (December 2019): 587–592: "We conclude that tribal bias is a natural and nearly in-eradicable feature of human cognition and that no group—not even one's own—is immune" (p. 587). As journalist David Ropeik puts it, "Society, in a very real way, is survival. We have belonged to tribes for as long as modern humans have been around, and we have depended on our tribes for our very existence—for food and for protection. We have evolved to be keenly attuned to how our tribes are doing, because the better the tribe is doing, the better our chances are, and vice versa. So we tend to adopt behaviors and attitudes and perceptions of risk that reinforce the beliefs of the tribe, that reinforce cohesion in the tribe, and that also strengthen our acceptance by other members of the tribe." David Ropeik, *How Risky Is It, Really? Why Our Fears Don't Always Match the Facts* (New York: McGraw-Hill, 2010), 143.

9. Thankfully, there are dissenters from this consensus. Many of the most insightful thinkers have recognized and avoided ideological essentialism. See Nassim Taleb, *The Black Swan: The Impact of the Highly Improbable* (New York: Random House, 2007); Philip Tetlock, *Expert Political Judgment* (Princeton: Princeton University Press, 2006); Crispin Sartwell, *Entanglements: A System of Philosophy* (Albany: State University of New York Press, 2017); Thomas Chatterton Williams, "An Incoherent Truth," *Harper's* (February 2020), https://harpers.org/archive/2020/02/an-incoherent-truth/; Jason Weeden and Rob Kurzban, *The Hidden Agenda of the Political Mind: How Self-Interest Shapes Our Opinions and Why We Won't Admit It* (Princeton: Princeton University Press, 2014); Michael Lind, *The New Class War: Saving Democracy from the Managerial Elite* (New York: Penguin, 2020); Timothy Ferris, *The Science of Liberty* (New York: HarperCollins, 2010); and Jonathan Rauch, "Rethinking Polarization," *National Affairs* 45 (Fall 2019), https://www.nationalaffairs.com/publications/detail/rethinking-polarization?smid=nytcore-ios-shar. French intellectual Raymond Aron saw the lack of essence in French ideologies, saying in his memoirs, "I did not deny the fact that there was a distinction between the right and the left in the national assembly. What I denied was that there was an eternal left, the same in various historical circumstances, inspired by the same values, united in the same aspirations." Raymond Aron, *Memoirs: Fifty Years of Political Reflection* (New York: Holmes & Meier, 1990), 220.

10. Peter Wehner, *The Death of Politics: How to Heal Our Frayed Republic after Trump* (New York: HarperCollins, 2019), 30.

11. See, e.g., Vernon L. Parrington, *The Colonial Mind, 1620–1800* (New York: Harcourt Brace Jovanovich, Inc., 1927); Charles A. Beard, *The American Party Battle* (New York: Macmillan, 1928); Richard Hofstadter, *The American Political Tradition* (New York: Alfred Knopf, 1948); Schlesinger, *The Vital Center*; Louis Hartz, *The Liberal Tradition in America* (New York: Harcourt Brace & Co., 1955); Mary C. Brennan, *Turning Right in the Sixties: The Conservative Capture of the GOP* (Chapel Hill: University of North Carolina Press, 2000); Bruce J. Schulman and Julian Zelizer, eds., *Rightward Bound: Making America Conservative in the 1970s* (Cambridge, MA: Harvard University Press, 2008); Kim Phillips-Fein, "Conservatism: A State of the Field," *Journal of American History* 98, no. 3 (December 2011): 723–743; and Nancy MacLean, *Democracy in Chains: The Deep History of the Radical Right's Stealth Plan for America* (New York: Penguin Books, 2018).

12. Most introductory U.S. history textbooks, for instance, claim that the country "turned right-ward" in the 1980s.

13. For an overview of this literature, see Michael Barber and Nolan McCarty, "Causes and Consequences of Polarization," in *Negotiating Agreement in Politics*, ed. Jane Mansbridge and Cathie Jo Martin (Washington, DC: American Political Science Association, 2013), 19–53.

14. For example, John Gerring appropriately eschewed the left–right framework in his historical look at *Party Ideologies in America* (New York: Cambridge University Press, 1998) and instead simply divided Whig-Republican Party ideology into two phases (a "national epoch" and a

"neoliberal epoch") and Democratic Party ideology into three phases (a "Jeffersonian epoch," a "populist epoch," and a "universalist epoch"). Gerring recognized the mutability of labels like "left," "right," "liberal," and "conservative," and so used more useful descriptors: "The problem with conservatism, as with liberalism, is that the labels apply to too many things. The analysis of American party ideologies rightly begins, therefore, with the identification of concepts that can be more clearly delineated in time and space." Gerring, *Party Ideologies in America*, 14. John Lapinski also usefully disaggregates Congressional lawmaking into substantive policy issue areas rather than assuming that "left" and "right" naturally bundle together disparate issue positions and that ideology makes the nature of representation and lawmaking homogeneous across issue areas. John S. Lapinski, *The Substance of Representation: Congress, American Political Development, and Lawmaking* (Princeton: Princeton University Press, 2014). David Karol's 2009 book, *Party Position Change in American Politics* (New York: Cambridge University Press, 2009), similarly challenged the political science discipline's party-stasis view by showing how the two major parties have frequently switched positions on a variety of important political issues over time. While Downs, Poole, and Rosenthal believed that the parties would, and did, move left and right over time in search of a majority of the electorate, they did not—like Karol—allow for the possibility that the parties would completely switch places in ideological space. While Karol made this important contribution to our understanding of the evolutionary character of party ideologies, he did not take the next step to point out that, in changing their issue positions, the parties also changed the meanings of "liberal" and "conservative." Several other recent books have usefully chronicled how intra-party factions, social movements, and dissident groups have constantly transformed the ideologies of the two major parties, but they stop short of pointing out that these transformations also changed the meanings of "left" and "right." See Daniel DiSalvo, *Engines of Change: Party Factions in American Politics, 1868–2010* (New York: Oxford University Press, 2012); Daniel Schlozman, *When Movements Anchor Parties: Electoral Alignments in American History* (Princeton: Princeton University Press, 2016); Ruth Bloch Rubin, *Building the Bloc: Intraparty Organization in the U.S. Congress* (New York: Cambridge University Press, 2017); and Sidney M. Milkis and Daniel J. Tichenor, *Rivalry and Reform: Presidents, Social Movements, and the Transformation of American Politics* (Chicago: University of Chicago Press, 2018).

15. Hans Noel's 2012 book, *Political Ideologies and Political Parties in America* (Cambridge University Press, 2013), shows how liberalism and conservatism were first socially constructed as ideologies in America by journalists in the first half of the twentieth century, and how liberalism became associated with the Democratic Party and conservatism with the Republican Party during this period. However, Noel did not see that, once these ideologies were created and became associated with the two major parties, the parties themselves would be agents of changing the meaning and content of "liberalism" and "conservatism." Recent years have seen the production of more American political development (APD) scholarship that takes a nuanced view of parties and ideologies in American history, but none of it points out the fallacy of the essentialist theory of ideology and the myth of the left–right spectrum.

16. Charles Forcey, *The Crossroads of Liberalism: Croly, Weyl, Lippmann, and the Progressive Era, 1900–1925* (New York: Oxford University Press, 1967); Nancy Cohen, *The Reconstruction of American Liberalism, 1865–1914* (Chapel Hill: University of North Carolina Press, 2002); John E. Moser, *Right Turn: John T. Flynn and the Transformation of American Liberalism* (New York: New York University Press, 2007); Gary Gerstle, "The Protean Character of American Liberalism," *American Historical Review* 99, no. 4 (October 1994): 1043–1073.

17. We sometimes get the critique that we are attacking a "straw man" and that few people really believe in ideological essentialism, but virtually every pundit, activist, politician, and academic talks about left and right as if they were enduring essences. Most people who identify as "liberal" or "conservative" erroneously believe that their various issue positions are bound together by an essence. Very few people who identify as "liberal" or "conservative" admit that their various issue positions are bound together by socialization. Political psychologist John T. Jost, for instance, says that his research identifies the "core features of liberalism and conservatism." John T. Jost, "The End of the End of Ideology," *American Psychologist* 61, no. 7 (October 2006): 654. These "core features" are what we mean by "ideological essence." For more examples of scholarly invocations of ideological essentialism, see chapter 4. Anytime

someone argues that an individual or group moved "to the left" or "to the right" over time, they are assuming (whether consciously or not) that left and right have some enduring essential character. Otherwise, such a statement would be nonsense. See, e.g., Colin Wright, "Elon Musk Tweeted My Cartoon," *Wall Street Journal*, May 2, 2022, https://www.wsj.com/artic les/elon-musk-tweeted-my-cartoon-woke-progressive-left-wing-media-right-viral-twitter-politics-culture-liberal-center-11651504379?mod=hp_opin_pos_5#cxrecs_s. Essentialism is hardly a "straw man" when millions of Americans, including many academics and data scientists, talk about "ideological polarization" and get into arguments about which party has moved farther toward "left" or "right" essences.

Chapter 1

1. According to Jost, ideology is an "interrelated set of attitudes." John T. Jost, "The End of the End of Ideology," *American Psychologist* 61, no. 7 (October 2006): 653. Whatever it is that "relates" these "interrelated" attitudes is the essence. We, claim, by contrast, that there is no inherent relationship between these attitudes. An attitude that favors free markets, for instance, has no necessary relationship to an attitude that favors militarism. They are not, as Jost maintains, interrelated (as the militarism of socialists such as Stalin, Mao, and Hitler make clear).

2. An "essentialist" in this book is someone who accepts the essentialist theory of ideology.

3. John R. Alford, John R. Hibbing, and Kevin B. Smith, *Predisposed: Liberals, Conservatives, and the Biology of Political Differences* (New York: Routledge, 2014), 12.

4. Marcel Gauchet, "Right and Left," in *Realms of Memory: The Construction of the French Past*, Vol. 1: Conflicts and Divisions, ed. Lawrence D. Krtizman and trans. Arthur Goldhammer (New York: Columbia University Press, 1996), 241–298.

5. This is what Robert Kurzban and Jason Weeden call the "General Orientations Model" in *The Hidden Agenda of the Political Mind* (Princeton: Princeton University Press, 2014).

6. According to the Merriam-Webster dictionary, conservatives tend to "maintain existing views, conditions, or institutions" while "left-winger," "liberal," and "progressive" are antonyms to "conservative." Merriam-Webster Dictionary online, "Conservative," https://www.merr iam-webster.com/dictionary/conservative, accessed May 25, 2022. The terms "progressive" and "conservative" themselves indicate that progressives want to progress and conservatives want to conserve. Also see, e.g., Jost, "End of the End of Ideology," 654; and John T. Jost, Jack Glaser, Arie W. Kruglanski, and Frank J. Sulloway, "Political Conservatism as Motivated Social Cognition," *Psychological Bulletin* 129, no. 3 (2003): 339–375. Although change-preservation is the most commonly proposed essence, it is by no means the only one. We address many of the other proposed essences in chapter 4.

7. See Matthew Continetti, *The Right: The Hundred Year War for American Conservatism* (New York: Basic Books, 2022). Continetti's is a prominent work of recent scholarship declaring that the tie uniting all the various conservative types is opposition to progressive change, but this sentiment goes back to the beginning. The editors of *National Review*, the magazine generally recognized to have birthed the conservative movement, declared in the inaugural issue that their goal was to stand "athwart history yelling 'stop.'" William F. Buckley Jr., "Publisher's Statement," *National Review* 1, no. 1 (November 1955): 5.

8. A variant of essentialism says that the essence is the one issue that defines ideology when all others are stripped away—a "key issue" rather than a "master issue." So, for instance, some argue that a preference for free markets defines the right across time and space, and that other issues associated with the right (e.g., nationalism, militarism, regulation of abortion, capital punishment) are only incidental to the ideology. Whether we talk in terms of a master issue or a key issue, the one, defining issue that we model on the political spectrum is the "essence." As we will show, there is no issue (including free markets) that has persisted across time in defining ideology, and therefore "key issue" essentialism is as mistaken as "master issue" essentialism.

9. Jonathan Haidt, *The Righteous Mind* (New York: Pantheon, 2012), 290.

10. And just as teams can change composition, so ideologies can change composition. Cleveland Cavaliers fans stopped cheering for LeBron James when he switched teams in 2010, and liberals stopped cheering for laissez-faire capitalism when it switched teams in the early

twentieth century. See Charles Forcey, *The Crossroads of Liberalism: Croly, Weyl, Lippmann, and the Progressive Era, 1900–1925* (New York: Oxford University Press, 1967) and Nancy Cohen, *The Reconstruction of American Liberalism, 1865–1914* (Chapel Hill: University of North Carolina Press, 2002), 47–50, 56–57.

11. Numerous studies have confirmed that tribal identity requires no underlying ideal, value, goal, or unifying principle to create coherence. The tribe alone is enough. Children sorted at random into two tribes with nothing connecting them other than the tribal assignment will immediately show hostility to those of the other tribe. They will even reduce their own absolute well-being in order to inflict damage on the outgroup. If this sounds like contemporary politics, it is because both have the same psychological roots. See Muzafer Sherif et al., *The Robbers Cave Experiment: Intergroup Conflict and Cooperation* (Middletown, CT: Wesleyan University Press, 1988); Henri Tajfel et al., "Social Categorization and Intergroup Behavior," *European Journal of Social Psychology* 1, no. 2 (April–June 1971): 149–178; Marilynn B. Brewer, "Ingroup Bias in the Minimal Intergroup Situation: A Cognitive Motivational Analysis," *Psychological Bulletin* 86, no. 2 (March 1979): 307–324; and Jim Sidanius et al., "Vladimir's Choice and the Distribution of Social Resources: A Group Dominance Perspective," *Group Processes & Intergroup Relations* 10, no. 2 (April 2007): 257–265. To those who ask, "If principle does not unite an ideological tribe, then what does?" the answer is (strangely), "The tribe unites the tribe."

12. See Robert Sapolsky, "This Is Your Brain on Nationalism: The Biology of Us and Them," *Foreign Affairs* 98, no. 2 (March/April 2019): 42–47. Just as nations are not bound by an essence but are "imagined communities," so the social theory says that today's ideologies are not bound by an essence but are equally "imagined communities." Anderson, *Imagined Communities.*

13. Stanley Feldman and Christopher Johnston, "Understanding the Determinants of Political Ideology: Implications of Structural Complexity," *Political Psychology* 35, no. 3 (June 2014): 337–358, https://doi.org/10.1111/pops.12055; and Jason Weeden, "If Being Routinely Liberal or Conservative is a Human Universal, Why Is It True Only of Recent College-Educated Whites?" *We the Pleeple,* June 30, 2014, https://pleeps.org/files/lege-educa ted-whites_uhu76v7eqhe0dwvrqu3efc/. Malko and Soto found that the messages inherent in political discourse cause the coherence of many different positions from the ideological menu and that "left" or right" coherence is a function of socialization: "Those high in political engagement are more likely to adopt a consistently conservative or consistently liberal package of attitudes." Ariel Malka and Christopher J. Soto, "Rigidity of the Economic Right? Menu-Independent and Menu-Dependent Influences of Psychological Dispositions on Political Attitudes," *Current Directions in Psychological Science* 24, no. 2 (April 1, 2015): 137–142, https://doi.org/10.1177/0963721414556340. Those who would argue that ideologies do not cohere except among elites because only elites are smart enough to "discover" the essential connection between many diverse issues fail to realize that it is political engagement and socialization, not education or some other marker of intelligence, that correlates with having a coherent set of left or right views. It is socialization into the tribe, not "discovery" of an essence, that explains the unity of views considered liberal or conservative.

14. Ariel Malka, Christopher J. Soto, Michael Inzlicht, and Yphtach Lelkes, "Do Needs for Security and Certainty Predict Cultural and Economic Conservatism? A Cross-National Analysis," *Journal of Personality and Social Psychology* 106 (2014): 1031–1051; Jason Weeden and Robert Kurzban, "Do People Naturally Cluster into Liberals and Conservatives?" *Evolutionary Psychological Science* 2 (2016): 47–57; Philip E. Converse, "The Nature of Belief Systems in Mass Publics (1964)," *Critical Review* 18, nos. 1–3 (2006): 1–74; Weeden and Kurzban, *Hidden Agenda of the Political Mind*; and Christopher M. Federico and Paul Goren, "Motivated Social Cognition and Ideology: Is Attention to Elite Discourse a Prerequisite for Epistemically Motivated Political Affinities?" in *Social and Psychological Bases of Ideology and System Justification*, ed. John T. Jost, Aaron C. Kay, and Hulda Thorisdottir (New York: Oxford University Press, 2009), 267–291.

15. Donald Kinder and Nathan Kalmoe, *Neither Liberal nor Conservative: Ideological Innocence in the American Public* (Chicago: University of Chicago Press, 2017), 114.

16. Eric D. Gould and Esteban F. Klor, "Party Hacks and True Believers: The Effect of Party Affiliation on Political Preferences," *Journal of Comparative Economics* 47, no. 3 (September 2019): 504–524.

17. Michael Barber and Jeremy C. Pope, "Does Party Trump Ideology? Disentangling Party and Ideology in America," *American Political Science Review* 113, no. 1 (February 2019): 38–54. For a summary of similar findings, see Brian Resnick, "Nine Essential Lessons from Psychology to Understand the Trump Era," *Vox*, January 10, 2019, https://www.vox.com/science-and-health/2018/4/11/16897062/political-psychology-trump-explain-studies-research-science-motivated-reasoning-bias-fake-news.

18. We give a fuller discussion of the relationship between party and ideology in later chapters.

19. Geoffrey L. Cohen, "Party over Policy: The Dominating Impact of Group Influence on Political Beliefs," *Journal of Personality and Social Psychology* 85 (2003): 811.

20. Lilliana Mason, "Ideologues without Issues: The Polarizing Consequences of Ideological Identities," *Public Opinion Quarterly* 82, no. S1 (2018): 866–887. Mason notes that "these findings demonstrate how Americans can use ideological terms to disparage political opponents without necessarily holding constrained [i.e., principled] sets of policy attitudes," and that "identity-based elements of ideology are capable of driving heightened levels of affective polarization against outgroup ideologues, even at low levels of policy attitude extremity or constraint." Furthermore, "identification with liberals or conservatives reliably predicts substantial social distancing from ideological outgroups" but doesn't predict support for any given issue position.

21. Gabriel S. Lenz, *Follow the Leader? How Voters Respond to Politicians' Policies and Performance* (Chicago: University of Chicago Press, 2012).

22. Michael Macy, Sebastian Deri, Alexander Ruch, and Natalie Tong, "Opinion Cascades and the Unpredictability of Partisan Polarization," *Science Advances* 5, no. 8 (August 2019): 28.

23. Ibid.: "The unpredictability suggests that what appear to be deep-rooted partisan divisions in our own world may have arisen through a tipping process that might just as easily have tipped the other way."

24. Dan Kahan, "Fixing the Communications Failure," *Nature* 463 (2010): 296–297.

25. Donald Green, Bradley Palmquist, and Eric Schickler, *Partisan Hearts and Minds: Political Parties and the Social Identities of Voters* (New Haven: Yale University Press, 2002), 28–29.

26. Philip E. Tetlock and Dan Gardner, *Superforecasting: The Art and Science of Prediction* (New York: Crown, 2015), 162.

27. Barber and Pope conclude that "the fact that stronger conservatives are the ones most likely to react to the treatment—regardless of the ideological direction of the treatment—suggests that the nearly ubiquitous self-placed ideology measure is less a measure of principled conviction and more of a social identity." Barber and Pope, "Does Party Trump Ideology?," 47–48.

28. Extreme L.A. Lakers fans were extremely against LeBron James until he joined the team in 2018, at which point extreme Lakers fans became extremely in favor of LeBron James. In the same way and for the same reason, extreme conservatives were extremely against militarism until militarism joined the conservative team in the fifties, at which point conservatives became extremely militaristic.

29. For examples of such storytelling, see Russell Kirk, *The Conservative Mind* (Chicago: Regnery, 1953); Norman Cantor, *The American Century: Varieties of Culture in Modern Times* (New York: HarperCollins, 1997); Patrick Allitt, *The Conservatives: Ideas and Personalities throughout American History* (New Haven: Yale University Press, 2009); and Continetti, *The Right.*

30. Joyce Applebee, *The Relentless Revolution: A History of Capitalism* (New York: W. W. Norton, 2010). Notice also that the "extreme right-wing" Unabomber's manifesto was explicitly anti-capitalist. See "Industrial Society and Its Future," *Washington Post*, September 22, 1995, https://www.washingtonpost.com/wp-srv/national/longterm/unabomber/manifesto.text.htm.

31. Some have assumed that because Hitler hated communism, he must have loved capitalism, but, in reality, he hated both capitalism and communism. To either system he preferred his own nationalist, racialist variety of socialism. The same was true of Hitler's "right-wing" allies in Japan and Italy.

32. Upholding "change versus preservation" as the essence of left versus right often depends upon circular reasoning. John Jost, for instance, says that conservatives hold "favorable attitudes toward groups that uphold the status quo," including "Big Business." But what is it that makes "Big Business" conservative of the status quo and not, say, "big government"? The fact that conservatives support it. See Jost, "End of the End of Ideology," 657.

33. Jutta Proch, Julia Elad-Strenger, and Thomas Kessler, "Liberalism and Conservatism, for a Change! Rethinking the Association Between Political Orientation and Relation to Societal Change," *Political Psychology* 40, no. 4 (August 2019): 877–903; and Jennifer Burns, "Godless Capitalism: Ayn Rand and the Conservative Movement," *Modern Intellectual History* 1, no. 3 (November 2004): 1–27.

34. Jeff Greenberg and Eva Jonas, "Psychological Motives and Political Orientation—The Left, the Right, and the Rigid: Comment on Jost et al. (2003)," *Psychological Bulletin* 129, no. 3 (May 2003): 376–382.

35. According to Patrick Allitt, conservatives from Alexander Hamilton to George W. Bush have been united by their "backward-directed" political values. Allitt, *The Conservatives*, 2–3.

36. Note that "left-wing" President Obama dismissed Senator Paul Ryan's budget reforms on the grounds that they introduced too much change in society and would, he believed, "lead to a fundamentally different America than the one we've known throughout most of our history." Barack Obama, "Remarks by the President on Fiscal Policy," George Washington University, April 13, 2011, http://www.whitehouse.gov/the-press-office/2011/04/13/remarks-presid ent-fiscal-policy. One of the most vocal advocates for preserving "endangered values" has been liberal ex-President Jimmy Carter, who claims that conservatives threaten such permanent American ideals as civil liberties, economic opportunity, environmental stewardship, and the separation of church and state. Jimmy Carter, *Our Endangered Values: America's Moral Crisis* (New York: Simon & Schuster, 2005).

37. See Levin, *The Fractured Republic* (New York: Basic Books, 2016); and Lindsey, *The Age of Abundance* (New York: HarperCollins, 2007).

38. Katherine Mangu-Ward, "Wikipedia and Beyond: Jimmy Wales' Sprawling Vision," *Reason* (June 2007), http://reason.com/archives/2007/05/30/wikipedia-and-beyond; and Peter Thiel, "The Education of a Libertarian," *Cato Unbound*, April 13, 2009, http://www.cato-unbound.org/2009/04/13/peter-thiel/the-education-of-a-libertarian/.

39. Greenberg and Jonas note that "all political movements borrow from the past in some way. At the very least, leftists rely on the long-dead Karl Marx, and often on a myth of prehistoric egalitarian communalism." Greenberg and Jonas, "Psychological Motives and Political Orientation," p. 377. Some say that conservatives want to go back to the individualism of the past while liberals want to go forward to the communalism of the future, but the hunter-gatherer and feudal-agricultural economies of the past were far more communal than the capitalist economy of the present, meaning that anti-capitalist communitarians are far more backward-looking than capitalist individualists.

40. Ronald Reagan, "Address Accepting the Presidential Nomination at the Republican National Convention in Detroit," The American Presidency Project, July 17, 1980, https://www.pre sidency.ucsb.edu/documents/address-accepting-the-presidential-nomination-the-republi can-national-convention-detroit.

41. Newt Gingrich, *Winning the Future: A Twenty-First Century Contract with America* (Washington, DC: Regnery, 2005). Gingrich also conducted an admiring interview of Toffler for C-Span. Newt Gingrich interview with Alvin Toffler, C-Span's *After Words*, May 21, 2006, http://www.c-spanvideo.org/program/Alvi&showFullAbstract=1. Futurist Herman Kahn was an inspiration for current-day neoconservatives and a fellow at the conservative Hudson Institute.

42. Liberal historian Daniel T. Rodgers, in *The Age of Fracture* (Cambridge: Belknap Press, 2011), laments the intellectual shifts of the last generation and yearns for an earlier era when Americans thought big instead of small. Liberal sociologist Alan Wolfe applauds the nostalgia of Rodgers's book, saying, "I live in a different country than the one into which I was born in 1942. . . . If more thinkers wrote books like this, the country in which I live may once again resemble the one in which I was born. How sweet that would be"—backward-looking sentiments indeed from one of America's leading liberal intellectuals. Wolfe, "The

Big Shrink: Review of 'The Age of Fracture' by Daniel T. Rodgers," *The New Republic Online*, March 10, 2011, http://www.tnr.com/book/review/age-fracture-daniel-rodgers.

43. Karl Popper, *The Poverty of Historicism* (Boston: Beacon, 1957). Moreover, "backward looking" is often a matter of opinion and perspective. Since we only know the direction of history after it has happened, it is impossible to determine beforehand which political positions will predominate in the future. Recall, e.g., how often opponents of both Soviet communism and Nazi fascism were told they were on the "wrong side of history." The term "forward-looking" is not an objective descriptor of ideology but a compliment we pay to opinions we favor. Kierkegaard wisely noted that "life can only be understood backwards; but it must be lived forwards." Unfortunately, we often mistake our certainty about the past for certainty about the future. We only know the "wrong side of history" about history that has already happened, so it's impossible to know who will be on the "wrong side of history" in the future. The much-repeated Martin Luther King Jr. quote "The long arc of history bends towards justice" is a statement of faith, not a statement of fact—King was a clergyman after all—and even if this statement is correct, there is no way to know for certain which policies today will lead to that millennial justice.

44. If those on the left are optimistic believers in progress by definition (as the synonym "progressive" indicates), why has the language of decline been, over the course of the past century, far more characteristic of the political left than the political right? See Arthur Herman, *The Idea of Decline in Western History* (New York: The Free Press, 1997).

45. An astrologer, for instance, would maintain that courage is an essential Leo characteristic and then make up stories showing how a Leo who fought in the Iraq War was "courageous" for joining the military, but also how a Leo who didn't join the military was "courageous" for refusing to follow the government into an unjust war. It's "heads I win, tails you lose" storytelling that makes both astrology and the essentialist theory immune from falsification and therefore non-rational.

46. See Weeden and Kurzban, "Do People Naturally Cluster?" and Weeden, "Routinely Liberal or Conservative." Political scientist Michael Lind has also shown that there is no correlation between the "right wing" position on government social safety net spending and the "right wing" position on immigration: those in favor of expanding the social safety net are also more likely to favor immigration restriction, as both are perceived to help the American working class. Michael Lind, *The New Class War: Saving Democracy from the Managerial Elite* (New York: Penguin, 2020), 70–71.

47. If anything, there is a more natural tie between militarism and socialism, since wars necessarily expand state power. This explains why the most notorious socialist dictators of the last century (e.g., Stalin, Hitler, Mao, Kim) have also been militarists while the most famous libertarians have also been pacifists. See, e.g., Brian Doherty, *Radicals for Capitalism: A Freewheeling History of the Modern American Libertarian Movement* (New York: Public Affairs, 2007); Bruce Porter, *War and the Rise of the State* (New York: Free Press, 1994); Francis Fukuyama, *America at the Crossroads: Democracy, Power and the Neoconservative Legacy* (New Haven: Yale University Press, 2006); Friedrich Hayek, *The Road to Serfdom* (Chicago: University of Chicago Press, 1945); and Ludwig von Mises, *Omnipotent Government: The Rise of the Total State and Total War* (New Haven: Yale University Press, 1944).

48. "If one looks at data from the U.S. General Social Survey over the past 35 years on opinions on abortion and on government reduction of income differences, in fact the correlation is basically zero." Weeden, "Routinely Liberal or Conservative."

49. Like any metaphor, this one has its limits. Teenagers, unlike political actors, are not involved in the zero-sum world of competing for a monopoly on coercive power, but the analogy still works to illuminate the basic problems inherent in a unidimensional political model.

50. Christopher R. Weber and Christopher M. Federico, "Moral Foundations and Heterogeneity in Ideological Preferences," *Political Psychology* 34, no. 1 (February 2013): 107–126, https://doi.org/10.1111/j.1467-9221.2012.00922.x.

51. Weeden and Kurzban have found that the views associated with left and right only correlate among those who believe in and conform to the political spectrum. It's as if we found a correlation between astrological signs and the characteristics of those signs *only* among those steeped in astrology—this would not confirm the truth of astrology, only the tendency

of humans to conform to socially constructed stereotypes. Weeden and Kurzban, *Hidden Agenda.*

52. See Sherif et al., *The Robbers Cave Experiment;* Henri Tajfel et al., "Social Categorization and Intergroup Behavior"; Brewer, "Ingroup Bias"; and Sidanius et al., "Vladimir's Choice."

53. Back in 2007, Philip Tetlock correctly noted that tribal partisans "are vulnerable to occasional bouts of ideologically induced insanity." Philip Tetlock, "Why Foxes Are Better Forecasters Than Hedgehogs," The Long Now Foundation: Seminars about Long-Term Thinking, January 26, 2007, https://longnow.org/seminars/02007/jan/26/why-foxes-are-better-forecasters-than-hedgehogs/. Sadly, the "ideologically induced insanity" has only increased since then.

54. Lilliana Mason summed up these findings well: "More often than not, citizens do not choose which party to support based on policy opinion; they alter their policy opinion according to which party they support. Usually they do not notice that this is happening, and most, in fact, feel outraged when the possibility is mentioned. All citizens want to believe that their political values are solid and well-reasoned. More often, though, policy attitudes grow out of group-based defense." Mason, *Uncivil Agreement: How Politics Became Our Identity* (Chicago: University of Chicago Press, 2018), 20–21.

55. Cory J. Clark et al., "Tribalism Is Human Nature," *Current Directions in Psychological Science* 28, no. 6 (December 2019): 587–592; Kinder and Kalmoe, *Neither Liberal nor Conservative.*

56. It turns out that political theorist Michael Oakeshott was correct when he said, "Far from a political ideology being the quasi-divine parent of political activity, it turns out to be its earthly stepchild . . . political activity comes first and a political ideology follows after." Michael Oakeshott, "Political Education *(LSE, 1951),*" in *The Study of Politics: A Collection of Inaugural Lectures,* ed. Preston King (London: Frank Cass, 1977), 79. Similarly, journalist Kevin Williamson noted that "people do not choose political parties based on their ideologies; more often it is the case that they acquire ideological orientations through preexisting political affiliations, which is to say, through preexisting social identities." Kevin Williamson, *The Smallest Minority* (Washington, DC: Regnery, 2019), chap. 10.

Chapter 2

1. Marcel Gauchet, "Right and Left," in *Realms of Memory: The Construction of the French Past, Vol. 1: Conflicts and Divisions,* ed. Lawrence D. Kritzman and trans. Arthur Goldhammer (New York: Columbia University Press, 1996), 241–298.

2. The fact that many on the left still invoke the "right side of history" rhetoric shows that although essential principles do not persist across time, the narrative strategies often do. Even as the principles of left and right constantly reverse, there is a continuity in the stories essentialists tell about those of the same ideology just as there is continuity in the stories astrologers tell about those of the same astrological sign.

3. Notice, for instance, that in Webster's 1828 dictionary, the terms "liberal" and "conservative" had no political or ideological connotations while the terms "left-wing" and "right-wing" do not even show up and were not in general use until a century later. American Dictionary of the English Language, Webster's Dictionary 1828, http://www.webstersdictionary1828.com.

4. See Charles A. Beard, *The American Party Battle* (New York: Macmillan, 1928); Vernon L. Parrington, *The Colonial Mind, 1620–1800* (New York: Harcourt Brace Jovanovich, Inc., 1927); Richard Hofstadter, *The American Political Tradition* (New York: Alfred Knopf, 1948); Arthur M. Schlesinger Jr., *The Vital Center: The Politics of Freedom* (Boston: Houghton-Mifflin, 1949); and Louis Hartz, *The Liberal Tradition in America* (New York: Harcourt Brace & Co., 1955). For an example of journalism that referred to the Founders as "left wing," see Louis M. Hacker, "Revolutionary America," *Harper's Monthly Magazine* 170 (February 28, 1935): 431. To Carl Becker, the American revolutionaries were "radicals," while those opposed to it were "conservatives." Carl Becker, *Our Great Experiment in Democracy: A History of the United States* (New York: Harper, 1920), 40–45, 109–111.

5. At the time of the ratification debates over the U.S. Constitution, the "left-wing" Anti-Federalists believed that democracies needed to be demographically homogeneous, and that the requisite virtues of the citizenry must come from religion. This preference for homogeneity caused them to advocate for small, agrarian, insular republics that would not be corrupted by

cities with their diverse populations and factions. The "right-wing" Federalists, on the other hand, argued for more demographic diversity, more national government power, higher taxes, more spending, and more economic regulation. Some recent scholars have claimed that the Anti-Federalists, like the Southern Democrats of the Jim Crow era and the Goldwater Republicans of the postwar era, were really "conservatives," and that the Federalists, like the Northern Republicans of the Civil War era and the Democrats of the New Deal era, were really "liberals," but this simply reinforces the point that applying the labels "conservative" and "liberal" anachronistically is arbitrary and confusing. Jeffrey K. Tulis and Nicole Mellow, *Legacies of Losing in American Politics* (Chicago: University of Chicago Press, 2018). The fact that historians can't agree on who in the past shared which essence is strong evidence against their entire essentialist framework. We should stop arguing over who were the "liberals" and "conservatives" in history and simply describe them as they described themselves. We need to abandon the strange quest to recruit the heroes of history into our side of current-day political battles when they had radically different policy views (e.g., recruiting the small government Thomas Jefferson into the "progressive" cause of expanding government power by labeling him a "progressive" is misleading).

6. Beard, *American Party Battle*, 51.
7. The "highly conservative views" of the Federalist Party, says historian Robert Remini, "included support for a strong central government, payment of national and state debts by the central government, and the establishment of a national bank." Remini, *John Quincy Adams* (New York: Times Books, 2002), 22. If the Federalists were indeed "conservatives," then Bush's "big-government conservatism" was not an apostasy from "true conservatism" but a restoration of what conservatism had been at the beginning of the republic in which case Goldwater and Reagan were actually "left wingers." Such are the absurdities we run into when we embrace ideological essentialism.
8. Gordon Wood, the leading historian of the American founding, presents this standard "Jefferson-left, Hamilton-right" view in "The Founding Liberal and the Founding Conservative," *Wall Street Journal*, October 13, 2017, https://www.wsj.com/articles/the-founding-liberal-and-the-founding-conservative-1507905412; and Carl Becker claimed that "the [Jeffersonian] Republicans were what would today be called a radical party, the Federalists a conservative party." Becker, *Our Great Experiment*, 109.
9. See Arthur M. Schlesinger Jr., *The Age of Jackson* (Boston: Little, Brown, and Co., 1945); and Remini, *John Quincy Adams*.
10. Lewis et al., "Congress at a Glance: Major Party Ideology," Voteview, https://voteview.com/parties/all, accessed May 10, 2022.
11. Erik B. Alexander, "'The Wisest Counsel of Conservatism': Northern Democrats and the Politics of the Center, 1865–1968," *Civil War History* 66, no. 3 (September 2020): 295–315.
12. Charles Forcey, *The Crossroads of Liberalism: Croly, Weyl, Lippmann, and the Progressive Era, 1900–1925* (New York: Oxford University Press, 1967).
13. Theda Skocpol, *Protecting Soldiers and Mothers: The Political Origins of Social Policy in the United States* (Cambridge, MA: Harvard University Press, 1992).
14. "The Eclipse of Liberalism," *The Nation*, August 9, 1900, in *The Libertarian Reader: Classic and Contemporary Writings from Lao-Tzu to Milton Friedman*, ed. David Boaz (New York: Free Press, 1997), 324–25. Also see Tom G. Palmer, *Realizing Freedom: Libertarian Theory, History, and Practice* (Washington, DC: Cato Institute, 2009), 32. Godkin's liberals ("Mugwumps") notoriously bolted the Republican party to support the more "liberal" candidate, Democrat Grover Cleveland, since the "conservative" Republican Party pursued higher taxes and more intervention in the economy.
15. See, e.g., "Fighting Gets Fiercer on the Western Front; No Rest for Soldiers: Germans Incessantly Bombard Allied Left Wing Near Ypres," *The Atlanta Constitution*, January 24, 1915, p. 1; "The Army's Right Wing," *The Bayonet* 1, no. 49 (September 27, 1918): 4; "Bulgars in Balkans Are on Offensive: Left Wing Advances, Driving Back British and French on the Struma," *San Francisco Chronicle*, August 23, 1916, p. 2; "Marching on Bridge City: Left Wing of Rumanian-Russian Army Badly Defeated at Coast Base," *New York Times*, October 24, 1916, p. 1; Theodore M. Fisher, "Two Houses Built for Less Than $1500," *Ladies' Home Journal* 28, no. 4 (February 15, 1911): 12; William B. Stout, "Modern Aeroplanes—Burgess-Wright

Biplane," *Chicago Daily Tribune*, August 4, 1911, p. 7; "Yale Expects to Strengthen Its Hockey Seven," *The Christian Science Monitor*, January 26, 1915, p. 20; and Melville E. Webb Jr., "Tufts Beats Harvard: Football Victory over Crimson, 7-3, after Wait of 41 Years," *Boston Daily Globe*, October 8, 1916, p. 1.

16. For the earliest references to Henry George as "left wing," see H. N. Brailsford, "English Land Tax is Wiped Out by Tories," *Baltimore Sun*, May 27, 1934, p. 9; and George R. Geiger, "The Forgotten Man: Henry George," *The Antioch Review* 1, no. 3 (Fall 1941): 291, which said, "George's support came from a powerful but amorphous collection of all the left-wing elements in the city." For examples of articles that referred to Bryan as a "radical" when he was a presidential candidate, but never a "left-winger," see Richard Linthicum, "William Jennings Bryan," *Outlook* 54, no. 4 (July 25, 1896): 135; "Silver Men Alert," *Chicago Daily Tribune*, May 6, 1898, p. 7; and "Nominated Mr. Bryan," *Austin Daily Statesman*, July 26, 1896, p. 1. For later references to Bryan as "left wing," see Robert Kuttner, "Who Owns Populism? Common Men, Left and Right," *The New Republic* 194, no. 23 (June 9, 1986): 12; Melvin Maddocks, "'Populists' Hope to Turn Nation's Mood into Victory," *The Austin Statesman*, May 18, 1972, p. A27; Hacker, "Revolutionary America," 431; Patrick Reddy, "Can Occupy Wall Street Succeed?" *Buffalo News*, November 20, 2011, p. G1; and Rodney A. Smolla, "Monkey Business," *New York Times Book Review*, October 5, 1997, p. 21.

17. See, e.g., "Radicals Form Part of Danger to New Russia," *Chicago Daily Tribune*, March 18, 1917, p. 5, which references "socialists of the left wing" and alludes to the French Revolution. The article, "City's Bolsheviki Disown All Order," *New York Times*, December 3, 1917, p. 6, makes reference to "extreme left wing radicals." Also see "Russ Assembly Opens with Slaughter by Red Guard," *San Francisco Chronicle*, January 20, 1918, p. 2A; "Democrats Will Fight Bolshevism," *The Statesman*, November 30, 1918, p. 1; and "German Soldiers Fight Bolshevism: Bulk of Troops Said to Be Opposed to 'Red' Methods," *The Atlanta Constitution*, November 18, 1918, p. 1; "Lenin Develops Strength in Early Soviet Elections," *Chicago Daily Tribune*, June 27, 1918, p. 4; and Arthur Ransome, "Bolshevist Rule Menaced by Foes-Social Revolutionists in Majority," *New York Times*, January 15, 1918, p. 1. In Ransome's words, "The socialist revolutionaries consequently have it in their control. It is uncertain how many of their left wing will vote with the Bolsheviki and how many of their right will not attend." The fact that the spectrum was only used to refer to infighting among socialists helps explain why Hitler's "National Socialist" party would have been considered "right wing" in 1930s Europe, even while the term "right wing" referred to anti-government libertarianism in the United States at the time.

18. Steffens publicized the writing of Bolshevik leader Leon Trotsky for an American audience and wrote introductions to his articles and pamphlets. See Lincoln Steffens, introduction to Leon Trotzky, "The Bolsheviki and World Peace," *The Atlanta Constitution*, January 14, 1918, p. 1; and Peter Hartshorn, *I Have Seen the Future: A Life of Lincoln Steffens* (Berkeley: Counterpoint, 2011). For more on the Marxist importation of the political spectrum, see "Left Wing Put Out by Socialist Party: Radicals Refused Admittance to Chicago Convention—Threaten to Join Communist Party. John Reed Leading Them," *New York Times*, August 31, 1919, p. 5; and "Radicals Split Off from Main Socialist Body: Discord Increased by Rift in Right Wing Delegates to Emergency Convention," *San Francisco Chronicle*, September 2, 1919, p. 22.

19. Max Eastman, "The International Class Struggle," *The Liberator* 2, no. 6 (June 1919): 6. Also in 1919, socialist Upton Sinclair wrote that he had withdrawn from the "left wing" of the socialist movement in America. Sinclair, "Good News," *The Liberator* 1, no. 12 (February 1919): 13. In 1918, the year of its founding, *The Liberator* always used "left wing" to refer to European socialist factions, never Americans. See, e.g., John Reed, "With Gene Debs on the Fourth," *The Liberator* (September 1918): 7–9.

20. "Growth of 'Left-Wing' Movement among Labor," *Women's Wear* 18, no. 42 (February 20, 1919): 36; "Socialist Use of Political Action," *The Christian Science Monitor*, April 21, 1919, p. 1; Mitchell Palmer, "The Case against the 'Reds,'" *Forum* (February 1920): 173; and "Bail Is Refused for Buffalo Reds; Captured Communists' Applications Will Be Heard Tomorrow. Union Leader Arrested; Campbell, Former 'Left Wing' Socialist, Is the Most Prominent of the Prisoners," *New York Times*, January 4, 1920, p. 2.

21. "Socialist Factions Name Two Tickets: Right and Left Wing Contest Reduces the Party's Strength in Primaries," *New York Times*, August 7, 1919, p. 9; "Socialist Party Left Wing Splits: One Group, Calling Itself the Communist Party of America, Forms a New Organization, with Headquarters in Chicago Fusion to Defeat Socialists," *The Christian Science Monitor*, August 5, 1919, p. 1; "Socialist Party Control at Issue: Conflict between Old Line Membership and Left Wing to Be Settled at Convention," *The Christian Science Monitor*, August 1, 1919, p. 14; "The Socialist Quarrel," *New York Times*, June 25, 1919, p. 18; "Socialist Lefts and Rights Mix Left and Right: Battle Opens Convention as Somebody Nabs Olive Branch," *Chicago Daily Tribune*, August 31, 1919, p. 12; "Socialist Status in United States: As Result of Chicago Conventions Movement Has Well-Defined Right, Left, and Center," *The Christian Science Monitor*, September 9, 1919, p. 5; "Rift Widens in Socialist Party: Right Wing Charges Left Wing with Trying to Dominate," *The Christian Science Monitor*, June 30, 1919, p. 13; and Gordon S. Watkins, "The Present Status of Socialism in the United States," *The Atlantic Monthly* 124, no. 6 (December 1919): 821. Watkins spoke of "The Socialist Party on the Extreme Right" and the "Communist Party on the Extreme left." As of 1919, "extreme right" didn't yet refer in any sense to advocates of laissez-faire capitalism but was applied exclusively to non-radical socialists.

22. Benjamin Stolberg, "The Third Party Movement," *The Independent* 112, no. 3864 (March 15, 1924): 142; "Third Party Keynote Speaker Flays Both of Old Parties: Calls Them, in Chicago Speech, 'Right and Left Wings of Same Bird of Prey,' and Products of Wall Street—Fires Hot Shot at Palmer," *The Baltimore Sun*, July 11, 1920, p. 2; and "Radicals Wreck Unity Plans of Third Partyites: Forty-Eighters and Single Taxers Unable to Travel with Socialists of the Left Wing," *The Austin Statesman*, July 14, 1920, p. 1.

23. "Lafollette Sends Word He Will Lead: Wants Third Party Platform to Meet His Views and It Will Be Changed. Committee of 48 Yields to Labor Party," *New York Times*, July 14, 1920, p. 1; and "After La Follette, What?" *Chicago Daily Tribune*, September 28, 1924, p. 8. A reporter for *The Boston Globe* spoke of the "left wing" followers of Bob LaFollette and his "right wing" opponents within the Republican Party in "Plan New Drive on La Follette: Strict Republicans Meet to Choose a Rival. Three to Eight Men Will Run for Senate in Wisconsin. Son of Progressive Chief Sees Principles Winning," *Boston Daily Globe*, September 17, 1925, p. 2.

24. See "Radicalism Rebuked," *The Atlanta Constitution*, November 9, 1924, p. C2; and "By-Products," *New York Times*, March 1, 1925, p. E4. In the 1920s, the terms "left" and "right" even began to be applied to congressional legislation. See "Tax Revision Plans of Many Varieties for New Congress," *New York Times*, November 11, 1922, p. 1.

25. Beard, *American Party Battle*; Parrington, *The Colonial Mind*, and Becker, *Our Great Experiment*.

26. Arthur Sears Henning, "Morris to Face Split Nebraska Sets of Bolters," *Chicago Daily Tribune*, October 16, 1930, p. 11; "By-Products," *New York Times*, November 8, 1931, p. E1; Frank R. Kent, "The Great Game of Politics: Public Psychology," *The Baltimore Sun*, November 8, 1931, p. 1; and J. P. Essary, "Senate Will Press For Liberal To Take Justice Holmes' Place: President Will Face Contest Over Confirmation If He Names Conservative To Supreme Court—Democrat May Be Selected For Vacancy," *The Baltimore Sun*, January 13, 1932, p. 1.

27. Franklin D. Roosevelt, "Address Accepting the Presidential Nomination at the Democratic National Convention in Chicago," July 2, 1932, in *The American Presidency Project*, ed. Gerhard Peters and John T. Woolley, www.presidency.ucsb.edu/ws/?pid=75174.

28. Journalist Arthur Sears Henning, for instance, spoke of the "Left wing elements of both parties" in the 1932 election and was uncertain about which direction president-elect Roosevelt was leaning. Arthur Sears Henning, "Roosevelt Sweeps All U.S.: Gains Victory in 42 States; Whole of West," *Chicago Daily Tribune*, November 9, 1932, p. 1.

29. See S. K. Ratcliffe, "President Roosevelt's Team," *The Spectator* 150, no. 5463 (March 10, 1933): 328; Arthur Krock, "Roosevelt Seen Veering"; "Senate Liberal Bloc Weakened: Rougher Road Seen for New Deal Legislation," *Daily Boston Globe*, November 10, 1938, p. 14; Joseph Alsop, "The Capital Parade: Conservative Democrats Fall Back into Line," *Daily Boston Globe*, November 18, 1938, p. 1; J. Fred Essary, "Stay Liberal Roosevelt Warns Party: Cautions Young Democrats against Maneuvers of Conservatives. Invites 'Reactionaries' to Go over into Camp of Enemies," *The Baltimore Sun*, April 20, 1939, p. 1; Charles Groves, "Wheeler Is Boosted to

Head '40 Ticket: Liberal Montana Senator Urged by Colorado's Johnson as Man Suited to Unite Split Party," *Daily Boston Globe*, July 2, 1939, p. B1; Charles Groves, "President Affirms His Right to Combat Foes in Primaries: His Address Includes Virtual Appeal to Nation to Vote for 'Liberal' Candidates Next Fall," *Daily Boston Globe*, June 1938, p. 1. In a 1938 poll, "Right wing" was used as a synonym for "conservative" and "anti–New Deal." Those polled who wanted a "conservative Democrat" were also those who wanted the Democrats to turn against the New Deal. This was even the case in the South, indicating once again that social issues such as race were not included in the left–right, liberal–conservative conceptual schema of the time. George Gallup, "Poll Shows New Deal Leads in Kentucky: Barkley Tops Chandler Almost 2 to 1 in Most Recent Survey of Contest for U.S. Senate," *Daily Boston Globe*, May 15, 1938, p. 23.

30. Ronald Rotunda, *The Politics of Language: Liberalism as Word and Symbol* (Iowa City: University of Iowa Press, 1986).

31. See, e.g., the polling data in "Majority of Voters Are Conservatives: Vote Cuts Party Lines, But Poll Shows Nation Is Opposed to Forming New Right and Left Parties," *Daily Boston Globe*, June 21, 1936, p. B5. By the end of the decade, this taxonomy had only become more entrenched. However, having observed the tyrannies of "extreme left" communism in the Soviet Union and "extreme right" fascism in Nazi Germany, the early Cold War generation of historians argued that America's two major parties were engaged in a relatively mild battle between a "center-left" represented by the Democratic Party and a "center-right" represented by the Republican Party. See Hofstadter, *American Political Tradition*; Schlesinger, *Vital Center*; and Hartz, *Liberal Tradition*. What put both anti-government "conservatives" in the United States and totalitarian National Socialists in Germany on the same "right wing" of the political spectrum? Only convoluted essentialist stories that ultimately amount to "I dislike Hitler and I dislike opponents of the New Deal, ergo, opponents of the New Deal are on the same side as Hitler."

32. Felix Belair Jr., "Roosevelt Scorns Party Lines in Plea to Elect 'Liberals': Says He Prefers Republicans with Views Like His to Conservative Democrats," *New York Times*, September 3, 1938, p. 1; "Comment on President's Views on a 'Good Liberal,'" *The Baltimore Sun*, September 3, 1938, p. 2; David Lewis, "Landslide Buries F.D.R.'s Attempt to Purge Tydings: Conservative Democrat Takes 20 of Maryland's 23 Counties from President's Man," *The Atlanta Constitution*, September 14, 1938, p. 1.

33. Al Smith, "The Facts in the Case," American Liberty League Pamphlets no. 97 (Washington, DC: American Liberty League, 1936).

34. For evidence of the sorting of the parties (conservatives leaving the Democrats and liberals leaving the Republicans) that occurred in Roosevelt's first term, see, Chapin Hall, "Upton Sinclair Out for Governor: Starts Energetic Campaign in California and Scares Both Parties. Runs as a Democrat. Liberals in Republican Party Running Out—Rolph Seeks Renomination," *New York Times*, April 1, 1934, p. E6; John Merrill, "Politics and Politicians," *Daily Boston Globe*, May 6, 1934, p. A19; Frank R. Kent, "The Great Game of Politics: All in the New Deal Bed," *The Baltimore Sun*, August 30, 1934, p. 1; "L. W. Douglas Quits Budget Post over U.S. Fiscal Policies: Resignation Is Accepted by Roosevelt," *The Baltimore Sun*, September 1, 1934, p. 1; and Chesly Manly, "Douglas Quits Budget Place; Assistant Out: New Deal Fiscal Policy Is Reported Cause," *Chicago Daily Tribune*, September 2, 1934, p. 3. Even Roosevelt's future progressive vice president, Henry Wallace, sorted himself out of the Republican Party at this time. Arthur Krock, "In the Nation: Hyde Park Conferees Reflect Parties' Mix-Up," *New York Times*, August 4, 1936, p. 18.

35. See Arthur Krock, "Roosevelt Seen Veering to Farmer-Labor Left: Colloquy with Gov. Benson Gives Rise to View that New Alignment Jettisons Old Liberalism. 'Mr. C.' Supplanting 'A' and 'B.' Benson as a 'B' or 'C.' Trend to the Left Vote of the Farmers Loss of Old Liberals, *New York Times*, September 11, 1938, p. 77; and "Senate Liberal Bloc Weakened," p. 14. In the words of one anti–New Dealer, "True liberals, today as always are those who are making a determined fight against centralization of government powers." Felix Belair Jr., "Roosevelt Scorns Party Lines in Plea to Elect 'Liberals.' Opposes the Word 'Purge.' Realignment Aim Is Seen. Hamilton Defines 'True Liberals.' Barbour Hails Statement," *New York Times*, September 3, 1938, p. 1. Also see "Comment on President's Views on a 'Good Liberal,'" *The Baltimore Sun*,

September 3, 1938, p. 2, which says, "The traditional liberal would be inclined to pin his hopes of progress" on opponents of the New Deal.

36. William F. Buckley Jr.'s first book, *God and Man at Yale: The Superstitions of Academic Freedom* (Chicago: Regnery, 1951), referred to his preferred political philosophy as "individualism," and the anti–New Deal student organization of the 1950s called itself the Intercollegiate Society of Individualists. Also see George Nash, *The Conservative Intellectual Movement in America, since 1945* (New York: Basic Books, 1976); and James T. Patterson, *Mr. Republican: A Biography of Robert A. Taft* (Boston: Houghton-Mifflin, 1972).

37. See, e.g., Isabel Paterson, *The God of the Machine* (New York: G. P. Putnam's Sons, 1943); Rose Wilder Lane, *The Discovery of Freedom: Man's Struggle against Authority* (New York: John Day, 1943); and Ayn Rand, *The Fountainhead* (New York: Bobbs-Merrill, 1943).

38. Peter Viereck, *Conservatism Revisited: The Revolt against Revolt, 1815–1949* (New York: Scribner, 1949).

39. Political scientist Clinton Rossiter made a similar case six years later in his book *Conservatism in America* (New York: Knopf, 1955).

40. In this way, Viereck staked out a position similar to Arthur M. Schlesinger Jr.'s in *The Vital Center*, published in the same year, in which Schlesinger identified "liberalism" as the philosophy of freedom in between the tyrannies of communism on the extreme left and fascism on the extreme right. This underscores the flexible nature of the "liberal" and "conservative" narratives—both stories were used to justify identical policies.

41. Russell Kirk, *The Conservative Mind* (Chicago: Regnery, 1953).

42. For the definitive account of this topic, see Nash, *The Conservative Intellectual Movement*.

43. See Arnold Kling, *The Three Languages of Politics* (Washington, DC: Cato Institute, 2017).

44. In the 2000s, those Democrats who believed the unpopular label "liberal" was costing them votes began to revive the term "progressive" to describe their views.

45. Emily J. Charnock, "More than a Score: Interest Group Ratings and Polarized Politics," *Studies in American Political Development* 32, no. 1 (April 2018): 49–78.

46. "Mr. Dies Scores," *New York Times*, February 5, 1939, p. E1. Contrary to popular perception, "conservative Democrats" were not Democrats who adhered to a conservative philosophy, but simply dissenters from the party line (the same was true of "liberal Republicans"). For example, in the 1938 party primaries, FDR tried to campaign against Democrats who dissented from the New Deal. Having failed to purify the party, he discussed with Wendell Willkie, in 1944, the possibility of forming a "Liberal Party" separate from the Democratic and Republican Parties. After FDR's death, the American Political Science Association took up his cause by calling for a "responsible two-party system" divided between a "liberal" party and a "conservative" party. Despite FDR's (and political scientists') frustrations with "conservative" (small government) Democrats voting with Republicans to hold back New Deal and Fair Deal legislation, it was clear to the general public that one party (the Democratic Party) was more in favor of entrusting the national government with greater control of the economy and was therefore the more "liberal" of the two.

47. Sam Rosenfeld, *The Polarizers: Postwar Architects of Our Partisan Era* (Chicago: University of Chicago Press, 2018). Also see, Charles Groves, "G. O. P. Platforms Denounce New Deal," *Daily Boston Globe*, September 30, 1934, p. A47.

48. See Charles Groves, "Recent Events Seen as Boost to Vandenberg Coalition Plan: La Follette Move and Pepper Victory Provide Impetus for Nation's Conservative Bloc," *Daily Boston Globe*, May 8, 1938, p. C9; "West Ponders Effect of Roosevelt's Tour: In Regions Which He Has Traversed Little Evidence Is Discovered of Change in Public Attitude," *New York Times*, October 3, 1937, p. C7; "Party Lines Fall in Relief Dispute: Return of Administration to States Is Demanded by Congress 'Coalition,'" *The Atlanta Constitution*, May 10, 1937, p. 7; "Liberals In House Back Third Term," *New York Times*, December 24, 1939, p. 10; "F. D.'s Popularity Today," *Daily Boston Globe*, June 1, 1938, p. 16; "Strife Menaces Party in Power: Liberty League Divides Democratic Leaders," *Daily Boston Globe*, January 2, 1936, p. 16; "New Dealers Lead Primary," *Daily Boston Globe*, August 10, 1938, p. 1; "Senator Pope Creeps Ahead in Idaho Vote," *Daily Boston Globe*, August 10, 1938, p. 4; "Result in Idaho Is High Point of Four Primaries," *The Christian Science Monitor*, August 11, 1938, p. 3; and "New Deal Acts for Showdown by House Foes," *The Christian Science Monitor*, August 3, 1939, p. 1.

49. See, e.g., George Gallup, "Survey Sees Trend to Conservatism," *New York Times,* June 29, 1938, p. 7; and "Majority of Voters Are Conservatives," *Daily Boston Globe,* June 21, 1936, p. B5.
50. Christopher R. Weber and Christopher M. Federico, "Moral Foundations and Heterogeneity in Ideological Preferences," *Political Psychology* 34, no. 1 (February 2013): 107–126, https://doi.org/10.1111/j.1467-9221.2012.00922.x.
51. Indeed, the most prominent "conservative Democrats" early in the New Deal were northern foes of segregation, such as Alfred E. Smith of New York, Henry Breckinridge of Illinois, and Peter Gerry of Rhode Island. See Frank R. Kent, "The Great Game of Politics: The Road to Coalition," *The Baltimore Sun,* August 1, 1935, p. 1; W. R. Huff, "Senators Reveal Deep Hostility to House Tax Bill: Conservative Finance Committee in Belligerent Mood as Hearings Get Started," *Wall Street Journal,* July 31, 1935, p. 1; "Macy Calls Nye Type to Run for President: Says He Is Amused by 'Tories' in Party Who Would Nominate a 'Reactionary Democrat,'" *New York Times,* June 9, 1935, p. 3; Uncle Dudley, "Looking Forward," *Daily Boston Globe,* September 4, 1935, p. 14; "Davis Denounces Aims of New Deal: In Sweeping Attack He Tells State Bar Present Policy Leads to Autocracy. Defends Supreme Court. Conservative Democrat Leader Criticizes Officials Who Take Oaths Lightly," *New York Times,* January 25, 1936, p. 1; and Frank R. Kent, "The Great Game of Politics: The Political View," *Wall Street Journal,* April 16, 1935, p. 2. Those who opposed Justice Hugo Black because of his background in the Ku Klux Klan were considered "conservatives" because Black was a supporter of the New Deal. See William Fulton, "Klan Issue as N.Y. Holds Its Primary Today: New York Votes in Mayoralty Primary Today. Black Klan Charges Help Copeland. New York Mayoralty Candidates," *Chicago Daily Tribune,* September 16, 1937, p. 1.
52. In fact, the Democratic Party had a political incentive to keep other issues, like civil rights for African-Americans, off the table so as to avoid splintering their winning New Deal coalition. Segregationist Huey Long was considered to be "to the left" of Roosevelt, as was the anti-Semitic, fascist sympathizer Father Coughlin. Felix Belair Jr., "Radical Party Wedge Goes with Huey Long: Roosevelt Democrats No Longer Fear Leftist Cut into Vote," *New York Times,* September 15, 1935, p. E3.
53. See Willard Edwards, "New Deal Senate Stalwart Raps Third Term Hope: Would Defeat Party, Says Johnson of Colorado," *Chicago Daily Tribune,* July 2, 1939, p. 7; and "Stay Liberal Roosevelt Warns Party," p. 1.
54. Google Books Ngram Viewer, https://books.google.com/ngrams/graph?content=left-wing%2Cright-wing&year_start=1800&year_end=2019&corpus=26&smoothing=3&direct_url=t1%3B%2Cleft%20-%20wing%3B%2Cc0%3B.t1%3B%2Cright%20-%20wing%3B%2Cc0, accessed May 26, 2022.

Chapter 3

1. Herbert Croly's progressive bible, *The Promise of American Life* (New York: Macmillan, 1909), was both highly nationalistic and militaristic, as was his progressive political hero, Theodore Roosevelt.
2. In his anthology of pre–World War II conservative writing, Robert Crunden shows that his subjects were bound together not only by a distrust of the state but by their anti-interventionism in foreign affairs. Robert M. Crunden, ed., *The Superfluous Men: Conservative Critics of American Culture, 1900–1945* (Austin: University of Texas Press, 1977). According to one encyclopedia of conservatism, "From the 1930s to the early 1950s, conservatives were strong in isolationist ranks." See Bruce Frohnen, Jeremy Beer, Jeffrey O. Nelson, eds., *American Conservatism: An Encyclopedia* (Wilmington: ISI Books, 2006), 444. Conservative Senate leader Robert Taft even opposed the Cold War doctrine of containment as an overly aggressive foreign policy, and the leader of the postwar American Right, William F. Buckley Jr., had been an anti-war isolationist. Sam Tanenhaus, "Athwart History: How William F. Buckley, Jr. Turned against the War—and His Own Movement," *The New Republic* (March 19, 2007): 32; and John Judis, *William F. Buckley Jr.: Patron Saint of the Conservatives* (New York: Simon & Schuster, 1988). The "war as a pretext for power grab" charges that F. A. Hayek levied against American liberals of his time are the same charges that American liberals of the George W. Bush era levied against conservatives. See Joe Conason, *It Can Happen Here: Authoritarian Peril in the Age of*

Bush (New York: Thomas Dunne Books, 2007); and Naomi Wolf, *The End of America: Letter of Warning to a Young Patriot* (White River Junction, VT: Chelsea Green Publishing, 2007).

3. Even as late as 1957, anti-militarism was still associated with the right. In his first book, political scientist Samuel P. Huntington took it as a given that Eisenhower's drawdown of military spending was in line with the Republican Party's anti–New Deal ideology. Samuel P. Huntington, *The Soldier and the State* (Cambridge: Harvard University Press, 1957), 371–373.

4. Brian Doherty, *Radicals for Capitalism: A Freewheeling History of the Modern American Libertarian Movement* (New York: Public Affairs, 2007). Doherty notes that during World War II, "Most of the antiwar forces ended up opposing Roosevelt fully, not limiting themselves to his foreign policy" (pp. 60–61). Senators Bennett Champ Clark, Walter F. George, and other anti-war isolationists were considered "conservative Democrats." See "Senator Clark, Presidential Timber, Addresses Georgia Press Tonight: Conservative Democrat Will Be Guest of Constitution at Institute," *The Atlanta Constitution*, February 22, 1939, p. 1; and "Roosevelt 'War Scare' Hit; Congress Has Ear to Ground: Bridges Opens Attack, George Intervenes," *The Christian Science Monitor*, April 14, 1939, p. 2. The "conservative Democrat," Senator Walter F. George, charged President Roosevelt with being responsible for an "unjustified war scare," and George was "highly resolved" to "keep America out." It is clear that throughout the first half of the twentieth century, militarism was associated with liberalism, not conservatism.

5. William F. Buckley Jr., *God and Man at Yale: The Superstitions of Academic Freedom* (Chicago: Regnery, 1951); and Whittaker Chambers, *Witness* (New York: Random House, 1952).

6. William F. Buckley Jr. and L. Brent Bozell, *McCarthy and His Enemies: The Record and Its Meaning* (Chicago: Regnery, 1954); Willmoore Kendall, "The 'Open Society' and Its Fallacies," *American Political Science Review* (December 1960): 972–979; and Kendall, *The Conservative Affirmation* (Chicago: Regnery, 1963). For more on conservatives and domestic anti-communism in the 1950s, see George Nash, *The Conservative Intellectual Movement in America since 1945* (New York: Basic Books, 1976). Note also that the first anti-communist red hunts in American history were undertaken by progressive Democrat Woodrow Wilson at the end of World War I.

7. Eastman, "I Acknowledge My Mistakes," *National Review* (February 22, 1956): 11–14.

8. At the beginning of the 1950s, both of the leading Republican presidential candidates ("conservative" isolationist Robert Taft and "moderate" Dwight D. Eisenhower) were criticizing liberal Harry Truman for his militarism (manifest in the intervention in Korea), but by decade's end, Republican presidential candidate Richard Nixon was criticizing his liberal opponent John F. Kennedy for not being militaristic enough. Both Nixon and Kennedy jockeyed to "out-hawk" each other in their famous 1960 presidential debates.

9. But even so, this "more versus less militarism" dimension is still fickle. Generally, support for military action largely depends on which tribe is launching the war. Verlan Lewis, *Ideas of Power: The Politics of American Party Ideology Development* (New York: Cambridge University Press, 2019), chapter 4. When Bill Clinton undertook military actions in the 1990s, liberals were more interventionist than conservatives; when George W. Bush undertook military actions in the early 2000s, conservatives were more interventionist than liberals. Which side is more hawkish at a given moment depends upon whether a Democrat or Republican is in power. "When it comes to the issue of foreign intervention, the meanings of 'liberalism' and 'conservatism' have switched positions several times in recent decades. . . . To say that the Democratic Party has become more 'liberal,' and the Republican Party has become more 'conservative' since 1988 tells us nothing about the two parties' ideologies with respect to foreign interventionism." Verlan Lewis, "The Problem of Donald Trump and the Static Spectrum Fallacy," *Party Politics*, September 16, 2019, https://journals.sagepub.com/doi/10.1177/1354068819871673.

10. Many neoconservatives identify McGovern's pacifist 1972 presidential campaign as the moment that the left lost them. Jacob Heilbrunn, *They Knew They Were Right: The Rise of the Neocons* (New York: Doubleday, 2008); Paul Ehrman, *The Rise of Neoconservatism: Intellectuals and Foreign Affairs, 1945–1994* (New Haven: Yale University Press, 1994); Gary J. Dorrien, *The Neoconservative Mind: Politics, Culture, and the War of Ideology* (Philadelphia: Temple University Press, 1993); and Francis Fukuyama, *America at the Crossroads: Democracy,*

Power and the Neoconservative Legacy (New Haven: Yale University Press, 2006). Also see Charles Krauthammer, *Things that Matter: Three Decades of Passions, Pastimes, and Politics* (New York: Crown, 2013).

11. See Thomas C. Leonard, *Illiberal Reformers: Race, Eugenics, and American Economics in the Progressive Era* (Princeton: Princeton University Press, 2017); Edward G. Carmines and James A. Stimson, *Issue Evolution: Race and the Transformation of American Politics* (Princeton: Princeton University Press, 1991); and Lewis, *Ideas of Power*, 10.

12. This is a fact that some historians, in a move away from Schlesinger's interpretation of the Jacksonian era, have begun to realize. See Daniel Walker Howe, *What Hath God Wrought: The Transformation of America, 1815–1848* (New York: Oxford University Press, 2007).

13. "While conservatism in the first half of the twentieth century tended to focus on the size of government and was frequently associated with an isolationist foreign policy posturing, it was not until after the civil rights movement and the emergence of race as a salient political concern that liberals and conservatives began to consistently differ on domestic social policy." Christopher R. Weber and Christopher M. Federico, "Moral Foundations and Heterogeneity in Ideological Preferences," *Political Psychology* 34, no. 1 (February 2013): 107–126, https://doi.org/10.1111/j.1467-9221.2012.00922.x. In other words, the three pillars of conservative ideology—libertarianism, hawkishness, and traditionalism—were not associated with one another before the 1960s and became disassociated once again in the 2000s. When we say those three pillars constitute the "consistently conservative principles" (see Nash, *Conservative Intellectual Movement*, and Lilliana Mason, "Ideologues without Issues: The Polarizing Consequences of Ideological Identities," *Public Opinion Quarterly* 82, no. S1 (2018): 866–887), we are incorrectly assuming that the Reaganite iteration of conservatism is the authentic conservatism, when in fact it only defined conservatism for a single generation. Conservatism prior to 1950 had no hawkish associations, and conservatism since Reagan has moved away from libertarianism.

14. This became visible with Goldwater's 1964 rejection of civil rights legislation and became an important part of "conservatism" with Nixon's "southern strategy."

15. Koopman, "Religion and American Political Parties," in *In God We Trust: Religion and American Political Life*, ed. Corwin E. Smidt (Grand Rapids: Baker Academic, 2001), 157. For more on the religious nature of the early twentieth-century left, see Lyman Kellstedt et al., "Faith Transformed: Religion and American Politics from FDR to George W. Bush," and George M. Marsden, "Afterword: Religion, Politics, and the Search for an American Consensus," both in *Religion and American Politics: From the Colonial Period to the Present*, ed. Mark Noll and Luke E. Harlow (New York: Oxford University Press, 2007). For Catholicism's connection to liberalism in the early twentieth century, see Kevin E. Schmiesing, *Within the Market Strife: American Catholic Economic Thought from Rerum Novarum to Vatican II* (Lanham, MD: Lexington Books, 2004), 15–17. The 1930s, says historian John McGreevy, "were a high point for the Catholic Liberal alliance" because of their common vision of economic cooperation. McGreevy, *Catholicism and American Freedom: A History* (New York: Norton, 2003), 153. Note also that Reinhold Niebuhr was at once the most prominent American theologian of the 1950s and a staunch New Deal Democrat. He gave the fullest theological justification for his political views in *The Children of Light and the Children of Darkness: A Vindication of Democracy and a Critique of Its Traditional Defense* (New York: Charles Scribner's Sons, 1944). On the fading of liberal Protestantism, see Mark Noll and Lyman Kellstedt, "Religion, Voting for President, and Party Identification, 1948–1984," in *Religion and American Politics*, 355–379. Noll and Kellstedt show that among religious Americans at large, and especially regular "church-attenders," the percentage voting Democratic steadily declined from 1960 onward. Also see Robert Handy, "Protestant Theological Tensions and Political Styles in the Progressive Period," in *Religion and American Politics*, 281–301. Three of the most prominent right-wing critics of the New Deal, Max Eastman, H. L. Mencken, and Ayn Rand, were also outspoken atheists.

16. See Max Eastman, "Am I Conservative?," *National Review* (January 28, 1964): 57; E. Merrill Root, "What about Ayn Rand?," *National Review* (January 30, 1960): 76–77; Murray Rothbard to the Editor, *National Review* (January 25, 1958): 95; John Chamberlain, "An Open Letter to Ayn Rand," *National Review* (February 2, 1958): 118; and Priscilla Buckley,

Living It Up with National Review: A Memoir (Dallas: Spence Publishing, 2005), 182. Also see Hyrum Lewis, "The Conservative Capture of Anti-Relativist Discourse in Postwar America," *Canadian Journal of History* 43 (Winter 2008): 51–475.

17. See, e.g., Frank S. Meyer, ed., *What Is Conservatism?* (New York: Holt, Rinehart and Winston, 1964); William F. Buckley Jr., ed., *Did You Ever See a Dream Walking? Conservative Thought in the Twentieth Century* (New York: Bobbs-Merrill Co., 1967); and Buckley, "A Long Way from Rome," *New York Times Book Review,* May 14, 1967, p. 8. For more on the essentialist stories ideologues began to tell, see chapter 4.

18. For the view that free speech was an essential principle of left-liberalism, see, e.g., Kendall, "The Open Society and Its Fallacies"; and James Burnham, *Suicide of the West: An Essay on the Meaning and Destiny of Liberalism* (New Rochelle, NY: Arlington House, 1964). For the Democrat reversal on free speech, see Amy Mitchell and Mason Walker, "More Americans Now Say Government Should Take Steps to Restrict False Information Online than in 2018," Pew Research Center, August 18, 2021, https://www.pewresearch.org/fact-tank/2021/08/18/more-americans-now-say-government-should-take-steps-to-restrict-false-information-online-than-in-2018/. For a typical view that such speech restriction constitutes a move "to the left," see Colin Wright, "Elon Musk Tweeted My Cartoon," *Wall Street Journal,* May 2, 2022, https://www.wsj.com/articles/elon-musk-tweeted-my-cartoon-woke-progressive-left-wing-media-right-viral-twitter-politics-culture-liberal-center-11651504379?mod=hp_opin_pos_5#cxrecs_s.

19. See, e.g., Suzanne McGee, "How Barry Goldwater Brought the Far Right to Center Stage in the 1964 Presidential Race," *History,* October 20, 2020, https://www.history.com/news/barry-goldwater-1964-campaign-right-wing-republican. According to McGee, "While his own bid for the White House flamed out, the embers of Goldwater's political philosophy—championing small government and individual freedoms—would ignite the party's conservative wing for decades to come." If McGee were correct, then big-government George W. Bush would have been considered "left wing" and opposed by "conservatives."

20. See, e.g., Anna Lührmann, Juraj Medzihorsky, Garry Hindle, and Staffan I. Lindberg, "New Global Data on Political Parties: V-Party," *V-Dem Institute Briefing Paper,* No. 9, October 26, 2020, https://www.v-dem.net/static/website/img/refs/vparty_briefing.pdf ; Chris Walker, "Study Shows GOP Has Moved to Extreme Right over Past 20 Years," *Truthout,* October 26, 2020, https://truthout.org/articles/study-shows-gop-has-moved-to-extreme-right-over-past-20-years/; Anne Applebaum, *Twilight of Democracy* (New York: Doubleday, 2020); and "Trump Delivers Another Nod to Right-Wing Extremists," MSN, September 30, 2020, https://www.msn.com/en-us/news/world/trump-delivers-another-nod-to-right-wing-extremists/ar-BB19Aiif. According to historian Alan Brinkley's widely respected and assigned American history textbook, "George W. Bush governed as a staunch conservative." Alan Brinkley, *The Unfinished Nation: A Concise History of the American People,* 5th ed. (New York: McGraw-Hill, 2008), 926–927.

21. See Norman Ornstein and Thomas Mann, *It's Even Worse than It Looks: How the American Constitutional System Collided with the New Politics of Extremism* (New York: Basic Books, 2012); James Mann, *George W. Bush* (New York: Macmillan, 2015); Peter Beinart, *The Good Fight* (New York: Harper Perennial, 2008); and Sam Tanenhaus, *The Death of Conservatism: A Movement and Its Consequences* (New York: Random House, 2010).

22. See Max Burns, "Donald Trump and the New Isolationism," *The Hill,* September 24, 2019, https://thehill.com/opinion/international/462787-donald-trump-and-the-new-isolationism; Heather Hurlburt and Elena Souris, "Isolationism in the Trump Era of 'America First'," *New America,* August 24, 2017, https://www.newamerica.org/weekly/edition-174/isolationism-trump-era-america-first/. For earlier isolationism among Republicans being considered "right wing," see James T. Patterson, *Mr. Republican: A Biography of Robert A. Taft* (Boston: Houghton-Mifflin, 1972); and Doherty, *Radicals for Capitalism.*

23. See, e.g., Cas Mudde, *The Far Right Today* (Hoboken, NJ: Wiley, 2019); Simon Kuper, "Why Rightwing Populism Has Radicalised," *Financial Times,* September 11, 2019, https://www.ft.com/content/0fcafba6-d428-11e9-8367-807ebd53ab77; and Oscar Wineburg, "Insult Politics: Donald Trump, Right-Wing Populism, and Incendiary Language," *European Journal of American Studies* 12, no. 2 (Summer 2017): 1–15. According to David French, "The left

moves left, and the right moves right. We are moving away from each other at increasing speed." Of course French, like everyone who uses the political spectrum, is quickly caught in self-contradiction. At times he says Trump followers are not authentic conservatives, and at other times he says they belong to the "extreme right" which would make them "extreme" conservatives. David French, *Divided We Fall: America's Secession Threat and How to Restore Our Nation* (New York: St. Martin's Press, 2020), 89. For more on Reagan as representing the "far right," see Rick Perlstein, *Reaganland: America's Right Turn, 1976–1980* (New York: Simon & Schuster, 2020).

24. Jonathan Rauch is one of the few political commentators to have recognized this. He notes that Republicans haven't moved "to the right" in the sense of becoming more extreme on certain fixed principles but have only become more tribal and hostile to the outgroup. "Polarization has not only grown sharper but has even become its own justification." Jonathan Rauch, "Rethinking Polarization," *National Affairs* 45 (Fall 2019), https://www.nationalaffa irs.com/publications/detail/rethinking-polarization?smid=nytcore-ios-shar.

25. See Brad Nathan, Ricardo Perez-Truglia, and Alejandro Zentner, "Is the Partisan Divide Real? Polarization in Preferences for Redistribution," *AEA Papers and Proceedings* 112 (May 2022): 156162; and Hyrum Lewis, "Has the Republican Party Really Moved to the Right?," *RealClearPolitics*, May 16, 2018, https://www.realclearpolitics.com/articles/2018/05/16/has_the_republican_party_really_moved_to_the_right_137048.html.

26. Mann and Ornstein, *It's Even Worse Than It Looks*; Mann, *George W. Bush*; Beinart, *The Good Fight*; and Peter Beinart, "The Rise of Right-Wing Foreign Policy in America," *The Atlantic*, March 15, 2018, https://www.theatlantic.com/international/archive/2018/03/trumps-fore ign-policy-gop/555644/.

27. Had Ron Paul been president, they also would have said the Republicans moved "to the right" even though Paul had opposite policy views from Bush on the main issues of the day (Paul opposed the Iraq War, opposed Bush's big spending, opposed Bush's surveillance state, opposed Bush's immigration proposal, opposed Bush's drug policy, etc.). See Debra J. Saunders, "Ron Paul Is So Far Right, He Intrigues Left," *Los Angeles Daily News*, December 22, 2011, https://www.dailynews.com/2011/12/22/debra-j-saunders-ron-paul-is-so-far-right-he-intrigues-left-2/.

28. Under George W. Bush and a "conservative" Congress, government spending rose from 18% to 25% of GDP (the biggest increase since FDR). Under Reagan and a "liberal" congress, it decreased from 21% to 18%. The idea that Bush's big spending was out of his control or mostly military-related isn't backed up by the facts: domestic discretionary spending increased faster under Bush than under any president since Lyndon Johnson. Furthermore, he created a new entitlement program, pushed through the largest expansion of federal spending on education in history (No Child Left Behind), and vastly increased funding for farm subsidies, the arts, humanities, foreign aid, etc. See Ryan Sager, *The Elephant in the Room: Evangelicals, Libertarians, and the Battle to Control the Republican Party* (Hoboken, NJ: Wiley, 2006); Stephen Slivinski, *Buck Wild: How Republicans Broke the Bank and Became the Party of Big Government* (New York: HarperCollins, 2006); Michael D. Tanner, *Leviathan on the Right: How Big-Government Conservatism Brought Down the Republican Revolution* (Washington, DC: Cato, 2007); Veronique de Rugy, "Spending under President George W. Bush," George Mason University Mercatus Center Working Paper, March 2009, https://www.mercatus.org/publications/government-spending/spending-under-president-george-w-bush; and Chris Edwards, "George W. Bush: Biggest Spender Since LBJ," Cato Institute, December 19, 2009, https://www.cato.org/blog/george-w-bush-biggest-spender-lbj.

29. When Woodrow Wilson, FDR, and Truman were pushing for more American involvement in foreign wars, their interventionism was considered "liberal," so why was Bush's interventionism "conservative"? Because Bush was a conservative. If the essentialists claim that foreign interventionism is essentially "conservative," then they are stuck with the demonstrably false proposition that Wilson, FDR, and Truman were considered "conservative" in their time. And if Bush was "far right" for advocating the Iraq War, does that make Donald Trump "far left" for repudiating it? Given the historical record on foreign interventionism, we have to conclude that the social theory is correct: "left-wing" is whatever those in the left-wing tribe are doing, and "right-wing" is whatever those in the right-wing tribe are doing.

30. See, e.g., Lee Edwards, *The Conservative Revolution: The Movement that Remade America* (New York: Free Press, 1999); Steven Hayward, *The Age of Reagan: The Fall of the Old Liberal Order, 1964–1980* (Roseville, CA: Forum, 2001); Godfrey Hodgson, *The World Turned Right Side Up: A History of Conservative Ascendancy in America* (Boston: Mariner Books, 1997); Jonathan Schoenwald, *A Time for Choosing: The Rise of Modern American Conservatism* (New York: Oxford University Press, 2001); Donald T. Critchlow, *The Conservative Ascendancy: How the GOP Right Made Political History* (Cambridge, MA: Harvard University Press, 2007); Rick Perlstein, *The Invisible Bridge: The Fall of Nixon and the Rise of Reagan* (New York: Simon & Schuster, 2014); and Rick Perlstein, *Before the Storm: Barry Goldwater and the Unmaking of the American Consensus* (New York: Hill and Wang, 2001).

31. See the 2006 HBO documentary *Mr. Conservative: Goldwater on Goldwater*. See Michael Lind, *The New Class War: Saving Democracy from the Managerial Elite* (New York: Penguin, 2020), 107. "Right-wing" Senator Robert Taft also supported tax increases and complained that the Democrats' 1941 tax bill, "the largest single revenue bill in American history . . . did not raise enough." Patterson, *Mr. Republican*, 236.

32. Hyrum Lewis, "Historians and the Myth of American Conservatism," *Journal of the Historical Society* 12, no. 1 (March 2012): 27–45.

33. For more on big-government conservatism, see Fred Barnes, *Rebel in Chief: Inside the Bold and Controversial Presidency of George W. Bush* (New York: Three Rivers Press, 2006); and Anthony Nadler, A. J. Bauer, and Magda Konieczna, "Report on the Values and Practices of Online Journalists on the Right," *TOW Report*, March 31, 2020, https://www.cjr.org/tow_center_reports/conservative-newswork-report-on-the-values-and-practices-of-online-jour nalists-on-the-right.php#_ftn17. For more on the libertarian nature of midcentury conservatism, see Nash, *Conservative Intellectual Movement*.

34. David Brody, "Why Donald Trump Won't Touch Your Entitlements," *The Daily Signal*, May 21, 2015, https://www.dailysignal.com/2015/05/21/why-donald-trump-wont-touch-your-entitlements/. Also see Alan Rappeport, "Donald Trump Proposes to Double Hillary Clinton's Spending on Infrastructure," *New York Times*, August 2, 2016, https://www.nyti mes.com/2016/08/03/us/politics/trump-clinton-infrastructure.html?_r=0.

35. Government spending information available at the Congressional Budget Office website, https://www.cbo.gov/, accessed May 24, 2022. Also see Maya MacGuineas, "The Debt Is Huge Because Trump Kept His Promises," *Washington Post*, October 5, 2020, https://www.washingtonpost.com/opinions/2020/10/05/debt-is-huge-because-trump-kept-his-promises/.

36. Pew Research Center, "The Partisan Divide Grows Even Wider," October 5, 2017, https://www.pewresearch.org/politics/2017/10/05/5-homosexuality-gender-and-religion/.

37. See, e.g., Walker, "Study Shows GOP Has Moved to Extreme Right," and Katherine Pickering Antonova, "The GOP Is No Longer a 'Conservative' Party: They've Become Radical, and They Want to Remake America," *The Huffington Post*, July 25, 2017, https://www.huffpost.com/entry/republicans-no-longer-conservative-party_n_59767dd6e4b0e201d5776f8c. If "change" is the essence of the left, then wouldn't the fact that Republicans want to "remake America" put them on the "extreme left"?

38. Harold Hotelling, "Stability in Competition," *The Economic Journal* 39, no. 153 (March 1929): 41–57; Anthony Downs, *An Economic Theory of Democracy* (New York: Harper & Row, 1957).

39. Ironically, in 1957 Downs assumed that the Democratic Party was farther to the right than the Republican Party. *Economic Theory of Democracy*, 131. Clearly, he was falling victim to the private language fallacy, using the terms "right" and "left" in ways that went against public meaning.

40. Keith T. Poole and Howard Rosenthal, *Congress: A Political-Economic History of Roll Call Voting* (New York: Oxford University Press, 1997).

41. Since the publication of Poole and Rosenthal's DW-NOMINATE data, an entire "polarization literature" has emerged based on the assumption that left and right have fixed meanings and arguing that America's political parties are moving to the poles of the "extreme left" and/or the "extreme right." Jacob Hacker and Paul Pierson, *Off Center: The Republican Revolution and the Erosion of American Democracy* (New Haven: Yale University Press,

2005); Barbara Sinclair, *Party Wars: Polarization and the Politics of National Policymaking* (Norman: Oklahoma University Press, 2006); Nolan McCarty, Keith T. Poole, and Howard Rosenthal, *Polarized: The Dance of Ideology and Unequal Riches* (Cambridge, MA: MIT Press, 2006); Alan Abramowitz, *The Disappearing Center: Engaged Citizens, Polarization, and American Democracy* (New Haven: Yale University Press, 2010); Mann and Ornstein, *It's Even Worse Than It Looks*; Matt Grossman and David A. Hopkins, *Asymmetric Politics: Ideological Republicans and Interest-Group Democrats* (New York: Oxford University Press, 2016); and Justin Buchler, *Incremental Polarization: A Unified Spatial Theory of Legislative Elections, Parties, and Roll Call Voting* (New York: Oxford University Press, 2018). Most of this literature marshals DW-NOMINATE as evidence of this partisan movement to the poles. While some have argued that Americans have "sorted" rather than "polarized," there is very little questioning of the assumption that the "poles" of left and right have fixed and enduring content. Morris P. Fiorina, Samuel J. Abrams, and Jeremy Pope, *Culture War? The Myth of a Polarized America* (New York: Pearson Longman, 2005).

42. The inadequacy of DW-NOMINATE as a measure of ideology is underscored by the fact that it codes Alexandria Ocasio-Cortez as a "conservative" Democrat simply because she often votes against other members of her own party, believing they don't go far enough in the direction of what the party stands for. Verlan Lewis, "Is AOC the Most Conservative Democrat in Congress?," *The Hill*, June 28, 2019, https://thehill.com/opinion/campaign/450651-is-aoc-the-most-conservative-democrat-in-congress.

43. Pew Research Center, "Political Polarization in the American Public," June 12, 2014, https://www.pewresearch.org/politics/2014/06/12/political-polarization-in-the-american-public/.

44. It's also easy to misinterpret poll data as indicating a move toward extremism. For example, slightly fewer Republicans today than in the past believe "The government should do more for the needy," but this change has occurred even as government anti-poverty spending has risen substantially—meaning that someone with the same beliefs would answer the question differently given the changing circumstances. This would not indicate they had "moved rightward." Such questions about Republican views on government spending do not measure fixed ideology, but relative attitudes toward changing government policy. See Pew Research Center, "Majorities Say Government Does Too Little for Older People, the Poor and the Middle Class," *Pew U.S. Politics and Policy*, January 30, 2018, https://www.pewresearch.org/politics/2018/01/30/majorities-say-government-does-too-little-for-older-people-the-poor-and-the-middle-class/

45. "Ideology and partisanship are highly correlated and have become even more so over time." Michael Barber and Jeremy C. Pope, "Does Party Trump Ideology? Disentangling Party and Ideology in America," *American Political Science Review* 113, no. 1 (February 2019): 39. Notice that when the Republicans reversed their position on free trade, essentialists didn't say they had moved "to the left," they simply redefined "the right" to fit their new position (e.g., calling Donald Trump an "extreme right-wing populist"). See Robert Samuelson, "Trump's Risky Nationalism," *The Washington Post*, December 4, 2016, https://www.washingtonpost.com/opinions/trumps-risky-nationalism/2016/12/04/dabc8f66-b8bd-11e6-a677-b608fbb3aaf6_story.html.

46. See, e.g., Ted Van Green, "Republicans Increasingly Critical of Several Major U.S. Institutions, Including Big Corporations and Banks," Pew Research Center, August 20, 2021, https://www.pewresearch.org/fact-tank/2021/08/20/republicans-increasingly-critical-of-several-major-u-s-institutions-including-big-corporations-and-banks/; and Tyler Cowen, "Republicans Will Regret Their Breakup with Big Business," *Bloomberg*, April 16, 2021, https://www.bloomberg.com/opinion/articles/2021-04-16/republicans-will-regret-their-breakup-with-big-business. Since conservatives have recently become less favorable to big business than liberals, essentialists, such as John T. Jost, who have long claimed that support for big business is an essential characteristic of "the right" must either conclude that the Republican Party has moved "to the left" over the past decade or that they were wrong about the essence of the right. John T. Jost, "The End of the End of Ideology," *American Psychologist* 61, no. 7 (October 2006): 657. For a summary of the ubiquity of ideological flip-flopping based on tribal attachments, see Elaine Kamarck and Alexander R. Podkul, "Role Reversal: Democrats and Republicans Express Surprising Views on Trade, Foreign Policy, and Immigration," *Brookings*

Primaries Project, October 25, 2018, https://www.brookings.edu/blog/fixgov/2018/10/25/role-reversal-democrats-and-republicans-express-surprising-views-on-trade-foreign-policy-and-immigration/. These reversals are only "surprising" to those who subscribe to the essentialist theory.

47. "Public Uncertain, Divided over America's Place in the World," Pew Research Center, May 5, 2016, https://www.people-press.org/2016/05/05/1-americas-global-role-u-s-superpower-status/; and "The Partisan Divide on Political Values Grows Even Wider," Pew Research Center, October 5, 2017, http://www.people-press.org/2017/10/05/3-foreign-policy/.

48. "In Shift from Bush Era, More Conservatives Say 'Come Home, America,'" Pew Research Center, June 16, 2011, https://www.people-press.org/2011/06/16/in-shift-from-bush-era-more-conservatives-say-come-home-america/. Also see Lewis, *Ideas of Power*.

49. "Continued Partisan Divides in Views of the Impact of Free Trade Agreements," Pew Research Center, April 24, 2017, https://www.pewresearch.org/fact-tank/2017/04/25/support-for-free-trade-agreements-rebounds-modestly-but-wide-partisan-differences-remain/ft_17-04-24_freetrade_usviews_2/; John LaLoggia, "As New Tariffs Take Hold, More See Negative than Positive Impact for the U.S.," Pew Research Center, July 19, 2018, http://www.pewresearch.org/fact-tank/2018/07/19/as-new-tariffs-take-hold-more-see-negative-than-positive-impact-for-the-u-s/?utm_source=AdaptiveMailer&utm_medium=email&utm_campaign=17-07-19%20FT%20Tariffs&org=982&lvl=100&ite=2890&lea=643075&ctr=0&par=1&tr; and Bradley Jones, "Support for Free Trade Agreements Rebounds Modestly, but Wide Partisan Differences Remain," Pew Research Center Fact Tank, April 27, 2017, https://www.pewresearch.org/fact-tank/2017/04/25/support-for-free-trade-agreements-rebounds-modestly-but-wide-partisan-differences-remain/. Also see Greg Ip, "Democrats Could Be Free Trade's Protector," *The Wall Street Journal*, July 19, 2018, p. A2. Lewis, "The Problem of Donald Trump": "Trump's tariffs have only increased the Republican appetite for government regulation of international trade. According to the Pew Research Center, in less than two years, support for free trade fell among self-identified Republicans by nearly 50%. As you might expect, Democrats opposed to Trump are becoming increasingly in favor of free trade."

50. For more on the increasing references to the Republican Party as "far right" since the advent of Trump, see David Rozado and Eric Kaufmann, "The Increasing Frequency of Terms Denoting Political Extremism in U.S. and U.K. News Media," *Social Sciences* 11, no. 4 (April 6, 2022), 167; https://doi.org/10.3390/socsci11040167. Barber and Pope point out that, "remarkably, in less than two years, support for a bedrock principle of conservatism [free trade] fell by nearly 50% among members of the Republican party." Barber and Pope, "Does Party Trump Ideology?," 4. Barber and Pope are correct that tribal attachments cause conservatives to change their views, but they are wrong to consider free trade or anything else as "a bedrock principle of conservatism." Such principles don't exist. To say Trump is not "conservative" because he doesn't adhere to what the right believed in the Bush years assumes that Bush defined conservative principles for all times and places. This is incorrect. The conservatism of Bush was much different from the conservatism of Reagan which was, in turn, much different from the conservatism of Goldwater which was, in turn, much different from the conservatism of Taft, and so on. Since there is no essential conservatism, there are no "bedrock conservative principles."

51. Dean of historians of the right, George Nash, believed opposition to Russian aggression was the "glue" that bound the diverse strands of conservatism together, and political theorist James Burnham maintained that an anti-Russian foreign policy was a defining issue of the right. Nash, *Conservative Intellectual Movement*; and James Burnham, *Containment or Liberation? An Inquiry into the Aims of United States Foreign Policy* (New York: J. Day, 1953), 9. This anti-Russian tendency on the right continued all the way through the presidential candidacy of Mitt Romney, whom President Obama criticized for having a retrograde approach to foreign affairs. Jillian Rayfield, "Obama: The '80s Called, They Want Their Foreign Policy Back," *Salon*, October 23, 2012, https://www.salon.com/2012/10/23/obama_the_80s_called_they_want_their_foreign_policy_back/.

52. Pollster Lydia Saad notes, "As recently as 2016 there was no difference between the parties in mentions of Russia as the top enemy. However, as federal investigations into Russia's possible involvement with Donald Trump's presidential campaign have revealed Russian efforts

to influence the 2016 election, views have grown more partisan. Nearly half of Democrats (46%) versus 14% of Republicans now view Russia as the country's top enemy." Lydia Saad, "Majority of Americans Now Consider Russia a Critical Threat," Gallup, February 27, 2019, https://news.gallup.com/poll/247100/majority-americans-consider-russia-critical-threat. aspx. Also see R. J. Reinhart, "Republicans More Positive on U.S. Relations with Russia," Gallup, July 13, 2018, https://news.gallup.com/poll/237137/republicans-positive-relations-russia.aspx; and Margaret Vice, "Public Worldwide Unfavorable Toward Putin, Russia," Pew Research Center, August 16, 2017, https://www.pewresearch.org/global/2017/08/16/publ ics-worldwide-unfavorable-toward-putin-russia/.

53. See, e.g., William J. Bennett, *The Death of Outrage: Bill Clinton and the Assault on American Ideals* (New York: The Free Press, 1998).

54. Evangelical Protestants constitute one of the base demographics of the American right, and yet on the importance of the character of politicians, "No group has shifted their position more dramatically than white evangelical Protestants. More than seven in ten (72%) white evangelical Protestants say an elected official can behave ethically even if they have committed transgressions in their personal life—a 42-point jump from 2011, when only 30% of white evangelical Protestants said the same." Brookings Institution, "Backing Trump, White Evangelicals Flip Flop on Importance of Candidate Character," PRRI/Brookings Survey, October 19, 2016, https://www.prri.org/research/prri-brookings-oct-19-poll-politics-elect ion-clinton-double-digit-lead-trump/. Also see Danielle Kurtzleben, "White Evangelicals Have Warmed to Politicians Who Commit 'Immoral' Acts," NPR, October 23, 2016, https://www.npr.org/2016/10/23/498890836/poll-white-evangelicals-have-warmed-to-politici ans-who-commit-immoral-acts.

55. Jeffrey M. Jones, "Partisans Switch Sides in Presidential Attributes Trade-Off," Gallup, November 14, 2019, https://news.gallup.com/poll/268331/partisans-switch-sides-presi dential-attributes-trade-off.aspx?et_rid=850609425&s_campaign=arguable:newsletter.

56. John Zaller, *The Nature and Origins of Mass Opinion* (New York: Cambridge University Press, 1992).

57. Mason, "Ideologues without Issues."

58. Even James Hohmann, a former aide to Trump, admitted that the Trump campaign was not about policy but tribalism. James Hohmann, "The Daily 202: Trump's Pollster Says He Ran a 'Post-Ideological' Campaign," *Washington Post*, December 5, 2016, https://www.washing tonpost.com/news/powerpost/paloma/daily-202/2016/12/05/daily-202-trump-s-polls ter-says-he-ran-a-post-ideological-campaign/5844d166e9b69b7e58e45f2a/?utm_term= .80807b45e480.

59. For extensive data on the constant flip-flopping of left and right on "fundamental" issues, see Lewis, "The Problem of Donald Trump."

60. Lewis, "Historians and the Myth."

61. Barber and Pope, "Does Party Trump Ideology?," 39. Michael Lind has found the same in his analysis of the terms "very liberal" and "strong Democrat." Lind, *New Class War*, 102. For more on how the "rightward" shift of Republicans is rhetorical rather than substantive, see Lewis, "Has the Republican Party Really Moved to the Right?"; and Lilliana Mason, "The Rise of Uncivil Agreement: Issue Versus Behavioral Polarization in the American Electorate," *American Behavioral Scientist* 57, no. 1 (2013): 140–159, http://journals.sagepub.com/doi/ pdf/10.1177/0002764212463363.

62. Dan M. Kahan et al., "Motivated Numeracy and Enlightened Self-Government," *Behavioural Public Policy* 1, no. 1 (May 2017): 54–86, https://doi.org/10.1017/bpp.2016.2.

63. Christopher D. Johnston and Julie Wronski, "Personality Dispositions and Political Preferences across Hard and Easy Issues," *Political Psychology* 36, no. 1 (February 2015): 35–53, https://doi.org/10.1111/pops.12068.

64. Political philosopher Alan Ryan notes that policies are offered to the public in bundles and "The bundle of policies is constantly reconstructed in response to pressures." Alan Ryan, *On Politics: A History of Political Thought from Herodotus to the Present* (New York: Norton, 2012), 966.

65. For instance, although lower levels of openness are today associated with "the right" (see chapter 5), in 1940 lower levels of openness were associated with "the left." See David O. Sears

and Jonathan L. Freedman, "Selective Exposure to Information: A Critical Review," *Public Opinion Quarterly* 31, no. 2 (Summer 1967): 194–213, https://doi.org/10.1086/267513. The party demographics have switched and therefore so have the character trait correlations associated with each ideology.

66. For more on the application of the left–right labels to these figures, see Arthur M. Schlesinger Jr., *The Age of Jackson* (Boston: Little, Brown, and Co., 1945); Charles A. Beard, *The American Party Battle* (New York: Macmillan, 1928); Vernon L. Parrington, *The Colonial Mind, 1620–1800* (New York: Harcourt Brace Jovanovich, Inc., 1927); and Carl Becker, *Our Great Experiment in Democracy: A History of the United States* (New York: Harper, 1920).

67. Jonah Goldberg, "Today's Conservative Divide Pits Anti-State against Anti-Left," *National Review Online*, January 24, 2020, https://www.nationalreview.com/2020/01/conservative-divide-anti-state-against-anti-left/.

68. Ezra Klein, "For Elites, Politics Is Driven by Ideology. For Voters, It's Not," *Vox*, November 9, 2017, https://www.vox.com/policy-and-politics/2017/11/9/16614672/ideology-liberal-conservatives. Of course, Klein's error is thinking that there is "true ideology" to which elites adhere. It's not that elites are ideological while the masses are tribal, it's that elites are more likely to be "sticky ideologues" loyal to a previous tribe (see chapter 4).

69. Andrew Ferguson, "The Groaning Shelves," *The Weekly Standard* 24, no. 6 (October 2018), https://www.washingtonexaminer.com/weekly-standard/the-groaning-shelves.

Chapter 4

1. Robert Saldin and Steve Teles, *Never Trump: The Revolt of the Conservative Elites* (New York: Oxford University Press, 2020).

2. Jeff Flake, *Conscience of a Conservative* (New York: Random House, 2017).

3. Stephen Dinan, "Anti-Trumpers Rest in Peace at CPAC, Times Poll Shows," *The Washington Times*, February 24, 2018, https://www.washingtontimes.com/news/2018/feb/24/cpac-times-poll-conservatives-love-trump-but-not-s/.

4. Journalist Jonah Goldberg calls Trump followers "CINOS" (conservatives in name only). Goldberg, "Burn, Baby, Burn: Thoughts on the NeverTrump Divide," *The Dispatch*, July 31, 2020, https://gfile.thedispatch.com/p/burn-baby-burn. Senator Ben Sasse argues that Trump is not a "true conservative" because Trump believes in concentrating power in Washington. "In under 90 Seconds, Sen. Ben Sasse Defines Conservatism," *The Daily Signal*, January 29, 2016, https://www.dailysignal.com/2016/01/29/in-under-90-seconds-sen-ben-sasse-defines-conservatism/.

5. Donald Kinder and Nathan Kalmoe, *Neither Liberal nor Conservative: Ideological Innocence in the American Public* (Chicago: University of Chicago Press, 2017), 3–7, 120.

6. Lilliana Mason, "Ideologues without Issues: The Polarizing Consequences of Ideological Identities," *Public Opinion Quarterly* 82, no. S1 (2018):866–887. According to Mason, "'Ideology' can be understood separately as a set of issue positions and as an identity, and this article finds that it is the 'otherness' of ideological opponents, more than issue-based disagreement, that drives liberal-versus-conservative rancor" (p. 867).

7. Ludwig Wittgenstein, *Philosophical Investigations* (New York: Routledge, 1991), §243–271.

8. Andrew Sullivan, "The Triumph of Obama's Long Game," *New York*, July 21, 2017, https://nymag.com/intelligencer/2017/07/the-triumph-of-obamas-long-game.html; and Bruce Bartlett, *Impostor: How George W. Bush Bankrupted America and Betrayed the Reagan Legacy* (New York: Doubleday, 2006). Also see David Swerdlick, "Barack Obama, Conservative," *Washington Post*, November 22, 2019, https://www.washingtonpost.com/outlook/2019/11/22/barack-obama-conservative/?arc404=true. Andrew Sullivan articulates his personal political philosophy, which he mistakes for a universal "true" conservatism, in *The Conservative Soul: How We Lost It, How to Get It Back* (New York: Harper, 2006). Sullivan believes that he and Obama share a political philosophy—which may be true—but it's pointless to insist that this philosophy is "truly conservative" when most conservatives abhorred Obama and his policies. For a notable example of a self-described liberal engaging in the same mistaken project, see Alan Wolfe, *The Future of Liberalism* (New York: Random House, 2009). Those like Sullivan and Wolfe would be far better off dropping the pretension that they know the

"true" meaning of the spectrum (while everyone else is in error), and instead articulate their preferred political philosophy without bringing in the language of left and right, liberal and conservative, to confuse matters.

9. Jonah Goldberg, *Liberal Fascism: The Secret History of the American Left from Mussolini to the Politics of Change* (New York: Crown, 2009); and Harry J. Ausmus, *Will Herberg: From Right to Right* (Chapel Hill: University of North Carolina Press, 1987). Also see Philip Cross, "The 'Anti-Fascist' Left Were the Real Fascists All Along," *Financial Post*, May 31, 2019, https://business.financialpost.com/opinion/philip-cross-the-anti-fascist-left-were-the-real-fascists-all-along.

10. See George Nash, *The Conservative Intellectual Movement in America since 1945* (New York: Basic Books, 1976). When pressed for a definition of conservatism, Nash correctly says, "Conservatism is as conservatism does." Also see Hyrum Lewis, "Historians and the Myth of American Conservatism," *Journal of the Historical Society* 12, no. 1 (March 2012): 27–45; and Verlan Lewis, *Ideas of Power: The Politics of American Party Ideology Development* (New York: Cambridge University Press, 2019).

11. For the Reaganite critique of Bush apostasy, see Bartlett, *Impostor*; Richard A. Viguerie, *Conservatives Betrayed: How George W. Bush and Other Big Government Republicans Hijacked the Conservative Cause* (Los Angeles: Bonus Books, 2006); and Stephen Slivinski, *Buck Wild: How Republicans Broke the Bank and Became the Party of Big Government* (New York: HarperCollins, 2006). For the Taft critique of Reaganite apostasy, see John J. Langdale III, *Superfluous Southerners: Cultural Conservatism and the South, 1920–1990* (Columbia: University of Missouri Press, 2012); Patrick J. Buchanan, *A Republic, Not an Empire* (Washington, DC: Regnery Publishing, 2002); and Paul Gottfried, *The Vanishing Tradition: Perspectives on American Conservatism* (Ithaca: Cornell University Press, 2020). Political scientist Samuel Huntington also fell into this error, arguing that militarist Republicans weren't "true conservatives," but that realist Democrats such as George Kennan and Reinhold Niebuhr were the "true conservatives." See Samuel P. Huntington, *The Soldier and the State* (Cambridge, MA: Harvard University Press, 1957), 457–466. Senator Jeff Flake's *Conscience of a Conservative* argues that Donald Trump apostatized from the true conservatism of Ronald Reagan, while John W. Dean's *Conservatives without Conscience* (New York: Penguin, 2006) argues that Ronald Reagan apostatized from the true conservatism of Barry Goldwater. Many in the NeverTrump movement are George W. Bush supporters who insist that Trump is not a "true conservative" because his big spending goes against "true conservative" principles. Those making this charge conveniently ignore Bush's record on spending, which was the largest in American history up to that point, meaning that if Trump and his supporters are not "true conservatives," then neither are Bush and his supporters, including many of those making the "not true conservative" charge.

12. E. L. Godkin, "The Eclipse of Liberalism," August 9, 1900, in *The Libertarian Reader: Classic and Contemporary Writings from Lao-Tzu to Milton Friedman*, ed. David Boaz (New York: Free Press, 1997), 324–325. Also see Nancy Cohen, *The Reconstruction of American Liberalism, 1865–1914* (Chapel Hill: University of North Carolina Press, 2002), 47–50, 56–57; and Charles Forcey, *The Crossroads of Liberalism: Croly, Weyl, Lippmann, and the Progressive Era, 1900–1925* (New York: Oxford University Press, 1967).

13. James T. Patterson, *Mr. Republican: A Biography of Robert A. Taft* (Boston: Houghton-Mifflin, 1972). Even William F. Buckley Jr., the central conservative intellectual of the late twentieth century, had been an anti-war isolationist in his youth. John Judis, *William F. Buckley Jr.: Patron Saint of the Conservatives* (New York: Simon & Schuster, 1988).

14. Deirdre McCloskey, *Why Liberalism Works: How True Liberal Values Produce a Freer, More Equal, Prosperous World for All* (New Haven: Yale University Press, 2019).

15. Al Smith, "The Facts in the Case," American Liberty League Pamphlets no. 97 (Washington, DC: American Liberty League, 1936).

16. Ronald Reagan, "Address Accepting the Presidential Nomination at the Republican National Convention in Dallas, Texas," The American Presidency Project, August 23, 1984, https://www.presidency.ucsb.edu/documents/remarks-accepting-the-presidential-nomination-the-republican-national-convention-dallas.

17. See, e.g., David Brooks, "What Happened to American Conservatism?" *The Atlantic*, January/ February, 2022, https://www.theatlantic.com/magazine/archive/2022/01/brooks-true-conservatism-dead-fox-news-voter-suppression/620853/.

18. Herbert Hoover, "True Liberalism," in *Addresses upon the American Road* (New York: Charles Scribner's Sons, 1938).

19. Flake, *Conscience of a Conservative*. For a similar book published thirty-six years earlier, see Alan Crawford, *Thunder on the Right: The "New Right" and the Politics of Resentment* (New York: Pantheon Books, 1981).

20. George F. Bishop, "The Effect of Education on Ideological Consistency," *The Public Opinion Quarterly* 40, no. 3 (Autumn, 1976): 337–348. For an example of the reasoning of a sticky ideologue, see Brooks, "What Happened to American Conservatism?"

21. Kinder and Kalmoe, *Neither Liberal nor Conservative*. Why is it that those of higher education are more likely to adhere to a particular iteration of an ideology? The answer is likely two-fold: they are more adept at *ex post* storytelling and more likely to have publicly declared their positions. "Social psychologists have long known that getting people to publicly commit to a belief is a great way to freeze it in place, making it resistant to change. The stronger the commitment, the greater the resistance." Philip E. Tetlock and Dan Gardner, *Superforecasting: The Art and Science of Prediction* (New York: Crown, 2015), 161.

22. Although it is possible for there to be an established taxonomy of natural phenomena that the masses get wrong out of ignorance—for instance, many people would incorrectly call a chimpanzee a "monkey" while zoologists would know better—there is no such established taxonomy when it comes to ideologies. Political scientists, for example, are just as likely to call Trump "right wing" as are the masses. To complicate matters further, humans (unlike chimpanzees) are involved in self-identification and it would make no sense, for instance, to claim that self-identifying members of the Catholic Church aren't "true Catholics" because they don't fit the private definition of "true Catholic" established by an academic researcher.

23. Obviously, they do this to connect those they hate by implication with Stalin or Hitler. If an essentialist calls someone "far left," they are implying that the person shares an essence with Stalin, only differing with the Soviet dictator in degree, not in kind. This is a great rhetorical strategy to delegitimize and silence others. It's a poor strategy for accuracy, understanding, and civility. See, e.g., David Rozado and Eric Kaufmann, "The Increasing Frequency of Terms Denoting Political Extremism in U.S. and U.K. News Media," *Social Sciences* 11, no. 4 (April 6, 2022), 167; https://doi.org/10.3390/socsci11040167.

24. Dean, *Conservatives without Conscience*. Since the majority of Americans supported the invasion of Iraq, then, by definition, it was not an extremist policy (although it was, in our opinion, a mistaken policy).

25. Nancy MacLean, *Democracy in Chains: The Deep History of the Radical Right's Stealth Plan for America* (New York: Penguin Books, 2018).

26. James Buchanan, *Why I, Too, Am Not a Conservative: The Normative Vision of Classical Liberalism* (Northampton, MA: Edward Elgar Pub., 2005), 8.

27. Anne Applebaum, *Twilight of Democracy* (New York: Doubleday, 2020).

28. Sullivan, "Obama's Long Game"; and Stanley Kurtz, *Radical-in-Chief: Barack Obama and the Untold Story of American Socialism* (New York: Simon & Schuster, 2010). Rather than trying to place Obama somewhere on a meaningless line, it would be far better to simply look at Obama's policies and judge them on their merits.

29. Senator McCarthy was a master of this method of political demonization, claiming that his opponents were "far left" and therefore guilty by some imagined association with an international communist conspiracy.

30. But isn't someone like Noam Chomsky objectively on the "far left"? No, because there is no objective, settled definition of "left." As a self-described "anarchist socialist," does Chomsky belong on the anti-government right or the redistributionist left? He's also a passionate defender of free speech (as evidenced by his signing of the infamous *Harper's* Letter), which has recently aligned him with the right-wing tribe and brought down the ire of those of the identity-politics left. Chomsky et al., "A Letter on Justice and Open Debate," *Harper's*, July 7, 2020, https://harpers.org/a-letter-on-justice-and-open-debate/.

31. This is the essence of ideology invoked by historians of the "progressive school." For Arthur M. Schlesinger Jr., for instance, both FDR and Andrew Jackson were essentially liberal since they were both on the side of the poor, even though they had opposite policy views (FDR in favor of more government, Jackson in favor of less). Arthur M. Schlesinger Jr., *The Age of Jackson* (Boston: Little, Brown, and Co., 1945).

32. This is a dubious claim given the big-spending record of conservative politicians on education and safety net programs in recent years. And if spending big on social programs were the essence of the left, then George W. Bush would have been considered the most "far left" president since FDR.

33. Some studies even suggest that self-described conservatives are more generous in their charitable giving than liberals (even controlling for income and other variables). Arthur Brooks, *Who Really Cares: The Surprising Truth about Compassionate Conservatism* (New York: Basic Books, 2006).

34. The most notable example was probably Charles A. Murray, *Losing Ground: American Social Policy, 1950–1980* (New York: Basic Books, 1984).

35. This spills over into views about government debt: some use the term "fiscally conservative" as synonymous with "deficit hawk"—that is, conservatives are concerned about the deficit while Keynesian liberals think deficits are good—but even a cursory look at the record of recent conservative presidents on debt and deficits (Reagan, Bush, and Trump) should put this myth to rest.

36. Bryan Caplan, "What's Wrong with the Thrive/Survive Theory of Left and Right," *EconLog*, September 12, 2017, https://www.econlib.org/archives/2017/09/whats_wrong_wit_23.html; and Kevin Williamson, "No, Weld Can't Beat Trump. But He's the Only Way Real Conservatives Can Dissent," *Washington Post*, April 22, 2019, https://www.washingtonpost.com/outlook/2019/04/22/no-weld-cant-beat-trump-hes-only-way-real-conservatives-can-dissent/.

37. Adam Kirsch, "American Patriotism Is Worth Fighting For," *Wall Street Journal*, October 18, 2019, https://www.wsj.com/articles/american-patriotism-is-worth-fighting-for-11571413398.

38. Mark R. Levin, *Liberty and Tyranny: A Conservative Manifesto* (New York: Threshold Editions, 2009); and Stuart Brand, *Whole Earth Discipline* (New York: Penguin, 2010), p. 148.

39. Philip Converse, "The Nature of Belief Systems in Mass Publics," in *Ideology and Discontent*, ed. David Apter (New York: Free Press, 1964), 206–261; Lloyd A. Free and Hadley Cantril, *The Political Beliefs of Americans: A Study of Public Opinion* (New Brunswick, NJ: Rutgers University Press, 1967); John R. Zaller, *The Nature and Origins of Mass Opinion* (New York: Cambridge University Press, 1992); James A. Stimson, *Public Opinion in America: Moods, Cycles, and Swings*, 2nd ed. (Boulder: Westview Press, 1999); Robert Crunden, ed., *The Superfluous Men: Conservative Critics of American Culture, 1900–1945* (Austin: University of Texas Press, 1977); Kenneth Whyte, *Hoover: An Extraordinary Life in Extraordinary Times* (New York: Alfred A. Knopf, 2017); and Kimberly Phillips-Fein, *Invisible Hands: The Making of the Conservative Movement from the New Deal to Reagan* (New York: W. W. Norton, 2009). According to Lilliana Mason, "Traditionally, ideology has been considered to be a broad worldview represented by a set of issue positions that can be consistent with each other to varying degrees, and this consistency generally has been understood to form along one dimension—liberal to conservative, left to right, or pro-government to anti-government." Mason, "Ideologues without Issues," p. 868.

40. See Buckley, *Happy Days Were Here Again: Reflections of a Libertarian Journalist* (New York: Random House, 1993); and Barry M. Goldwater, *The Conscience of a Conservative* (Shepherdsville, KY: Victor Pub. Co., 1960). Journalist Fareed Zakaria well sums up this view when he says, "The divide that has organized politics for centuries has been between left and right. The Left has advocated a larger role for the state in the economy. The Right has staunchly defended free markets." Fareed Zakaria, *Ten Lessons for a Post-Pandemic World* (New York: Norton, 2020), 35.

41. George W. Bush's Faith Based Initiatives, for instance, expanded government power for "conservative" purposes, but if small government were itself the conservative purpose, this would have been oxymoronic. The fact is that there are plenty of conservative purposes besides just

size of government—meaning that there are many issues, not just one, and the essentialist theory is false. And if conservatives are fundamentally pro-market, then why is it that liberals want to take a more laissez-faire approach to gambling, abortion, drugs, foreign labor, and prostitution? In his book, *Identity* (New York: Farrar, Straus, and Giroux, 2018), political scientist Francis Fukuyama correctly notes that left and right used to be about size of government, but that this is no longer the case in the post-Trump era. He is correct that politics is no longer unidimensional, but he is wrong on the timing: this change isn't new to the twenty-first century but came about in the mid-twentieth century. Politics became multidimensional long before Trump came along and the "more versus less" government political spectrum has been obsolete for decades.

42. Government spending as a percentage of GDP went from 18% to 25% under Bush, while under Clinton it went from 21% to 18%. Contrary to popular mythology, most of Bush's big spending was domestic and unrelated to the "War on Terror." Bush's big-government conservative agenda included No Child Left Behind, a new prescription drug entitlement, expansion of farm subsidies, increase in funding for the NEA, NEH, and so on. That part of the budget that Bush had the most control over—domestic discretionary spending—increased most of all. For government spending data, see the federal government's Office of Management and Budget reports at https://www.whitehouse.gov/omb/budget/historical-tables/, accessed May 24, 2022.

43. Richard Haass, *The World: A Brief Introduction* (New York: Penguin, 2020), 22. Similarly, the "far right" militarist government in 1930s Japan advanced an "Imperial Socialist" economic philosophy which "was anti-capitalist . . . opposed free enterprise, and favored rigid state controls over the economy." Huntington, *Soldier and the State*, p. 134.

44. Anarchists of the present, such as Noam Chomsky, are heroes to the left, as are anarchists of the past, such as Sacco and Vanzetti.

45. Paul Krugman, "On the Liberal Bias of Facts," *New York Times*, April 18, 2014, https://krugman.blogs.nytimes.com/2014/04/18/on-the-liberal-bias-of-facts/; and Ann Coulter, *If Democrats Had Any Brains, They'd Be Republicans* (New York: Crown Forum, 2007).

46. Ravi Iyer, Spassena Koleva, Jesse Graham, Peter Ditto, and Jonathan Haidt, "Understanding Libertarian Morality: The Psychological Dispositions of Self-Identified Libertarians" *Plos One*, August 21, 2012, https://journals.plos.org/plosone/article?id=10.1371/journal.pone.0042366. Also see Artur Nilsson, Arvid Erlandsson, and Daniel Västfjäll, "The Complex Relation between Receptivity to Pseudo-Profound Bullsh-t and Political Ideology," *Personality and Social Psychology Bulletin* 45, no. 10 (October 1, 2019): 1440–1454, https://doi.org/10.1177/0146167219830415.

47. Feng Shi et al., "The Wisdom of Polarized Crowds," *Nature Human Behaviour* 3 (2019): 329–336, https://www.nature.com/articles/s41562-019-0541-6. Also see Charlan Nemeth, *In Defense of Troublemakers: The Power of Dissent in Life and Business* (New York: Basic Books, 2018); James Surowiecki, *The Wisdom of Crowds* (New York: Doubleday, 2004); Philip Tetlock, *Expert Political Judgment* (Princeton: Princeton University Press, 2006); and Scott E. Page, *The Difference: How the Power of Diversity Creates Better Groups, Firms, Schools, and Societies* (Princeton: Princeton University Press, 2008). Also see Lee Jussim et al., "Political Diversity Will Improve Social Psychological Science," *The Behavioral and Brain Sciences* 38, no. 130 (2015), https://doi.org/10.1017/S0140525X14000430; and Christopher Freiman, "In Defense of Viewpoint Diversity," *Inside Higher Ed*, October 8, 2018, https://www.insidehighered.com/views/2018/10/08/why-its-vital-academe-have-more-viewpoint-diversity-opinion.

48. Thomas Sowell, *A Conflict of Visions* (New York: William Morrow and Co., 1987); and Steven Pinker, *The Blank Slate: The Modern Denial of Human Nature* (New York: Penguin, 2002)

49. Ben Sasse, *The Vanishing American Adult* (New York: St. Martin's Press, 2017), chapter 1. Elsewhere, Senator Sasse suggests that conservatism is defined by gratitude. If so, then according to the political spectrum, the far right must be defined by extreme gratitude. Does the word "grateful" come to mind when we think of "far right" politicians such as Adolf Hitler or Benito Mussolini?

50. Diggins, *Up from Communism: Conservative Odysseys in American Intellectual Development* (New York: Columbia University Press, 1994), 90, 159, 175, 196, 393, 451. Diggins singled

out four leading conservative figures—John Dos Passos, James Burnham, Will Herberg, and Max Eastman—as exemplary of the move from the utopian far left to the chastened realism of the right. Their disillusionment with Marxism, Diggins believed, was a disillusionment with human goodness in general—the essential characteristic of the conservative temperament.

51. Yuval Levin, *The Great Debate: Edmund Burke, Thomas Paine, and the Birth of Right and Left* (New York: Basic Books, 2014).

52. Conservative columnist Charles Krauthammer was more explicit about it, saying that liberals "suffer incurably from naïveté." Charles Krauthammer, "The Central Axiom of Partisan Politics," *Washington Post*, July 26, 2002, available at https://www.deseret.com/opinion/2018/7/8/20794360/charles-krauthammer-the-central-axiom-of-partisan-politics.

53. Also see James Burnham, *Suicide of the West: An Essay on the Meaning and Destiny of Liberalism* (New Rochelle, NY: Arlington House, 1964); and Charles Krauthammer, *The Point of It All: A Lifetime of Great Loves and Endeavors* (New York: Random House, 2018), 287.

54. Dewey, *Liberalism and Social Action* (New York: G. P. Putnam's Sons, 1935); and Arthur M. Schlesinger Jr., *The Vital Center: The Politics of Freedom* (Boston: Houghton-Mifflin, 1949).

55. Notable foreign-policy realists who opposed the Iraq War included political scientists John Mearsheimer and Samuel P. Huntington (and Huntington even maintained that his opposition was rooted in "conservatism"). See Brian Lamb interview with Samuel P. Huntington, C-Span Booknotes, May 6, 2004, https://www.c-span.org/video/?181499-1/who-we-ameri cas-national-identity.

56. George W. Bush, Second Inaugural Address, January 20, 2005, http://www.cbsnews.com/stories/2005/01/20/politics/main668129.shtml.

57. And the foreign policy association with realism and the left extends back to the twentieth century. Reinhold Niebuhr, Hans Morgenthau, and George Kennan were the most notable realist public intellectuals of the Cold War and were also leading lights in liberal Democratic circles.

58. For instance, Clinton advisor George Stephanopoulos based his liberal welfare-state views on pessimism. He believed that because we are naturally selfish, we need a government that compels us to give charitably. This view, he claimed, came from reading Niebuhr, the leading realist (and Democratic) theologian of the twentieth century. See George Stephanopoulos, *All Too Human: A Political Education* (New York: Hachette, 1999).

59. Xiaowen Xu, Caitlin M. Burton, and Jason E. Plaks, "Three Dimensions of American Conservative Political Orientation Differentially Predict Negativity Bias and Satisfaction with Life," *Social Psychological and Personality Science*, January 6, 2022, https://doi.org/10.1177/19485506211057976.

60. David Ropeik, *How Risky Is It, Really? Why Our Fears Don't Always Match the Facts* (New York: McGraw-Hill, 2010), 145. We have yet to meet an actual conservative who fits this caricature. Also see, e.g., John T. Jost, "The End of the End of Ideology," *American Psychologist* 61, no. 7 (October 2006): 654.

61. See, e.g., Jim Sidanius and Felicia Pratto, *Social Dominance: An Intergroup Theory of Social Hierarchy and Oppression* (New York: Cambridge University Press, 1999); John T. Jost et al., "Political Conservatism as Motivated Social Cognition," *Psychological Bulletin* 129, no. 3 (2003): pp. 339–375; and David Farber, *The Rise and Fall of Modern American Conservatism: A Short History* (Princeton: Princeton University Press, 2010). Steven Lukes made one of the most convincing cases for this essence in "Epilogue: The Grand Dichotomy of the Twentieth Century," in *The Cambridge History of Political Thought in the Twentieth Century*, ed. Terence Ball and Richard Bellamy (New York: Cambridge University Press, 2003), 602–626. Christian Gonzalez maintains that attitudes toward hierarchy are the "elusive definitions" of left and right. Christian Gonzalez and Ian Storey, "The Elusive Definitions of Conservatism and Liberalism," Heterodox Academy Podcast: Half Hour of Heterodoxy 84, April 27, 2020, https://heterodoxacademy.org/podcast/podcast-hhh-84-christian-gonza lez-ian-storey/. Russell Kirk declared that acceptance of hierarchy was one of his "six canons of conservative thought." Russell Kirk, *The Conservative Mind* (Chicago: Regnery, 1953). This definition has also appeared on Wikipedia's page on the political spectrum (Wikipedia, "Left–right political spectrum," https://en.wikipedia.org/wiki/Left–right_political_spect rum, accessed May 26, 2022). In the words of Jesse R. Harrington and Michele J. Gelfand, blue states are "loose" with "few strongly enforced rules and greater tolerance for deviance,"

while red states are "tight" with "strongly enforced rules and little tolerance for deviance." Jesse R. Harrington and Michele J. Gelfand, "Tightness–Looseness across the 50 United States," PNAS 111, no. 22 (June 3, 2014): 7990–7995; https://doi.org/10.1073/pnas.131 7937111. Blue state restrictions during the Covid-19 pandemic soundly falsify their claim, as does cross-dimensional analysis which shows that red states generally have fewer "strongly enforced" economic rules. Mark J. Perry, "Freedom in the 50 States, but Mostly in the Red States?" AEI Report, March 28, 2013, https://www.aei.org/carpe-diem/freedom-in-the-50-states-but-mostly-in-the-red-states/.

62. Jason Weeden and Rob Kurzban, *The Hidden Agenda of the Political Mind: How Self-Interest Shapes Our Opinions and Why We Won't Admit It* (Princeton: Princeton University Press, 2014).

63. See, e.g., the work of economists Ed Glaeser, Milton Friedman, and Arthur Brooks. Liberal resistance to school reform falsifies the "compassion vs. greed" essence but substantiates the social theory since teachers' unions—who have the most to lose with the implementation of school vouchers—are the faction of the left-wing tribe that causes it to oppose education reform for social-group reasons.

64. Amy Mitchell and Mason Walker, "More Americans Now Say Government Should Take Steps to Restrict False Information Online than in 2018," Pew Research Center, August 18, 2021, https://www.pewresearch.org/fact-tank/2021/08/18/more-americans-now-say-government-should-take-steps-to-restrict-false-information-online-than-in-2018/.

65. For more on the inadequacy of equality vs. inequality as a left–right essence, particularly as it relates to communist totalitarianism, see Jeff Greenberg and Eva Jonas, "Psychological Motives and Political Orientation—The Left, the Right, and the Rigid: Comment on Jost et al. (2003)," *Psychological Bulletin* 129, no. 3 (May 2003): 377–378.

66. See, e.g., Michael Lind, *The New Class War: Saving Democracy from the Managerial Elite* (New York: Penguin, 2020); Paul Embery, *Despised: Why the Modern Left Loathes the Working Class* (Medford, MA: Polity Press, 2020); Joel Kotkin, *The Coming of Neo-Feudalism: A Warning to the Global Middle Class* (New York: Encounter Books, 2020); and David Kaiser, *A Life in History* (Mount Greylock Books, LLC, 2018), 378.

67. Once again, liberals might protest that those on the right are wrong (or lying) about their policies leading to greater equality, but this is exactly what conservatives say about liberal policies. The welfare state, many conservatives maintain, is not really about helping the poor, but about gaining control and expanding the power of liberal politicians, intellectuals, and bureaucrats. According to conservative N. A. Halkides, "The Progressive rationalizes his desire to rule as a concern for human welfare" and "Inside every liberal is a little totalitarian screaming to get out." N. A. Halkides, "Inside the Progressive Mind," *FrontPage Magazine*, May 21, 2013, https://archives.frontpagemag.com/fpm/inside-every-liberal-totalitarian-screaming-get-frontpagemagcom/.

68. For more on McCarthyism as a populist attack on elites, see Michael Kimmage, *The Conservative Turn: Lionel Trilling, Whittaker Chambers, and the Lessons of Anti-Communism* (Cambridge, MA: Harvard University Press, 2009), 215, 228–229; and Richard Hofstadter, *The Paranoid Style in American Politics* (New York: Knopf, 1965).

69. Visible, for instance, in the recall of California Governor Gray Davis and the passage of anti-gay-marriage (Proposition 8) and anti-tax legislation (Proposition 13).

70. Lind, *New Class War*, p. 63

71. Ronald Reagan, "A Time for Choosing," October 27, 1964, *The American Presidency Project*, ed. Gerhard Peters and John T. Woolley, https://www.presidency.ucsb.edu/node/276 336; and Betsy Sinclair, Steven S. Smith, and Patrick D. Tucker, "'It's Largely a Rigged System': Voter Confidence and the Winner Effect in 2016," *Political Research Quarterly* 71 no. 4 (2018): 854–868.

72. Whittaker Chambers, *Witness* (New York: Random House, 1952); and Ann Coulter, *Godless: The Church of Liberalism* (New York: Crown Forum, 2006).

73. Michael Kazin, *A Godly Hero: The Life of William Jennings Bryan* (New York: Knopf, 2006); and Robert Caro, *The Path to Power*, vol. 1, The Years of Lyndon Johnson (New York: Random House, 1990), 38. The history of left-wing religiosity holds internationally as well. The "left-wing" Chinese Tai-Ping movement of the 1850s, for instance, sought to establish a Christian

socialist "kingdom of heavenly peace." See Jonathan Spence, *The Search for Modern China* (New York: W. W. Norton & Co., 1990), 170–178.

74. Edmund Morris, *Colonel Roosevelt* (New York: Random House, 2010), 223.

75. Forcey, *The Crossroads of Liberalism*. Also notice that "left-wing" anti-racism was once allied with nationalism: Martin Luther King Jr. appealed to American national values to overcome the regionalists who wanted to maintain southern segregation laws by invoking "states' rights." See Stephen B. Oates, *Let the Trumpet Sound: The Life of Martin Luther King, Jr.* (New York: Harper and Row, 1982). Jonah Goldberg uses the prevalence of nationalism and socialism among progressives in the early twentieth century to argue that Hitler's National Socialism was actually a movement of the left, rather than the right. Jonah Goldberg, *Liberal Fascism*. But it's not that nationalism is "truly left wing" (and therefore Hitler, a nationalist, was "left wing"), but that different principles are associated with different ideological tribes at different times and places. Lacking an essence, ideologies evolve, and nationalism, socialism, or any other value can mean "right wing" in one place and time and "left wing" in another place and time. This means that these terms are useful only to describe policies when they refer to those of a specific tribe at a specific time and place. Their only cross-contextual meaning is tribal.

76. Douglas R. Oxley et al., "Political Attitudes Vary with Physiological Traits," *Science* 321, no. 5896 (September 19, 2008): 1667–1670, https://science.sciencemag.org/content/321/5896/1667; and John R. Hibbing, Kevin B. Smith, and John R. Alford, "Differences in Negativity Bias Underlie Variations in Political Ideology," *Behavioral and Brain Sciences* 37, no. 3 (June 2014): 297–307.

77. See, e.g., Maja Grasoa, Fan Xuan Chen, and Tania Reynolds, "Moralization of Covid-19 Health Response: Asymmetry in Tolerance for Human Costs," *Journal of Experimental Social Psychology* 93 (March 2021), https://doi.org/10.1016/j.jesp.2020.104084.

78. Pew Research Center, "Most Americans Say Coronavirus Outbreak Has Impacted Their Lives," March 30, 2020, https://www.pewsocialtrends.org/2020/03/30/most-americans-say-coronavirus-outbreak-has-impacted-their-lives/.

79. Both sides liberally quoted Benjamin Franklin to justify their positions. See Eugene Volokh, "Liberty, Safety, and Benjamin Franklin," *The Washington Post*, November 11, 2014, https://www.washingtonpost.com/news/volokh-conspiracy/wp/2014/11/11/liberty-safety-and-benjamin-franklin/.

80. Zeeshan Aleem, "A New Poll Shows a Startling Partisan Divide on the Dangers of the Coronavirus: Most Democrats Are a Lot More Worried than Republicans," *Vox*, March 15, 2020, https://www.vox.com/2020/3/15/21180506/coronavirus-poll-democrats-republicans-trump.

81. Bert N. Bakker et al., "Conservatives and Liberals Have Similar Physiological Responses to Threats," *Nature Human Behaviour* 4 (2020): 613–621, https://www.nature.com/articles/s41562-020-0823-z.

82. Ritchie, *Science Fictions: The Epidemic of Fraud, Bias, Negligence and Hype in Science* (New York: Metropolitan Books, 2020), 240.

83. Bakker et al., "Conservatives and Liberals"; and Kevin B. Smith and Clarisse Warren, "Physiology Predicts Ideology. Or Does It? The Current State of Political Psychophysiology Research," *Current Opinion in Behavioral Sciences* 34 (August 2020): 88–93, https://doi.org/10.1016/j.cobeha.2020.01.001.

84. Christopher D. Johnston, Howard G. Lavine, and Christopher M. Federico, *Open versus Closed: Personality, Identity, and the Politics of Redistribution* (Cambridge: Cambridge University Press, 2017); and Ariel Malka et al., "Do Needs for Security and Certainty Predict Cultural and Economic Conservatism? A Cross-National Analysis," *Journal of Personality and Social Psychology* 106 (2014): 1031–1051. For a useful summary of the problems with the literature on conservatives having a higher fear response, see Jesse Singal, "Conservatives Might Not Have a More Potent Fear Response than Liberals After All," *Research Digest*, February 12, 2020, https://digest.bps.org.uk/2020/02/12/conservatives-might-not-have-a-more-potent-fear-response-than-liberals-after-all/. The same problems appear in those studies which purport to show that conservatives are more motivated by "disgust" than liberals. Julia Elad-Strenger, Jutta Proch, and Thomas Kessler, "Is Disgust a 'Conservative' Emotion?" *Personality*

and Social Psychology Bulletin 46, no. 6 (October 16, 2019): 896–912, https://doi.org/ 10.1177/0146167219880191. "The relations between political orientation and disgust sensitivity depend on the specific set of elicitors used" (p. 896).

85. Dane Gorman Wendell, "Neural Correlates of Political Attitudes: Emotion and Ideology in the Brain" (PhD dissertation, Loyola University Chicago, 2016), https://ecommons.luc. edu/cgi/viewcontent.cgi?referer=&httpsredir=1&article=3298&context=luc_diss. Also see Christopher M. Federico and Ariel Malka, "The Contingent, Contextual Nature of the Relationship between Needs for Security and Certainty and Political Preferences: Evidence and Implications," *Political Psychology* 39, no. S1 (February 2018): 348, https://doi.org/ 10.1111/pops.12477: "Relationships between needs for security and certainty and political preferences vary considerably—sometimes to the point of directional shifts—on the basis of (1) issue domain and (2) contextual factors governing the content and volume of political discourse individuals are exposed to" (p. 3).

86. The scholars who conducted the replication study told the story in a *Slate* article. Kevin Arceneaux et al., "We Tried to Publish a Replication of a *Science* Paper in *Science*. The Journal Refused," *Slate*, June 20, 2019, https://slate.com/technology/2019/06/science-replication-conservatives-liberals-reacting-to-threats.html.

87. John Bargh, "At Yale, We Conducted an Experiment to Turn Conservatives into Liberals. The Results Say a Lot about Our Political Divisions," *Washington Post*, November 22, 2017, https://www.washingtonpost.com/news/inspired-life/wp/2017/11/22/at-yale-we-conducted-an-experiment-to-turn-conservatives-into-liberals-the-results-say-a-lot-about-our-political-divisions/.

88. Keith E. Stanovich, *The Bias that Divides Us: The Science and Politics of Myside Thinking* (Cambridge, MA: MIT Press, 2021).

89. "If the vast majority of a community shares a political perspective, the important function of peer review—to hold claims to the harshest scrutiny possible—is substantially weakened." Ritchie, *Science Fictions*, p. 116. Also see Yoel Inbar and Joris Lammers, "Political Diversity in Social and Personality Psychology," *Perspectives on Psychological Science* 7, no. 5 (September 5, 2012): 496–503, https://doi.org/10.1177/1745691612448792.

90. Dana R. Carney et al., "The Secret Lives of Liberals and Conservatives: Personality Profiles, Interaction Styles, and the Things They Leave Behind," *Political Psychology* 29, no. 6 (2008): 807–840, https://onlinelibrary.wiley.com/doi/full/10.1111/j.1467-9221.2008.00668.x. "Conservatives," says John T. Jost, "venerate tradition and—most of all—order and authority." Jost, "End of the End," p. 654. Of course, this formulation would mean that anti-government libertarians, anti-tax Tea Partiers, dissidents against Covid-19 health authorities, or outright insurrectionists are "left-wing"—a characterization Jost would obviously deny, meaning that his proposed essence is false.

91. This is how the Rigidity of the Right model was summarized by Ariel Malka, Yphtach Lelkes, and Nissan Holzer, "Rethinking the Rigidity of the Right Model," in *Frontiers of Social Psychology: Politics of Social Psychology*, ed. Jarret T. Crawford and Lee Jussim (New York: Routledge, 2018), 116–135.

92. Theodor Adorno et al., *The Authoritarian Personality* (New York: Harper, 1950). Notice that the connections Adorno made between conservatives and fascists could just have easily been made between liberals and fascists simply by cherry-picking another set of personality traits (e.g., measuring belief in expanding state power among German fascists and then finding that belief also to be high among American liberals).

93. Jost et al., "Political Conservatism as Motivated Social Cognition"; and Jihye Junga and Vikas Mittalb, "Political Identity and the Consumer Journey: A Research Review," *Journal of Retailing* 96, no. 1 (March 2020): 55–73, https://www.sciencedirect.com/science/article/ pii/S0022435919300557#bib0400. According to Junga and Mittalb, "Conservatives engage in more heuristic, automatic, and stereotypical thinking due to their higher need for cognitive closure. In contrast, liberals engage in more deliberate, systematic, and effortful thinking due to their higher need for cognition and higher tolerance for uncertainty" (pp. 56–57). For economist Arnold Kling, "People with a temperament that is high on openness and low on conscientiousness are inclined toward the left and tend to be curious, tolerant, and willing to explore the world with a commitment to intellectual honesty. People with a temperament

that is low on openness and high on conscientiousness are inclined toward the right and tend to emphasize standards of decency, restraint, and good behavior." Kling, "Restoring Political Health, Left and Right," *Medium*, December 4, 2017, https://medium.com/@arnoldkling/restoring-political-health-left-and-right-9a8e5a68b2a2.

94. Philip Tetlock debunked these studies decades ago, showing that they depended upon cherry-picking only those issues that made one's ideological opponents look bad. See Tetlock, "A Value Pluralism Model of Ideological Reasoning," *Journal of Personality and Social Psychology* 50, no. 4, (1986): 819–827, https://doi.org/10.1037/0022-3514.50.4.819.

95. "In a recent meta-analysis, liberals and conservatives showed similar levels of partisan bias, and several pro-tribe cognitive tendencies often ascribed to conservatives (e.g., intolerance toward dissimilar other people) were found in similar degrees in liberals." Cory J. Clark et al., "Tribalism Is Human Nature," *Current Directions in Psychological Science* 28, no. 6 (December 2019): 587. Lucian Gideon Conway III et al., "Are Conservatives Really More Simple-Minded than Liberals? The Domain Specificity of Complex Thinking," *Political Psychology* 37, no. 6 (December 2016): 777–798, https://onlinelibrary.wiley.com/doi/full/10.1111/pops.12304; Nilsson, Erlandsson, and Västfjäll, "The Complex Relation"; and Jesse Singal, "How Social Science Might Be Misunderstanding Conservatives," *New York*, July 15, 2018, https://nymag.com/intelligencer/2018/07/how-social-science-might-be-misunderstanding-conservatives.html. Matthew Hutson, "Why Liberals Aren't as Tolerant as They Think," *Politico Magazine*, May 9, 2017, http://www.politico.com/magazine/story/2017/05/09/why-liberals-arent-as-tolerant-as-they-think-215114. Also see Jeff John Roberts, "Democrats Are 3 Times More Likely to Unfriend You on Social Media, Survey Says," *Fortune*, December 19, 2016, http://fortune.com/2016/12/19/social-media-election/. Studies that consider epistemic closure in an international context are also revealing. James Harman, "Ideology as Motivated Cultural Cognition: How Culture Translates Personality into Policy Preferences," *Political Studies Association*, September 2017, https://www.psa.ac.uk/sites/default/files/conference/papers/2017/Ideology%20as%20Motivated%20Cultural%20Cognition.pdf. According to Harmon, "Whilst need for closure is associated with support for free-market policies in the Netherlands, it is in fact associated with state socialism in Poland." This is also true of open-mindedness. Liberals are just as likely to selectively evaluate, choose, or re-member information in ways that support their own views as are conservatives. Peter H. Ditto et al., "At Least Bias Is Bipartisan: A Meta-Analytic Comparison of Partisan Bias in Liberals and Conservatives," *Perspectives on Psychological Science* 14, no. 2 (March 1, 2019): 273–291, https://journals.sagepub.com/doi/full/10.1177/1745691617746796. "The key is that open-mindedness leads individuals to attack the dominant ideas which they encounter: if prevailing orthodoxies happen to be left-wing, then open minded individuals may become right-wing in protest." Harman, "Ideology as Motivated Cultural Cognition," p. 2. Also see Brian Guay and Christopher D. Johnston, "Ideological Asymmetries and the Determinants of Politically Motivated Reasoning," *American Journal of Political Science* 66, no. 2 (April 2022): 285–301, https://doi.org/10.1111/ajps.12624: "Across all experimental outcomes, and for each operationalization of a respondent's left–right orientation, we find no evidence for the asymmetry hypothesis," that is, that conservatives are more closed-minded than liberals. "Liberals and conservatives are equally prone to politically motivated reasoning" (p. 285).

96. Michael Lind, *New Class War*, p. 104–105. Lind continues, "The C-Scale test, purporting to measure conservatism, created by Glenn Wilson and John Patterson in the 1960s, used attitudes toward jazz as a touchstone. Combining the work of Altemeyer, Wilson, and Patterson, we may conclude that individuals who dislike both jazz and nudist camps are au-thoritarian conservatives. (Ironically, Adorno himself wrote a number of essays expressing his deep loathing of jazz music, declaring that 'jazz can be easily adapted for use by fascism.')" (p. 105).

97. John Levi Martin, "The Authoritarian Personality, 50 Years Later. What Lessons Are There for Political Psychology?" *Political Psychology* 22, no. 1 (2001): 1.

98. Many of these flawed studies are documented in Stuart Ritchie, *Science Fictions*; and Jesse Singal, *The Quick Fix: Why Fad Psychology Can't Cure Our Social Ills* (New York: Farrar, Straus and Giroux, 2021).

99. Chadly Stern and Jarret T. Crawford, "Ideological Conflict and Prejudice: An Adversarial Collaboration Examining Correlates and Ideological (A)Symmetries," *Social Psychological and Personality Science* 12, no. 1 (January 1, 2021): 42–53; Timothy P. Collins, Jarret T. Crawford, and Mark J. Brandt, "No Evidence for Ideological Asymmetry in Dissonance Avoidance," *Social Psychology* 48 (2017): 123–134 Also see Ronald Bailey, "Tracking Down the Elusive Left-Wing Authoritarian," *Reason*, March 8, 2018, https://reason.com/2018/03/08/tracking-down-the-elusive-leftwing-autho/. "Left-wing authoritarians can be just as prejudiced, dogmatic, and extremist as right-wing authoritarians." Mark J. Brandt et al., "The Ideological-Conflict Hypothesis: Intolerance among Both Liberals and Conservatives," *Current Directions in Psychological Science*, February 3, 2014. As one research summary put it, "Conservatives are indeed more dogmatic on the religious domain; but liberals are more dogmatic on the environmental domain." Ronald Bailey, "Liberals Are Simple-Minded . . . and Often More Dogmatic than Conservatives, According to a New Study," *Reason*, January 15, 2016, https://reason.com/2016/01/15/liberals-are-simple-minded/.

100. Malka et al., "Needs for Security and Certainty"; Johnston, Lavine, and Federico, *Open versus Closed*; and Ariel Malka and Christopher J. Soto, "Rigidity of the Economic Right? Menu-Independent and Menu-Dependent Influences of Psychological Dispositions on Political Attitudes," *Current Directions in Psychological Science* 24, no. 2 (April 1, 2015): 137–142, https://doi.org/10.1177/0963721414556340. John T. Jost's contention that conservatives inherently venerate "order and authority" ("End of the End of Ideology," p. 654) is falsified by the extreme anti-authority approach that conservatives took to Covid-19 restrictions, as well as their longstanding anti-authority approach to taxes, regulation, and other elements of government economic control. For many essentialists, "trust of authority" defines the right, while for other essentialists, "distrust of authority" (government) defines the right. That intelligent people are postulating the opposite dispositions as "essential" to conservatism is a strong indicator that there is no essence to conservatism.

101. See, e.g., William F. Buckley Jr., *God and Man at Yale: The Superstitions of Academic Freedom* (Chicago: Regnery, 1951); William F. Buckley Jr. and L. Brent Bozell, *McCarthy and His Enemies: The Record and Its Meaning* (Chicago: Regnery, 1954); and Willmoore Kendall, "The 'Open Society' and Its Fallacies," *American Political Science Review* (December 1960): 972–979.

102. Pamela B. Paresky, "When Is Speech Violence and What's the Real Harm?" *Psychology Today*, August 4, 2017, https://www.psychologytoday.com/us/blog/happiness-and-the-pursuit-leadership/201708/when-is-speech-violence-and-what-s-the-real-harm; Greg Lukianoff and Jonathan Haidt, *The Coddling of the American Mind: How Good Intentions and Bad Ideas Are Setting Up a Generation for Failure* (New York: Penguin Press, 2018); Lisa Feldman Barrett, "When Is Speech Violence?" *New York Times*, July 14, 2017, https://www.nytimes.com/2017/07/14/opinion/sunday/when-is-speech-violence.html; and Jeffrey Aaron Snyder and Amna Khalid, "Not a False Alarm," *Inside Higher Ed*, January 23, 2019, https://www.insidehighered.com/views/2019/01/23/partisan-politics-keeps-those-political-left-seeing-threats-free-speech-opinion. One study at the University of North Carolina asked "whether it is appropriate to obstruct a speaker with whom one disagrees. Noticeably more liberals (19 percent) than moderates or conservatives (both 3 percent) said it was appropriate to do so." Timothy Ryan, "The Hidden Consensus on Free Expression," *Heterodox: The Blog*, February 20, 2020, https://heterodoxacademy.org/blog/viewpoint-diversity-hidden-consensus-free-expression/. For more on left-wing intolerance on campus, see "Largest Ever Free Speech Survey of College Students Ranks Top Campuses for Expression," *FIRE Newsdesk*, September 29, 2020, https://www.thefire.org/largest-ever-free-speech-survey-of-college-students-ranks-top-campuses-for-expression/. Their study found that "liberal students expressed a higher acceptance of violence. Students identifying as extremely liberal said violence to stop a speech or event from occurring on campus was 'always' or 'sometimes' acceptable at a rate double than students identifying as extremely conservative: 13% to 6%." According to the Pew Research Center, "19% say that knowing a friend backed Trump would strain their friendship, while only 7% say the same about learning a friend had voted for Hillary Clinton" and "Democrats feel more negatively about talking politics with people who have a different opinion of the president than do

Republicans. A large majority of Democrats and Democratic-leaning independents—nearly seven-in-ten (68%)—say they find it to be stressful and frustrating to talk to people with different opinions of Trump. Among Republicans and Republican-leaners, fewer (52%) say they find this to be stressful and frustrating." Pew Research Center, "Since Trump's Election, Increased Attention to Politics—Especially Among Women," July 20, 2017, http://www.people-press.org/2017/07/20/since-trumps-election-increased-attention-to-politics-especially-among-women/.

103. See Buckley, "Notes toward an Empirical Definition of Conservatism," October 10, 1963, in Buckley, *The Jeweler's Eye: A Book of Irresistible Political Reflections* (New York: Putnam's, 1969), 11; Buckley, "Introduction," in *Did You Ever See a Dream Walking? American Conservative Thought in the Twentieth Century* (New York: Bobbs Merrill, 1970), xvii; Frank S. Meyer, "Summing Up: Consensus and Divergence," in *What Is Conservatism?*, ed. Frank Meyer (New York: Holt, Reinhart, and Winston, 1964), 210; and Goldberg, "Cries and Whispers," The Remnant with Jonah Goldberg, episode 466 (March 12, 2022), https://podcasts.apple.com/us/podcast/cries-and-whispers/id1291144720?i=1000553780040.

104. Stuart Ritchie, *Science Fictions*, p. 150: "Everyone, especially scientists, is supposed to know that correlation is not causation. . . . If we find that drinking more coffee is correlated with having a higher IQ (which, by the way, it is), we can't conclude that 'coffee raises your IQ.' "

105. Ryota Kanai et al., "Political Orientations Are Correlated with Brain Structure in Young Adults," *Current Biology* 21, no. 8 (2011): 677–680, https://www.ncbi.nlm.nih.gov/pmc/articles/PMC3092984/. The authors are careful to point out that brain differences do not necessarily cause ideological differences, but they do suggest a causal explanation by drawing on the debunked "conservatives are more fearful" studies addressed earlier.

106. For an analogy, notice that fans of Utah Jazz guard Jordan Clarkson will have different characteristics than fans of Los Angeles Lakers guard LeBron James, but these characteristics are not what cause them to cheer for these players, and the incidental demographic characteristics of "conservatives" or "liberals" are not what cause them to cheer for the policies that currently fly under their tribal banner. Scholars citing such demographic characteristics as essential are mistaking demographic correlation for ideological causation.

107. Lewis, *Ideas of Power*.

108. Eric Litke, "Fact Check: Big Cities Have Crime and More Democrats, But It's a Stretch to Link Them," *USA Today*, June 24, 2020, https://www.usatoday.com/story/news/factcheck/2020/06/24/fact-check-linking-city-violence-democratic-politics-reach/3248102001/.

109. "More attractive individuals are. . . more likely to identify as conservative and Republican than less physically attractive citizens of comparable demographic backgrounds." Rolfe Peterson and Carl Palmer, "Effects of Physical Attractiveness on Political Beliefs," *Politics and the Life Sciences* 36, no. 2, (Fall 2017): 4, https://www.cambridge.org/core/journals/politics-and-the-life-sciences/article/effects-of-physical-attractiveness-on-political-beliefs/D5214D0CAE37EE5947B7BF29762547EE.

110. Lest we be tempted to believe that urban vs. rural is the essence of the spectrum, we must note that in the early twentieth century, American cities were far more Republican and "conservative" than the countryside, where radicals like William Jennings Bryan were popular. Furthermore, in Mao's China, urban residents were inherently suspect as "rightists" and routinely sent to the countryside for re-education.

111. Our current era in which religiosity is identified with free market economics is a historical anomaly.

112. John R. Alford, John R. Hibbing, and Kevin B. Smith, *Predisposed: Liberals, Conservatives, and the Biology of Political Differences* (New York: Routledge, 2014), 45; and John R. Alford, Carolyn L. Funk, and John R. Hibbing, "Are Political Orientations Genetically Transmitted?" *American Political Science Review* 99, no. 2 (May 2005): 153–167, https://doi.org/10.1017/S0003055405051579.

113. Stephen G. Morris, "Empathy and the Liberal-Conservative Political Divide in the U.S.," *Journal of Social and Political Psychology* 8 (February 2020), https://jspp.psychopen.eu/article/view/1102.

114. For a refutation of the empathy essence, see Paul Bloom, *Against Empathy: The Case for Rational Compassion* (New York: Ecco, 2016).

115. Jonathan Haidt, *The Righteous Mind* (New York: Pantheon, 2012); and Michael Barber and Jeremy C. Pope, "Does Party Trump Ideology? Disentangling Party and Ideology in America," *American Political Science Review* 113, no. 1 (February 2019): 38–54.

116. Tom Jacobs, "For Americans, Partisanship Trumps Values," April 10, 2019, *Pacific Standard*, https://psmag.com/news/partisanship-trumps-morality-for-todays-americans. Jacobs, reporting on a study of the immoral behavior of politicians, said that the researchers "found that Democrats responded to alleged [moral] violations more strongly than Republicans did." Just as the social theory predicts, the study found that "there are impulses even more foundational than our innate moral compasses: the desire to fit in with our group, and the instinct to distinguish between 'us' and 'them.'"

117. H. Michael Crowson, "Are All Conservatives Alike?" Crowson only found correlates between individual traits and individual policy domains, not between individual traits and ideologies in general (e.g., "economic conservatism" correlated with "epistemic openness" while "social conservatism" correlated with "epistemic closedness"). Although traits may have a one-to-many relationship to a *set* of related positions—e.g., someone against a higher sales tax is also likely to be against a higher property tax—they don't have a one-to-many relationship to unrelated positions (i.e., the social as opposed to economic domain of politics).

118. Weeden and Kurzban, *Hidden Agenda*.

119. Jesse Graham, Jonathan Haidt, and Brian A. Nosek, "Liberals and Conservatives Rely on Different Sets of Moral Foundations," *Journal of Personality and Social Psychology* 96, no. 5 (2009): 1029–1046, https://www.semanticscholar.org/paper/Liberals-and-conservatives-rely-on-different-sets-Graham-Haidt/469f40500c6fb37340c69967df95ad94b9285d16.

120. Christopher R. Weber and Christopher M. Federico, "Moral Foundations and Heterogeneity in Ideological Preferences," *Political Psychology* 34, no. 1 (February 2013): 107–126, https://doi.org/10.1111/j.1467-9221.2012.00922.x. Weber and Federico found that "different classes of conservatives rely on different constellations of moral considerations." Talking of the moral foundations of left and right is misleading, since different moral foundations are associated with different parts of the ideological package; e.g., "social conservatives" will have opposite moral foundations from "economic conservatives."

121. Jonathan Haidt, "The Moral Roots of Liberals and Conservatives," TED Talk, March 2008, https://www.ted.com/talks/jonathan_haidt_the_moral_roots_of_liberals_and_conser vatives?language=en#t-452012.

122. Ibid. Unsurprisingly for the social theory, conservatives are concerned with purity on conservative issues and liberals are concerned with purity on liberal issues. Some believe that moral foundations theory refutes our argument, but actually it bolsters it: there are many dimensions to morality (Haidt identifies five) and there are many dimensions to politics. Indeed, the most powerful criticism of moral foundations theory is that it doesn't offer enough dimensions to adequately cover the range of moral considerations. See Kurt Gray et al., "What Is 'Purity'? Conceptual Murkiness in Moral Psychology," PsyArXiv preprint, Feb 2, 2021, https://psyarxiv.com/vfyut/; and Oliver Scott Curry, "What's Wrong with Moral Foundations Theory, and How to Get Moral Psychology Right," *Behavioral Scientist*, March 26, 2019, https://behavioralscientist.org/whats-wrong-with-moral-foundations-the ory-and-how-to-get-moral-psychology-right/. Moral foundations theory would only falsify our argument if it showed that (1) moral foundations naturally clustered into two distinct packages independent of socialization, and (2) each package had a causal relationship to the many issues associated with its ideology. The evidence suggests the opposite. Also see Jacobs, "Partisanship Trumps Values": "Partisans of both parties express significantly greater negativity when a politician of the other party violates a moral foundation."

123. This falsifies not only the "individual autonomy" essence of liberalism put forward by Alan Wolfe in *The Future of Liberalism* but also the "liberty vs. order" essence of left and right that is so common. See, e.g., Yuval Levin, interview with Bari Weiss, March 18, 2022, *Honestly with Bari Weiss*, https://podcasts.apple.com/us/podcast/honestly-with-bari-weiss/id157 0872415?i=1000554465045. Levin says, "I think that there really is a basic difference between left and right that comes down to almost an anthropological difference. Do you start out thinking that the human person is just full of sin and vice and needs to be shaped in order to be a free citizen, or do you start out thinking that the human person is maybe not

perfect, but ready to be free and is born free, but, you know as Rousseau says, is everywhere in chains? Politics has to be about breaking chains . . . the trouble with the institutions of our society is that they oppress us, they keep pushing down on us. We need to get them off our backs . . . that is much more like the left's way of thinking of what institutions are for." If Levin were correct, we would have seen the left protesting Covid restrictions, high taxes, and greater economic regulations. Instead, groups that protested these were considered "right wing" (e.g., the "Tea Parties"). All essentialist stories, including Levin's, are quickly falsified once they are subjected to empirical testing.

124. Heiner Rindermann, David Becker, and Thomas R. Coyle, "Survey of Expert Opinion on Intelligence: Intelligence Research, Experts' Background, Controversial Issues, and the Media," *Intelligence* 78 (January–February 2020), article 101406, https://doi.org/10.1016/j.intell.2019.101406; and Stephen P. Schneider, Kevin B. Smith, and John R. Hibbing, "Genetic Attributions: Sign of Intolerance or Acceptance?," *The Journal of Politics* 80, no. 3 (July 2018): 1023–1027, https:// doi.org/10.1086/ 696860. Although many see genetic attribution as "right wing," it turns out that "conservatives are less likely than liberals to attribute people's life outcomes to genetics, particularly for moralized outcomes like sexual orientation and drug addiction." Kathryn Paige Harden, *The Genetic Lottery: Why DNA Matters for Social Equality* (Princeton: Princeton University Press, 2021), 206.

125. Weber and Federico, "Moral Foundations and Heterogeneity."

126. See Malka et al., "Needs for Security and Certainty"; Johnston, Lavine, and Federico, *Open versus Closed*; Malka and Soto, "Rigidity of the Economic Right?"; H. Michael Crowson, "Are All Conservatives Alike? A Study of the Psychological Correlates of Cultural and Economic Conservatism," *The Journal of Psychology* 143, no. 5 (2009): 449–463, https://www.tandfonline.com/doi/abs/10.3200/JRL.143.5.449-463; and Alexander Davidson and Derek A. Theriault, "How Consumer Experience Is Shaped by the Political Orientation of Service Providers," *Journal of Consumer Psychology* 31, no. 4 (October 2021): 792–800, https://doi.org/10.1002/jcpy.1233.

127. See Alford, Hibbing, and Smith, *Predisposed*; Alford, Funk, and Hibbing, "Are Political Orientations Genetically Transmitted?"; Pinker, *The Blank Slate*; Haidt, *The Righteous Mind*; Avi Tuschman, *Our Political Nature: The Evolutionary Origins of What Divides Us* (Amherst, NY: Prometheus Books, 2013); Carney et al., "Secret Lives"; and Marina Koren, "Study Predicts Political Beliefs with 83 Percent Accuracy," *Smithsonian Magazine*, February 14, 2013, https://www.smithsonianmag.com/science-nature/study-predicts-political-beliefs-with-83-percent-accuracy-17536124/. Again, these brain studies border on the tautological. They show that conservative brains light up with disgust at things conservatives don't like, while liberal brains light up with disgust at things liberals don't like. It's hardly remarkable that we can predict someone's politics as "conservative" when a photograph of Hillary Clinton activates the "disgust" regions of their brain. It just tells us what we already know: conservatives don't like Hillary Clinton. Brain scans indicate learned, social behaviors, and the social theory of ideology says that ideological hatreds are learned, social behaviors.

128. This view was satirized in Gilbert and Sullivan's "Iolanthe" (1882): "That every boy and every gal / That's born into the world alive. / Is either a little Liberal / Or else a little Conservative."

129. As Alford and Hibbing put it, "Research in behavioral genetics and elsewhere increasingly indicates a biological basis for the manner in which people behave in personal, interpersonal, and political situations, but this biological basis does not mean behavior in these three very different contexts is correlated." John R. Alford and John R. Hibbing, "Personal, Interpersonal, and Political Temperaments," *The Annals of the American Academy of Political and Social Science* 614, no. 1 (2007): 196, https://journals.sagepub.com/doi/abs/10.1177/0002716207305621. Also see Emily A. Willoughby et al., "Parent Contributions to the Development of Political Attitudes in Adoptive and Biological Families," *Psychological Science*, November 18, 2021, https://doi.org/10.1177/09567976211021844.

130. Malka and Soto, "Rigidity of the Economic Right?"

131. Stanley Feldman and Christopher Johnston, "Understanding the Determinants of Political Ideology: Implications of Structural Complexity," *Political Psychology* 35, no. 3 (June 2014): 337–358, https://doi.org/10.1111/pops.12055. As Malka and Soto put it in "The

Rigidity of the Economic Right?," "Sociocultural and economic political attitudes have different psychological bases" (p. 138)—the social and economic realms of politics are not "interrelated" as essentialists contend. For more on the psychological independence of the social and economic domains, see John Duckitt and Chris G. Sibley, "The Dual Process Motivational Model of Ideology and Prejudice," in *The Cambridge Handbook of the Psychology of Prejudice*, ed. Chris G. Sibley and Fiona Kate Barlow (New York: Cambridge University Press, 2017), 188–221, https://doi.org/10.1017/9781316161579.009.

132. According to biographer James Atlas, there was even a tendency among Marxist intellectuals of the early twentieth century to castigate homosexuality as a by-product of capitalism. James Atlas, *Delmore Schwartz: The Life of an American Poet* (New York: Farrar Straus Giroux, 1977), 61.

133. Mental illness has a genetic component and liberalism correlates with mental illness, but, as much as conservatives would like to argue that this is because all liberal positions are "crazy," it is actually a function of the demographics associated with the Democratic Party, who tend to be more susceptible to mental illness (the very poor) or willing to seek out treatment (young professionals). For the dataset on liberalism and mental illness, see Pew Research Demographic Trends, "Covid-19 Late March 2020," https://www.pewsocialtrends.org/dataset/covid-19-late-march-2020/. Also see Elizabeth Condra, "Over 50% of Liberal, White Women under 30 Have a Mental Health Issue. Are We Worried Yet?" *Evie*, April 12, 2021, https://www.eviemagazine.com/post/over-50-percent-white-liberal-women-under-30-mental-health-condition. For predictable conservative gloating about these findings, see Chris Menahan, "Pew Poll: White Liberals More Likely to Be Mentally Ill and Depressed," *InformationLiberation*, April 11, 2020, https://www.informationliberation.com/?id=61368. For more thoughtful commentary on the findings, see Tyler Cowen, "Claims about Politics (speculative)," *Marginal Revolution*, October 8, 2020, https://marginalrevolution.com/marginalrevolution/2020/10/claims-about-politics.html.

134. For instance, Alford, Funk, and Hibbing use twin studies to show that, despite being raised in different environments, identical twins tend to wind up in the same place ideologically. But even though their study controls for different parental environments, it does not control for different *tribal* environments—both twins are socialized by the same cultural-political context. To establish that left and right positions are intrinsically connected and inborn, they would need to show that these positions correlated *before* socialization. The data makes clear that the twins already had tribal identifications before participating in the study. Alford, Funk, and Hibbing, "Are Political Orientations Genetically Transmitted?" Also see Hibbing et al., *Predisposed*.

135. See Spence, *Search for Modern China*; and Jung Chang and Jon Halliday, *Mao: The Unknown Story* (New York: Anchor, 2006).

136. Amy Mackinnon, "What Actually Happens When a Country Bans Abortion," *Foreign Policy*, May 16, 2019, https:// foreignpolicy.com/ 2019/ 05/ 16/ what-actually-happens-when-a-country-bans-abortion-romania-alabama/.

Chapter 5

1. Thomas Reid, *Inquiry and Essays* (Indianapolis: Hackett, 1983), 112.
2. Karl Marx famously sought to reduce all the complexity of society to the single issue of class conflict. As Kevin Williamson explains, "When Copernicus and Galileo challenged the consensus model of the universe, it was not only the religious authorities who were scandalized: The philosophers and scientists were bent out of shape, too, because Galileo's observed universe was more disorderly and unruly than the one they deduced—and more complex. It was not only biblical astronomy but the Aristotelian taste for mathematical perfection (they mistook neatness for perfection) that left them too terrified to consider the truth: The heavens, Aristotle wrote, must be 'perfect and unchanging,' and to think otherwise was to invite anarchy into the world." Kevin Williamson, *The Smallest Minority* (Washington, DC: Regnery, 2019), chapter 10. Rejecting the simplistic Aristotelian model of the universe led to the scientific revolution, and rejecting the simplistic essentialist model of politics would also have beneficial results.

3. As Thomas Chatterton Williams puts it, "One of the outgrowths of the frenzied, justifiably Trump-panicked moment in which we find ourselves is a profound unease with ambiguity or multidimensionality of any sort—moral, intellectual, ideological, political, artistic." Thomas Chatterton Williams, "An Incoherent Truth," *Harper's* (February 2020), https://harpers.org/archive/2020/02/an-incoherent-truth/.

4. Andrew Hartz, "A Diagnosis for American Polarization," *Wall Street Journal*, November 3, 2020, https://www.wsj.com/articles/a-diagnosis-for-american-polarization-11604447133.

5. "Splitting is a term used in psychiatry to describe the inability to hold opposing thoughts, feelings, or beliefs. Some might say that a person who splits sees the world in terms of black or white—all or nothing. It's a distorted way of thinking in which the positive or negative attributes of a person or event are neither weighed nor cohesive." Kristalyn Salters-Pedneault, "Splitting and Borderline Personality Disorder: A Defense Mechanism Where Everything Is Black or White," *Verywell Mind*, February 16, 2021, https://www.verywellmind.com/what-is-splitting-425210.

6. Joris Lammers et al., "The Political Domain Appears Simpler to the Politically Extreme than to Political Moderates," *Social Psychological and Personality Science* 8, no. 6 (August 1, 2017): 612–622; Jason Weeden and Rob Kurzban, *The Hidden Agenda of the Political Mind: How Self-Interest Shapes Our Opinions and Why We Won't Admit It* (Princeton: Princeton University Press, 2014). According to Tetlock and Gardner, "The national security elites looked a lot like the renowned physicians from the prescientific era. They too overflowed with intelligence and integrity. But tip-of-your-nose delusions can fool anyone, even the best and the brightest—perhaps especially the best and the brightest." Philip E. Tetlock and Dan Gardner, *Superforecasting: The Art and Science of Prediction* (New York: Crown, 2015), 52.

7. Neil Gross and Solon Simmons, eds., *Professors and Their Politics* (Baltimore: Johns Hopkins University Press, 2014).

8. See, e.g., George F. Bishop, "The Effect of Education on Ideological Consistency," *The Public Opinion Quarterly* 40, no. 3 (Autumn, 1976): 337–348.

9. See Ariel Malka and Christopher J. Soto, "Rigidity of the Economic Right? Menu-Independent and Menu-Dependent Influences of Psychological Dispositions on Political Attitudes," *Current Directions in Psychological Science* 24, no. 2 (April 1, 2015): 137–142, https://doi.org/10.1177/0963721414556340; Christopher M. Federico and Paul Goren, "Motivated Social Cognition and Ideology: Is Attention to Elite Discourse a Prerequisite for Epistemically Motivated Political Affinities?," in *Social and Psychological Bases of Ideology and System Justification*, ed. John T. Jost, Aaron C. Kay, and Hulda Thorisdottir (New York: Oxford University Press, 2009), 267–291; and Weeden and Kurzban, *Hidden Agenda of the Political Mind*.

10. Hans Rosling, *Factfulness: Ten Reasons We're Wrong about the World—and Why Things Are Better than You Think* (New York: Flatiron Books, 2018).

11. As Weber and Federico put it, "While the simple liberal-conservative dimension may not fully capture the complexity of citizens' ideological attitude structures, it does have a great deal of predictive power and discursive relevance. As such, our goal is less to displace consideration of the left-right dimension than to illustrate some of the complexities behind it." Christopher R. Weber and Christopher M. Federico, "Moral Foundations and Heterogeneity in Ideological Preferences," *Political Psychology* 34, no. 1 (February 2013): 123, https://doi.org/10.1111/j.1467-9221.2012.00922.x.

12. Laith Al-Shawaf, "Should You Trust the Myers-Briggs Personality Test?," *Areo*, September 3, 2021, https://areomagazine.com/2021/03/09/should-you-trust-the-myers-briggs-personality-test/. What Al-Shawaf said of the Myers-Briggs personality types could also be said of essentialism: "By painting an inaccurate and crudely pixelated picture of human personality, [ideological essentialism] is an obstacle to a more accurate understanding. In this sense, it may be worse than nothing."

13. "Models are simplified descriptions of reality that strip away all of its complexity except for a few features thought to be critical to the understanding of the phenomenon under study." Turchin, *War and Peace and War: The Rise and Fall of Empires* (New York: Penguin, 2006), 291. When we strip away all but the critical features of politics, we find many dimensions, not one essential dimension.

14. "Although the left–right distinction is by no means airtight, it has been the single most useful and parsimonious way to classify political attitudes for more than 200 years." John T. Jost, "The End of the End of Ideology," *American Psychologist* 61, no. 7 (October 2006): 654.

15. Anup Gampa et al., "(Ideo)Logical Reasoning: Ideology Impairs Sound Reasoning," *Social Psychological and Personality Science* 10, no. 8 (November 1, 2019): 1075–1083; Barbara Mellers, Philip Tetlock, and Hal R. Arkes, "Forecasting Tournaments, Epistemic Humility and Attitude Depolarization," *Cognition* 188 (July 2019): 19–26; Drew Westen et al., "Neural Bases of Motivated Reasoning: An FMRI Study of Emotional Constraints on Partisan Political Judgment in the 2004 U.S. Presidential Election," *Journal of Cognitive Neuroscience* 18, no. 11 (2006): 1947–1958; Tetlock and Gardner, *Superforecasting*, 68; Peter H. Ditto et al., "At Least Bias Is Bipartisan: A Meta-Analytic Comparison of Partisan Bias in Liberals and Conservatives," *Perspectives on Psychological Science* 14, no. 2 (March 1, 2019): 273–291, https://journals.sagepub.com/doi/full/10.1177/1745691617746796; John Tooby, "What Scientific Term or Concept Ought to Be More Widely Known? Coalitional Instincts," Edge.org (2017), https://www.edge.org/response-detail/27168; Jan-Willem van Prooijen and André P. M. Krouwel, "Psychological Features of Extreme Political Ideologies," *Current Directions in Psychological Science* 28, no. 2 (April 1, 2019): 159–163; and Jarret T. Crawford and Lee Jussim, eds., *Politics of Social Psychology* (New York: Routledge, 2017).

16. Tooby, "What Scientific Term or Concept Ought to Be More Widely Known?"

17. Cory J. Clark et al., "Tribalism Is Human Nature," *Current Directions in Psychological Science* 28, no. 6 (December 2019): 587–592: "Because coalitional coordination and commitment were crucial to group success, tribes punished and ostracized defectors and rewarded loyal members with status and resources. . . . Tribalism, therefore, is natural," (p. 587) and a tribalism that expresses itself in left versus right political thinking is rewarded both in a deep evolutionary sense and in a current social sense. Also see Cass R. Sunstein and Robert H. Frank, *Conformity: The Power of Social Influences* (New York: New York University Press, 2019); and Edward O. Wilson, *The Social Conquest of Earth* (New York: Liveright, 2012).

18. David Ropeik, *How Risky Is It, Really? Why Our Fears Don't Always Match the Facts* (New York: McGraw-Hill, 2010), 225:

19. Michael Barber and Jeremy C. Pope, "Does Party Trump Ideology? Disentangling Party and Ideology in America," *American Political Science Review* 113, no. 1 (February 2019): 38–54.

20. Jonathan Haidt, *The Happiness Hypothesis: Finding Modern Truth in Ancient Wisdom* (New York: Basic Books, 2006); and Daniel Kahneman, *Thinking Fast and Slow* (New York: Farrar, Straus, and Giroux, 2011).

21. William Livingston, "Of Party Divisions (1753)," in *American Political Thought*, ed. Keith E. Whittington (New York: Oxford University Press, 2017), 47.

22. Publius, "The Federalist No. 10: Madison," *The Federalist Papers* (New York: Simon & Schuster, Inc.), 62.

23. George Washington, "Farewell Address (1796)," in *American Political Thought*, ed. Keith E. Whittington (New York: Oxford University Press, 2017), 184–185.

24. There was a period of exception, however. From the Jacksonian Era to the Progressive Era, during the "Golden Age of Parties," this anti-party sentiment subsided in American culture. During the nineteenth century—thanks to Martin Van Buren and others who created national party organizations—parties had a modest, but solid, respectability. Ordinary American citizens could take some limited measure of pride in their party identifications (as many also did, during this time, in their regional, religious, and ethnic identifications). James Ceaser, *Presidential Selection: Theory and Development* (Princeton: Princeton University Press, 1979).

25. Notable exceptions to the new rule include "neoconservatives," who switched from the Democratic Party to the Republican Party in the 1960s–1970s, "libertarians" who stopped supporting the Republican Party in the 1970s, environmental activists who formed the Green Party, and "NeverTrump conservatives" who switched from the Republican Party to the Democratic Party in the 2010s–2020s.

26. Barber and Pope, "Does Party Trump Ideology?"

27. Survey data finds that most Americans, when asked, will self-identify as "liberal" or "conservative," but when surveyors ask respondents if they are Democrats, Republicans, or Independents, the most common response is "Independent." See the American National

Election Studies (www.electionstudies.org). See also Bruce E. Keith et al., *The Myth of the Independent Voter* (Berkeley: University of California Press, 1992).

28. Kahneman, *Thinking Fast and Slow*.

29. Tali Sharot, *The Influential Mind: What the Brain Reveals about Our Power to Change Others* (New York: Picador, 2018), 24.

30. Robert Kurzban, John Tooby, and Leda Cosmides, "Can Race Be Erased? Coalitional Computation and Social Categorization," PNAS 98, no. 26 (December 18, 2001): 15387–15392, https://doi.org/10.1073/pnas.251541498; Adam Garfinkle, "The Darkening Mind," *American Purpose*, December 7, 2020, https://www.americanpurpose.com/articles/the-darkening-mind/; Haidt, *Righteous Mind*.

31. See Daniel Pipes, *Conspiracy: How the Paranoid Style Flourishes and Where It Comes from* (New York: Simon & Schuster, 1997); David Aaronovitch, *Voodoo Histories: The Role of Conspiracy Theory in Shaping Modern History* (London: Jonathan Cape, 2009); and Vincent Harinam and Rob Henderson, "Blame Modern Life for Political Strife," *Quillette*, November 6, 2018, https://quillette.com/2018/11/06/blame-modern-life-for-political-strife/.

32. For an in-depth discussion of thymos and its role in current politics, see Francis Fukuyama, *Identity: The Demand for Dignity and the Politics of Resentment* (New York: Farrar, Straus, and Giroux, 2018).

33. John Hart, "Is Ideology Becoming America's Official Religion?," *Forbes*, November 30, 2017, https://www.forbes.com/sites/johnhart/2017/11/30/is-ideology-becoming-americas-official-religion/?sh=2f5d2f6d164b.

34. Tribalism and partisanship existed long before the parties to the French Revolution sat on the left and right wings of the national assembly hall.

35. William J. Bennett, *The Death of Outrage: Bill Clinton and the Assault on American Ideals* (New York: The Free Press, 1998).

36. It is probably not a coincidence that the final major third-party challenge for the presidency—Teddy Roosevelt's "Bull Moose" 1912 campaign—happened in the last election before the importation of the left-right spectrum began in 1916.

37. Barry Goldwater, *The Conscience of a Conservative* (Shepardsville, KY: Victor Publishing Company, 1960), 16, 20.

38. Stephen Skowronek, "The Conservative Insurgency and Presidential Power: A Developmental Perspective on the Unitary Executive," *Harvard Law Review* 122, no. 8 (October 29, 2009): 2070–2103.

39. Most recently, conservatives have begun advocating for the federal government to break up and regulate large tech companies like Amazon, Twitter, and Facebook—not because conservatism is fundamentally defined by hostility to big business but because those companies recently censored claims made by conservatives about the 2020 presidential election being stolen from Donald Trump.

Chapter 6

1. Anup Gampa et al., "(Ideo)Logical Reasoning: Ideology Impairs Sound Reasoning," *Social Psychological and Personality Science* 10, no. 8, (November 1, 2019): 1075–1083; Charles S. Taber and Milton Lodge, "Motivated Skepticism in the Evaluation of Political Beliefs," *American Journal of Political Science* 50, no. 3 (2006): 755–769; Martin Bisgaard, "How Getting the Facts Right Can Fuel Partisan-Motivated Reasoning," *American Journal of Political Science* 63, no. 4 (October 2019): 824–839; Joris Lammers et al., "The Political Domain Appears Simpler to the Politically Extreme than to Political Moderates," *Social Psychological and Personality Science* 8, no. 6 (August 1, 2017): 612–622; Seth J. Hill, "Learning Together Slowly: Bayesian Learning about Political Facts," *The Journal of Politics* 79, no. 4 (2017): 1403–1418.

2. Cass R. Sunstein, "Democracy and Filtering," *Communications of the Association for Computing Machinery* 47, no. 12 (December 2004): 57–59; Drew Westen et al., "Neural Bases of Motivated Reasoning: An FMRI Study of Emotional Constraints on Partisan Political Judgment in the 2004 U.S. Presidential Election," *Journal of Cognitive Neuroscience* 18, no. 11 (2006): 1947–1958; and Peter H. Ditto et al., "At Least Bias Is Bipartisan: A Meta-Analytic Comparison of Partisan Bias in Liberals and Conservatives," *Perspectives on Psychological Science* 14, no.

2 (March 1, 2019): 273–291, https://journals.sagepub.com/doi/full/10.1177/174569161
7746796. Ideology is a major enabler of the kind of "non logical conduct" that Italian political
theorist Vilfredo Pareto identified in the early twentieth century. See James Burnham, *The
Machiavellians: Defenders of Freedom* (New York: John Day Company, Inc., 1943).

3. Philip E. Tetlock and Dan Gardner, *Superforecasting: The Art and Science of Prediction*
(New York: Crown, 2015), 68.

4. Leor Zmigrod, Peter Jason Rentfrow, and Trevor W. Robbins, "The Partisan Mind: Is
Extreme Political Partisanship Related to Cognitive Inflexibility?" *Journal of Experimental
Psychology: General* 149, no. 3 (August 2019): 1–12. The authors point out that "objectively
assessed cognitive inflexibility is related to greater ideological thinking" (p. 10).

5. Philip E. Tetlock, David Armor, and Randall S. Peterson, "The Slavery Debate in Antebellum
America: Cognitive Style, Value Conflict, and the Limits of Compromise," *Journal of
Personality and Social Psychology* 66, no. 1 (1994): 115–126, https://doi.org/10.1037/
0022-3514.66.1.115.

6. Artur Nilsson, Arvid Erlandsson, and Daniel Västfjäll, "The Complex Relation between
Receptivity to Pseudo-Profound Bullsh-t and Political Ideology," *Personality and Social
Psychology Bulletin* 45, no. 10 (October 1, 2019): 1440–1454, https://doi.org/10.1177/
0146167219830415.

7. Jeremy A. Frimer, Linda J. Skitka, and Matt Motyl, "Liberals and Conservatives Are Similarly
Motivated to Avoid Exposure to One Another's Opinions," *Journal of Experimental Social
Psychology* 72 (September 2017): 1–12.

8. This was the enduring theme of Sir Karl Popper's epistemological writings, but a number of
recent popular authors have reinforced his point. See, e.g., Adam Grant, *Think Again: The
Power of Knowing What You Don't Know* (New York: Viking, 2021); Tetlock and Gardner,
Superforecasting; and Nate Silver, *The Signal and the Noise* (New York: Penguin, 2012).

9. Jay Van Bavel and Andrea Pereira, "The Partisan Brain: An Identity-Based Model of Political
Belief," *Trends in Cognitive Sciences* 22, no. 3 (March 2018): 213–224.

10. Jeff Greenberg and Eva Jonas, "Psychological Motives and Political Orientation—The Left,
the Right, and the Rigid: Comment on Jost et al. (2003)," *Psychological Bulletin* 129, no. 3
(May 2003): 378.

11. Julia Galef, *The Scout Mindset: Why Some People See Things Clearly and Others Don't*
(New York: Penguin, 2021).

12. Karl Popper, *The Logic of Scientific Discovery* (1935; New York: Routledge, 2002).

13. Tragically, the cognitive impairment that comes from ideological thinking does not only affect
politics. There is an "epistemic spillover" effect as ideologues carry their dogmatic thinking
habits into non-political domains. Joseph Marks et al., "Epistemic Spillovers: Learning
Others' Political Views Reduces the Ability to Assess and Use Their Expertise in Nonpolitical
Domains," *Cognition* 188 (July 2019): 74–84.

14. Barbara Mellers, Philip Tetlock, and Hal R. Arkes, "Forecasting Tournaments, Epistemic
Humility and Attitude Depolarization," *Cognition* 188 (July 2019): 19–26.

15. Political scientists Howard G. Lavine, Christopher D. Johnston, and Marco R. Steenbergen
found that not only were political tribalists less able to see the world accurately, but they
were also less principled in making and communicating political choices. Howard G. Lavine,
Christopher D. Johnston, and Marco R. Steenbergen, *The Ambivalent Partisan: How Critical
Loyalty Promotes Democracy* (New York: Oxford University Press, 2012).

16. In his "Letter from Birmingham Jail," King identified several other moral heroes that he
sought to emulate, including Shadrach, Meshach, and Abednego, early Christians, Socrates,
and the American Revolutionaries.

17. Mellers, Tetlock, and Arkes, "Forecasting Tournaments."

18. Philip Tetlock, *Expert Political Judgment* (Princeton: Princeton University Press, 2006).

19. Ibid., and James Surowiecki, *The Wisdom of Crowds* (New York: Doubleday, 2004); Tetlock
and Gardner, *Superforecasting*.

20. Jonathan Haidt, "Why the Past 10 Years of American Life Have Been Uniquely Stupid," *The
Atlantic*, April 11, 2022, https://www.theatlantic.com/magazine/archive/2022/05/soc
ial-media-democracy-trust-babel/629369/. "The most pervasive obstacle to good thinking
is confirmation bias, which refers to the human tendency to search only for evidence that

confirms our preferred beliefs." Hence, the systematic checking of confirmation bias by seeking disconfirming evidence ("falsification") is at the heart of science.

21. Shanto Iyengar and Kyu S. Hahn, "Red Media, Blue Media: Evidence of Ideological Selectivity in Media Use," *Journal of Communication* 59, no. 1 (March 2009): 19–39; Christopher D. Johnston and Andrew O. Ballard, "Economists and Public Opinion: Expert Consensus and Economic Policy Judgments," *The Journal of Politics* 78, no. 2 (2016): 443–456; Rob Henderson, "Would People Agree about Everything If We Paid Them?" *Psychology Today*, June 19, 2017, available at: https://www.psychologytoday.com/intl/blog/after-service/201 706/would-people-agree-about-everything-if-we-paid-them; and Nilsson, Erlandsson, and Västfjäll, "The Complex Relation."

22. "People do not require an authoritarian state to ignore their own eyes and ears: partisan identities bias a broad range of judgments, even when presented with facts that contradict them." Jay Van Bavel and Andrea Pereira, "The Partisan Brain," p. 213.

23. Kabir Khanna and Gaurav Sood, "Motivated Responding in Studies of Factual Learning," *Political Behavior* 40, no. 1 (March 2018): 79–101; Steven J. Frenda et al. "False Memories of Fabricated Political Events," *Journal of Experimental Social Psychology* 49, no. 2 (March 2013): 280–286. For example, Frenda and his co-authors found that those who identify as left-wing are more likely to remember Bush vacationing during Katrina and those identifying as right-wing are more likely to remember Obama shaking hands with Iran's president. Neither happened.

24. Brendan Nyhan and Jason Reifler, "When Corrections Fail: The Persistence of Political Misperceptions," *Political Behavior* 32 (June 2010): 303–330.

25. Russell J. Dalton, "The Blinders of Partisanship?" in *Research Handbook on Political Partisanship*, ed. Henrik Oscarsson and Sören Holmberg (Northampton, MA: Edward Elgar, 2020), 74–88. Liberals are much better than conservatives at spotting errors in conservative thinking, and conservatives are much better than liberals at spotting errors in liberal thinking. Westen et al., "Neural Bases of Motivated Reasoning"; and Crystal L. Park, Making Sense of the Meaning Literature: An Integrative Review of Meaning Making and Its Effects on Adjustment to Stressful Life Events," *Psychological Bulletin* 136, no. 2 (2010): 257. Park found that ideologues create meaning frameworks that they use for epistemic closure at the expense of cognitive accuracy.

26. Christopher H. Achen and Larry M. Bartels, *Democracy for Realists: Why Elections Do Not Produce Responsive Government* (Princeton: Princeton University Press, 2016). Ideologues are also more likely to have a distorted understanding of basic political matters. Those in tribe-left, for instance, were far more likely to overestimate the risk of Covid-19 than non-ideologues. See Jonathan Rothwell and Sonal Desai, "How Misinformation Is Distorting Covid Policies and Behaviors," Brookings Report, December 22, 2020, https://www.brookings.edu/resea rch/how-misinformation-is-distorting-covid-policies-and-behaviors/.

27. Dan M. Kahan et al., "Motivated Numeracy and Enlightened Self-Government," *Behavioural Public Policy* 1, no. 1 (May 2017): 54–86, https://doi.org/10.1017/bpp.2016.2; and Dan M. Kahan et al., "The Polarizing Impact of Science Literacy and Numeracy on Perceived Climate Change Risks," *Nature Climate Change* 2 (2012): 732–735.

28. Steenbergen, *Ambivalent Partisan*, p. xiv.

29. Ibid.

30. Larry M. Bartels, "Beyond the Running Tally: Partisan Bias in Political Perceptions," *Political Behavior* 24, no. 2 (2002):117–150. Even informed journalists are misled by the myth of left and right into believing that Bush continued Reagan's small-government agenda. See, e.g., Sam Tanenhaus, *The Death of Conservatism: A Movement and Its Consequences* (New York: Random House, 2010).

31. Jean M. Twenge, "Young Americans Are Actually Not Becoming More Progressive," *Time*, August 22, 2017, https://time.com/4909722/trump-millennials-igen-republicans-voters/.

32. Glenn Kessler, "Greene's Ahistorical Claim That the Nazis Were Socialists," *Washington Post*, May 29, 2021, https://www.washingtonpost.com/politics/2021/05/29/greenes-ahistori cal-claim-that-nazis-were-socialists.

33. Jason Brennan, "Politics Makes Us Mean and Dumb," *Emotion Researcher*, February 2017, http://emotionresearcher.com/politics-makes-us-mean-and-dumb/.

34. Steven Webster and Matt Motta, "Many Americans Think That Climate-Change Deniers 'Get What They Deserve' When Disasters Strike," *Washington Post* January 24, 2019, https://www.washingtonpost.com/news/monkey-cage/wp/2019/01/24/many-americans-think-that-climate-change-deniers-get-what-they-deserve-when-disasters-strike/.

35. M. Keith Chen and Ryne Rohla, "The Effect of Partisanship and Political Advertising on Close Family Ties," *Science* 360, no. 6392 (June 1, 2018): 1020–1024, https://science.sciencemag.org/content/360/6392/1020; Christopher Freiman, *Why It's OK to Ignore Politics* (New York: Routledge, 2021); and Shanto Iyengar and Masha Krupenkin, "The Strengthening of Partisan Affect," *Political Psychology* 39, no. 1 (2018): 201–218.

36. Matthew S. Levendusky and Neil Malhotra, "(Mis)perceptions of Partisan Polarization in the American Public," *Public Opinion Quarterly* 80, no. 1 (2016): 378–391. Shanto Iyengar et al., "The Origins and Consequences of Affective Polarization in the United States," *Annual Review of Political Science* 22 (May 2019): 129–146.

37. Shanto Iyengar, Gaurav Sood, and Yphtach Lelkes, "Affect, Not Ideology: A Social Identity Perspective on Polarization," *Public Opinion Quarterly* 76:3 (Fall 2012): 405–431; and Pew Research Center, "Political Polarization in the American Public: How Increasing Ideological Uniformity and Partisan Antipathy Affect Politics, Compromise, and Everyday Life," June 12, 2014, https://www.pewresearch.org/politics/2014/06/12/political-polarization-in-the-american-public/.

38. Amanda Ripley, Rekha Tenjarla, and Angela He, "The Geography of Partisan Prejudice," *The Atlantic*, March 4, 2019, https://www.theatlantic.com/politics/archive/2019/03/us-counties-vary-their-degree-partisan-prejudice/583072/.

39. Amanda Taub, "The Real Story about Fake News Is Partisanship" *New York Times*, January 11, 2017, https://www.nytimes.com/2017/01/11/upshot/the-real-story-about-fake-news-is-partisanship.html.

40. Robert Sapolsky, *Behave: The Biology of Humans at Our Best and Worst* (New York: Penguin, 2017).

41. Shanto Iyengar and Sean J. Westwood, "Fear and Loathing across Party Lines: New Evidence on Group Polarization," *American Journal of Political Science* 59, no. 3 (July 2015): 690–707; and Nathan P. Kalmoe and Lilliana Mason, "Lethal Mass Partisanship: Prevalence, Correlates, & Electoral Contingencies," National Capital Area Political Science Association American Politics Meeting, 2019.

42. Vincent Harinman and Rob Henderson, "Blame Modern Life for Political Strife," *Quillette*, November 6, 2018, https://quillette.com/2018/11/06/blame-modern-life-for-political-strife/.

43. Karen Gift and Thomas Gift, "Does Politics Influence Hiring? Evidence from a Randomized Experiment," *Political Behavior* 37, no. 3 (2015): 653–675; and Christopher McConnell et al., "The Economic Consequences of Partisanship in a Polarized Era," *American Journal of Political Science* 62, no. 1 (2018): 5–18.

44. Thomas Edsall, "No Hate Left Behind: Lethal Partisanship Is Taking Us into Dangerous Territory," *The New York Times*, March 13, 2019, https://www.nytimes.com/2019/03/13/opinion/hate-politics.html.

45. Linton Weeks, "What Is Really Tearing America Apart," NPR, October 15, 2014, https://www.npr.org/sections/theprotojournalist/2014/10/15/356101335/what-is-really-tearing-america-apart.

46. Sean J. Westwood et al., "The Tie That Divides: Cross-National Evidence of the Primacy of Partyism," *European Journal of Political Research* 57 (2018): 333–354.

47. P. J. Henry and Jaime L. Napier, "Education Is Related to Greater Ideological Prejudice," *Public Opinion Quarterly* 81, no. 4 (Winter 2017): 930–942.

48. This definition was used in the 1993 film *Philadelphia*.

49. The 2018 movie *Vice*, for instance, portrays the libertarian Cato Institute as advocating the invasion of Iraq because it is a "right wing" think tank. Actually, Cato took a strong, official stance against the Iraq War from the beginning, but left–right thinking led the filmmakers to ignore reality in favor of false stereotyping. More recently, pundits have puzzled over the fact that the "right wing" billionaire Koch brothers have made common cause with "left wing" billionaire George Soros in establishing an institute for peace. But there is no puzzle: the Kochs are anti-war and so is Soros. It's that simple. Only bringing in left–right categories

makes their common enterprise seem mysterious, complicated, and contradictory. See Tom Embury-Dennis, "George Soros and Charles Koch to Fund New 'Anti-War' Think Tank," *The Independent*, July 1, 2019, https://www.independent.co.uk/news/world/americas/us-polit ics/george-soros-charles-koch-quincy-institute-think-tank-anti-war-a8982216.html.

50. Hitler was considered "right-wing" because he hated Jews and hated capitalism (as expressed in his book *Mein Kampf*) while economist George Gilder is considered "right-wing" because he loves Jews and loves capitalism (as expressed in his book *The Israel Test*). Such absurdities pile up quickly when we conceive of politics in left–right terms.

51. Jerey Berry and Sarah Sobieraj, *The Outrage Industry: Political Opinion Media and the New Incivility* (New York: Oxford University Press, 2014).

52. Thomas C. Leonard, *Illiberal Reformers: Race, Eugenics, and American Economics in the Progressive Era* (Princeton: Princeton University Press, 2016).

53. Yoni Appelbaum, "I Alone Can Fix It," *The Atlantic*, July 21, 2016, https://www.theatlantic. com/politics/archive/2016/07/trump-rnc-speech-alone-fix-it/492557/.

54. Arthur M. Schlesinger, Jr., *The Imperial Presidency* (New York: Houghton Mifflin, 2004).

55. Jerry Taylor, "The Alternative to Ideology," *The Niskanen Center*, October 29, 2018, https:// www.niskanencenter.org/the-alternative-to-ideology/.

56. Samuel P. Huntington, *The Clash of Civilizations and the Remaking of World Order* (New York: Simon & Schuster, 1996).

Chapter 7

1. Daniel Kahneman, *Thinking Fast and Slow* (New York: Farrar, Straus, and Giroux, 2011); Michael Lewis, *The Undoing Project: A Friendship that Changed Our Minds* (New York: W. W. Norton and Co., 2017).

2. Peter Novick, *That Noble Dream: The "Objectivity" Question and the American Historical Profession* (New York: Cambridge University Press, 1988).

3. Gordon Pennycook and David Rand, "Why Do People Fall for Fake News?," *New York Times*, January 19, 2019, https://www.nytimes.com/2019/01/19/opinion/sunday/fake-news.html.

4. Kahneman, *Thinking Fast and Slow*; Susan A. Ambrose et al., *How Learning Works: Seven Research-Based Principles for Smart Teaching* (San Francisco: Jossey-Bass, 2010), 190.

5. Julia Galef, *The Scout Mindset: Why Some People See Things Clearly and Others Don't* (New York: Penguin, 2021).

6. Jesse Singal, "The New Science of How to Argue—Constructively," *The Atlantic*, April 7, 2019, https://www.theatlantic.com/ideas/archive/2019/04/erisology-the-science-of-argu ing-about-everything/586534/.

7. Philip E. Tetlock and Dan Gardner, *Superforecasting: The Art and Science of Prediction* (New York: Crown, 2015).

8. Tim Harford, "Why Good Forecasters Become Better People: Forecasting, It Seems, Is an Antidote to Political Tribalism," *Financial Times*, November 24, 2018, https://www.ft.com/ content/1232d17c-ed90-11e8-89c8-d36339d835c0.

9. Robert Sapolsky, "Why Your Brain Hates Other People: And How to Make It Think Differently," *Nautilus*, June 16, 2017, https://nautil.us/why-your-brain-hates-other-people-rp-6877/.

10. See, e.g., Stanley Kurtz, "Obama's Radical-Left Ties Broad and Deep," CBS News, June 2, 2008, https://www.cbsnews.com/news/obamas-radical-left-ties-broad-and-deep/; and Rmuse, "Right Wing Haters for Christ Vow to Repeal the Affordable Care Act," *PoliticusUSA*, July 1, 2012, https://www.politicususa.com/2012/07/01/wing-haters-christ-vow-repeal-aff ordable-care-act.html.

11. Samuel P. Huntington, *Political Order in Changing Societies* (New Haven: Yale University Press, 1968).

12. See Norman Ornstein and Thomas Mann, *It's Even Worse Than It Looks: How the American Constitutional System Collided with the New Politics of Extremism* (New York: Basic Books, 2012).

13. Notice how many Republicans in the early 2000s supported the decision to invade Iraq, believing that it was a fundamental expression of their "conservative philosophy." They couldn't criticize the War without feeling like they were betraying their conservative

convictions and identity. Understanding that the invasion of Iraq wasn't part of a coherent "conservative" philosophy, but just a decision taken by a Republican president, could have made those millions of Republicans more skeptical of that decision.

14. Robert D. Putnam, *Bowling Alone: The Collapse and Revival of American Community* (New York: Simon & Schuster, 2000). Rejecting ideology can have literal health benefits for individuals. According to David Ropeik, "What feels fine may not be what is actually best for your health. If you want to think for yourself and make the most appropriate choice for your life, the challenge is to try to step outside the social pressure of your tribe(s)." David Ropeik, *How Risky Is It, Really? Why Our Fears Don't Always Match the Facts* (New York: McGraw-Hill, 2010), 235.

15. Alexis de Tocqueville recognized the value of American voluntary associations way back in the 1820s. Tocqueville, *Democracy in America*, trans. Harvey Mansfield and Delba Winthrop (Chicago: University of Chicago Press, 2002). Even non-believers can get the benefits of religious participation through churches or charitable secular associations. See, e.g., Robert Putnam and David Campbell, *American Grace* (New York: Simon & Schuster, 2012), 461; Harold G. Koenig, "Religion, Spirituality, and Health: The Research and Clinical Implications," *ISRN Psychiatry*, December 16, 2012, https://www.ncbi.nlm.nih.gov/pmc/articles/PMC3671693/; and Frank Newport, Sangeeta Agrawal, and Dan Witters, "Very Religious Americans Lead Healthier Lives," *Gallup*, December 23, 2010, https://news.gallup.com/poll/145379/religious-americans-lead-healthier-lives.aspx.

16. Putnam, *Bowling Alone*.

17. Robert Putnam and Shaylyn Romney Garrett, *The Upswing: How America Came Together a Century Ago and How We Can Do It Again* (New York: Simon & Schuster, 2020); Pew Research Center, "U.S. Public Becoming Less Religious," November 3, 2015, https://www.pewforum.org/2015/11/03/u-s-public-becoming-less-religious/.

18. Charlan Nemeth, *In Defense of Troublemakers: The Power of Dissent in Life and Business* (New York: Basic Books, 2018).

19. Brian Gallagher, "Wikipedia and the Wisdom of Polarized Crowds," *Nautilus*, March 14, 2019, https://nautil.us/issue/70/variables/wikipedia-and-the-wisdom-of-polarized-crowds; Anup Gampa et al., "(Ideo)Logical Reasoning: Ideology Impairs Sound Reasoning," *Social Psychological and Personality Science* 10, no. 8 (November 1, 2019): 1075–1083; Lee Jussim et al., "Political Diversity Will Improve Social Psychological Science," *The Behavioral and Brain Sciences* 38, no. 130 (2015), https://doi.org/10.1017/S0140525X14000430; Drew Westen et al., "Neural Bases of Motivated Reasoning: An FMRI Study of Emotional Constraints on Partisan Political Judgment in the 2004 U.S. Presidential Election," *Journal of Cognitive Neuroscience* 18, no. 11 (2006): 1947–1958; James Surowiecki, *The Wisdom of Crowds* (New York: Doubleday, 2004); Scott E. Page, *The Difference: How the Power of Diversity Creates Better Groups, Firms, Schools, and Societies* (Princeton: Princeton University Press, 2008); Adam Grant, *Originals: How Non-Conformists Move the World* (New York: Viking, 2016); Sian Beilock, "How Diverse Teams Produce Better Outcomes," *Forbes*, April 4, 2019, https://www.forbes.com/sites/sianbeilock/2019/04/04/how-diversity-leads-to-better-outcomes/#59a27f7f65ce.

20. Scott Page, *The Diversity Bonus: How Great Teams Pay Off in the Knowledge Economy* (Princeton: Princeton University Press, 2017).

21. Steven Johnson, "How to Make a Big Decision: Have No Fear. An Emerging Science Can Now Help You Choose," *New York Times*, September 1, 2018, https://www.nytimes.com/2018/09/01/opinion/sunday/how-make-big-decision.html.

22. Feng Shi et al., "The Wisdom of Polarized Crowds," *Nature Human Behaviour* 3 (2019): 329–336, https://www.nature.com/articles/s41562-019-0541-6.

23. On an individual level, we can do this by actively seeking out a diversity of political viewpoints. We can read both the *New York Times* and *Wall Street Journal* op-ed pages, consider policy papers from both the Brookings Institution and the American Enterprise Institute, and, most importantly, cultivate personal relationships with people of different political views. We can build collaboration with those who disagree ("adversaries") into the structure of our lives.

24. Tetlock found that epistemically pluralist "foxes" generally have better political judgment than monist "hedgehogs." Philip Tetlock, *Expert Political Judgment* (Princeton: Princeton University Press, 2006).

25. We often scoff at the "superstitious" peoples of earlier times who attributed divine infallibility to their leaders (Pharaohs in Egypt or emperors in Japan), and yet don't we in the twenty-first century do the same under the influence of ideology?

26. One of the fullest expressions of the value of openness for both science and society can be found in Karl Popper, *The Open Society and Its Enemies* (New York: Routledge, 2003).

27. Karl R. Popper, *In Search of a Better World* (New York: Routledge, 1994). With the rise of Trump, David French came to recognize the socially constructed, tribal nature of ideology and stopped identifying with "the right." He says, "I'm a man without a party. I have no 'tribe.' And I must confess that it has opened my eyes. I see things differently than I used to, and I understand the perspective of my political opponents better than I did before." David French, *Divided We Fall: America's Secession Threat and How to Restore Our Nation* (New York: St. Martin's Press, 2020), 3. This can be true of all of us.

28. Jon A. Shields and Joshua M. Dunn Sr., *Passing on the Right: Conservative Professors in the Progressive University* (New York: Oxford University Press, 2016).

29. Specificity instead of ideology would be crucial to adversarial collaboration in the academy. Just as lawyers are not assigned to a package of clients and causes, so we should not assign researchers based on ideological labels since people of opposite labels will often hold the same views on many issues. For instance, since both "left wing" Alexandria Ocasio-Cortez and "right wing" Bryan Caplan agree on open immigration, assigning them to jointly research the effects of immigration would not be "adversarial."

30. We must make clear that we refer to "contested political issues" here to pre-empt the ludicrous but predictable claim that adversarial collaboration would require inclusion of such ideas as the "flat earth" theory in geological research. We are asking for no such thing, but ideologues, believing that any view they don't hold is tantamount to belief in a flat earth love to bring this up to avoid listening to alternative viewpoints and engaging in the adversarial collaboration that would open their minds.

31. Patricia Limerick, the great historian of the American West, came to recognize the value of adversarial collaboration after years of experience: "Effectiveness as a public intellectual, contrary to what I used to think and to what many academics still think, works best when you deny yourself the initial fun of unrestrained expression, think strategically before speaking, listen respectfully to your critics, and even, now and then, admit that they have persuaded you to change your thinking." Patricia Limerick, *The Legacy of Conquest: The Unbroken Past of the American West* (New York: W. W. Norton and Co., 2011), 8.

Conclusion

1. The brilliant Danish astronomer Tycho Brahe is a notable example. See Victor E. Thoren, *The Lord of Uraniborg: A Biography of Tycho Brahe* (New York: Cambridge University Press, 1990).

INDEX

For the benefit of digital users, indexed terms that span two pages (e.g., 52–53) may, on occasion, appear on only one of those pages.

lack of correlation with other issues of, 14
left wing and, 57
liberalism and, 57, 134–35n.102
Republican Party and, 27, 29
right wing and, 27, 57, 126n.30
free trade. *See* economic policies
French, David, 118–19n.23, 147n.27
French Revolution, 17–18, 99–100, 102n.9
Friedman, Milton, 2–3, 12, 130n.63
Fukuyama, Francis, 127–28n.41
Funk, Carolyn, 138n.134

Gardner, Dan, 139n.6
Gelfand, Michele J., 129–30n.61
genetic correlates of ideology, 62–63
George, Henry, 20
Gerring, John, 102–3n.14
Gilder, George, 12, 145n.50
Gingrich, Newt, 12
Godkin, E. L., 19–20, 40, 41, 69
Goldberg, Jonah, 37, 40, 46–47, 122n.50, 131n.75,
    135n.103
Goldwater, Barry
    abortion and, 31
    conservatism and, 29, 30–31, 40, 42, 46–47, 73,
        125n.11
    essentialist theory and, 29, 30, 77, 92
    New Deal and, 36
    political extremism and, 77
    private language fallacy and, 42
    right wing and, 92, 120n.31
    size and role of government and, 29, 46–47, 73
Gould, Eric, 7
government size. *See* size and role of government
granularity
    abortion and, 88, 89, 90
    affirmative action and, 88
    American political development and, 89–90
    benefits of, 89–91
    economic policies and, 88
    essentialist theory counteracted by, 88–91
    ideology replaced by, 88–89
    language use and, 88–89, 91, 93, 94
greed vs. compassion essence, 45–46, 49
Greenberg, Jeff, 11–12, 107n.39

Haidt, Jonathan, 61, 67–68
Hamilton, Alexander, 23, 27–28, 92, 124n.66
Hamiltonian Federalists, 18
Hannity, Sean, 3, 83
harm of essentialist theory of ideology, 15, 38,
    66, 75–86
Harmon, James, 133n.95
Harrington, Jesse R., 129–30n.61
hawks. *See* foreign policy
Hayek, Friedrich, 28, 115–16n.2
Herberg, Will, 128–29n.50

heuristics, 66, 92, 95, 132–33n.93
Hibbing, John, 137n.129, 138n.134
hierarchy vs. equality essence, 50–52
high-mindedness, 35, 38, 69–71, 77, 86
historians. *See* scholarship and academia
Hitler, Adolf, 2–3, 11, 40, 47–48, 49, 126n.23,
    128n.49, 131n.75, 145n.50
Hofstadter, Richard, 51
Hoover, Herbert, 22, 40, 41
hostility. *See* partisan hostility
Hotelling, Harold, 31–32
House Un-American Activities Committee, 27
humility, intellectual, 76, 96
Huntington, Samuel, 85, 116n.3, 125n.11

idealism vs. realism essence, 48–50
identity
    abortion and, 7
    American political development and, 21
    conservatism and, 23
    essentialist theory and, 15, 76–77, 85, 88
    ideologues and, 8–9, 15, 39–40, 76
    ideology and, 1–2, 8–9, 70, 137n.130
    partisan hostility and, 15, 76
    political parties and, 70
    political spectrum and, 1–2
    social theory and, 8–9, 85
    tribalism and, 6, 7, 76, 79
ideological constraint, 48–50, 79
ideologism, 81–84
ideologues
    adversarial collaboration and, 98
    authentic ideologues, 39–43, 63
    cognitive biases and, 75, 77, 143n.26
    dogmatism and, 75–76, 78
    education level and, 78
    essentialist theory and, 35, 39–43, 63, 75–77,
        78, 85–86, 99–100
    forecasting and, 75–76, 89
    humility lacking in, 76
    identity and, 8–9, 15, 39–40, 76
    partisan hostility and, 15
    partisanship and, 35, 39–40
    principled ideologues, 35, 38
    private language fallacy and, 40
    scholarship and, 8–9, 35, 39–40, 75–76, 77, 78
    social theory and, 8–9, 77
    sticky ideologues, 9, 40, 41
    storytelling and, 38, 70, 78
    tribalism and, 8, 9, 39–40, 67, 76
    weak ideologues, 9
ideology. *See also* essentialist theory of ideology;
        social theory of ideology
    as about who rather than what, 3, 8, 15–16
    authentic ideologies and, 43–45
    definition of, 1, 104n.1, 127n.39
    detrimental role of, 1

political parties and, 22–25
reporting phase of, 20, 21
rise in America of, 19–21
rise in Europe of, 17
scholarship and, 4, 19, 21
social conception of, 2
standard view of, 1–4
tribalism and, 2–3, 6, 13, 14–15
political tribalism. *See* tribalism
political violence, 1, 82
Pol Pot, 51
Poole, Keith, 32, 102–3n.14, 120–21n.41
Pope, Jeremy, 7–8, 35, 67, 106n.27, 122n.50
populism, 42, 51–52, 69
prejudice, 2–3, 76, 78–79, 81, 82–83, 85–86
preservation vs. change essence, 5–6, 9–10, 11–13, 43–44, 45
principled commitment, 35, 38, 69–71, 77, 86
private language fallacy, 40, 42–43
Progressive Era, 19–20
Progressive Party, 52–53, 69
progressives
    American political development and, 20, 21, 22
    Democratic Party and, 3
    essentialist theory and, 6, 12, 51, 52–53, 55
    guilt by association and, 83
    New Deal and, 22
    racism and, 27–28
    Republican Party and, 21
    social issues and, 27–28
    storytelling and, 51
public debate, 1–3, 80–81, 83

quantification of ideology, 31–33

racism
    conservatism and, 27–28, 50, 83
    Democratic Party and, 36–37
    left wing and, 131n.75
    liberalism and, 27–28, 50
    progressives and, 27–28
Rand, Ayn, 28
Rand, David, 87
Rauch, Jonathan, 119n.24
Reagan, Ronald
    conservatism and, 30–31, 40, 41, 42, 122n.50
    elitism and, 52
    essentialist theory and, 12, 30
    foreign policy and, 29
    liberalism and, 41
    Republican Party and, 30, 42
    right wing and, 120n.31
    size and role of government and, 52, 119n.28
realism vs. idealism essence, 48–50
Red Scare, 27
Reed, John, 20–21
Reed, Ralph, 28

Reid, Thomas, 64
Reifler, Jason, 78
religiosity vs. secularism essence, 52–53
Religious Right, 7, 28
Remini, Robert, 110n.7
Republican Party
    abortion and, 35–37
    American political development and, 19, 22–25, 69
    anticommunism and, 27
    changing nature of, 28, 29, 33–34, 35, 73
    Cold War and, 41
    conservatism and, 24, 28–29, 30, 33–34, 37, 70, 73–74, 125n.11
    demographics of supporters of, 36, 58–59
    economic policies and, 27, 29, 33–34, 69, 121n.45, 124n.66
    essentialist theory and, 28–31, 37–38, 42, 58, 70, 72, 121n.45
    executive power and, 73
    foreign policy and, 26–27, 28, 29, 41, 73–74, 116n.9, 125n.11
    free speech and, 27, 29
    Iraq War and, 29
    language use and, 91–92, 93–94
    New Deal and, 23, 24, 28, 30, 116n.3
    party switching and, 41
    personal morality of officials and, 34
    political extremism and, 36–37, 120n.36
    progressives and, 21
    Religious Right in, 7, 28
    Russia and, 122–23n.52
    scholarship and, 8, 29–31, 35–36, 73
    shift to the right claims about, 29–31, 33–34, 36–37, 119n.24, 119n.27, 121–22n.46
    size and role of government and, 23, 24, 27, 28, 29, 30, 73, 116n.3, 119n.28
    social issues and, 27–28
    social theory and, 36
    storytelling and, 23–24
    as synonymous with conservative and right wing, 18–19, 22, 24, 33, 38, 70
    tribalism and, 37–38
    Vietnam War and, 27
research. *See* scholarship and academia
right wing
    abortion and, 7, 36–37, 63, 83
    American political development and, 19
    anticommunism and, 27
    changing nature of, 29, 120n.31
    cognitive biases and, 75–76, 77
    demographics of supporters of, 36, 58
    economic policies and, 9–10, 27, 43, 50
    education level and, 50
    elitism and, 51–52
    essentialist theory and, 3, 5–6, 7, 12–13, 15–16, 29, 48, 50, 56, 60, 62, 69–70, 77, 83